Contents

SOCIAL POLICY REVIEW 17

Edited by Martin Powell, Linda Bauld and
Karen Clarke

First published in Great Britain in June 2005 by

The Policy Press
University of Bristol
Fourth Floor, Beacon House
Queen's Road
Bristol BS8 1QU

Tel +44 (0)117 331 4054
Fax +44 (0)117 331 4093
e-mail tpp-info@bristol.ac.uk
www.policypress.org.uk

British Library Cataloguing in Publication Data
A catalogue record for this book is available from the British Library.

Library of Congress Cataloging-in-Publication Data
A catalog record for this book has been requested.

ISBN 1 86134 669 7 paperback
A hardback version of this book is also available.

Martin Powell is a Reader in Social Policy in the Department of Social and
Policy Sciences, University of Bath. **Linda Bauld** is a Senior Lecturer in Public
Policy in the Department of Urban Studies, University of Glasgow. **Karen Clarke**
is a Senior Lecturer in Social Policy in the School of Social Sciences, University of
Manchester.

Cover design by Qube Design Associates, Bristol.
Front cover: view of the Sage Gateshead from the Millennium Bridge, kindly
supplied by Nigel Young/Foster and Partners.
Printed and bound in Great Britain by MPG Books, Bodmin.

Notes on contributors

Adriana Castelli is a Research Fellow in the Health Policy team at the Centre for Health Economics, University of York.

John Clarke is Professor of Social Policy in the Department of Social Sciences, The Open University.

Daniel Clegg is a Marie-Curie Post-Doctoral Research Fellow at CEVIPOF (Centre d'Etude de la Vie Politique Française), Institut d'Etudes Politiques de Paris, France.

Diane Dawson is a Senior Research Fellow in the Health Policy team at the Centre for Health Economics, University of York.

Alexandra Dobrowolsky is Associate Professor in the Department of Political Science, St Mary's University, Halifax, Nova Scotia, Canada.

Stephen Driver is Principal Lecturer in the School of Business, Social Sciences and Computing, Roehampton University.

Hugh Gravelle is Professor in the National Primary Care Research and Development Centre, Centre for Health Economics, University of York.

Moira Hulme is a Senior Lecturer in Post-Compulsory Education, School of Education, University of Wolverhampton.

Rob Hulme is Principal Lecturer and Head of Social Studies in the Department of Applied Community Studies, Manchester Metropolitan University.

Jane Jenson is Professor in the Département de Science Politique, Université de Montréal, Canada.

Peter A. Kemp is Director and Professor of Social Policy in the Social Policy Research Unit, University of York.

Rudolf Klein is Visiting Professor at the London School of Economics and Political Science.

Eithne McLaughlin is Professor and Chair of Social Policy in the School of Sociology and Social Policy, Queen's University Belfast.

Peter Malpass is Professor of Housing Policy and Head of the School of Housing and Urban Studies in the Faculty of the Built Environment, University of the West of England.

Theodore Marmor is Professor of Public Policy and Management, Yale University School of Management, USA.

Ann Netten is Director of the Personal Social Services Research Unit, University of Kent.

Peter Robinson is a Senior Economist at the Institute for Public Policy Research, London.

Sally Ruane is a Senior Lecturer in the School of Applied Social Sciences, De Montfort University.

Nick Smith, at the time of writing, was a Research Associate in the Faculty of Social Sciences, The Open University.

Kate Stanley is Head of Social Policy at the Institute for Public Policy Research, London.

Andrew Street is a Senior Research Fellow in the Health Policy team, Centre for Health Economics, University of York.

Elizabeth Vidler, at the time of writing, was a Research Associate in the Faculty of Social Sciences, The Open University.

Fiona Williams is Professor of Social Policy in the Department of Sociology and Social Policy, University of Leeds.

Introduction

Martin Powell, Linda Bauld and Karen Clarke

This year's *Social Policy Review* follows the new structure introduced last year, with its three parts on the core areas of UK social policy, a wider exploration of policy issues, and a focused theme. As last year, we hope to combine a 'hot off the press' review of material by leading commentators from the UK and beyond, with personal analyses of issues from a variety of points of view.

Part One of this volume focuses on contemporary developments in social policy. It covers core areas of welfare in the UK, including social security, education, health, housing and the Personal Social Services. Each chapter has as its primary focus recent events and developments, particularly those that have taken place in 2004. While each of the five contributions in this section also attempts to place these developments in a wider context, the chapters vary in the extent to which they do this. To some extent this is driven by variation in the pace of change across policy areas. Developments in social security in 2004, for instance, were significant, in particular changes to pensions in the UK. Housing policy also witnessed a series of important developments in 2004. In contrast, a promised social services White Paper never materialised and due to this and other factors, the pace of change in the personal social services during this past year has been far slower and the focus is on a more gradual process of policy development.

Despite differences in style and scope between the chapters in Part One, each provides a valuable review of key recent policies and their impact that should be of interest to students, teachers and researchers alike.

Peter Kemp's chapter is the first in this section. He outlines recent developments in social security policy. His analysis begins with a review of key themes in welfare reform since 1997. He argues that New Labour has considerably reformed the social security system, driven by the need to adapt to societal changes and economic policy concerns. He then goes on to examine recent developments including those relating to welfare to work, Incapacity Benefit, policies for lone parents and pension reform, before considering emerging trends that could translate into major long-term reforms if Labour is returned to office in 2005.

Kemp's chapter is followed by Rob and Moira Hulme's analysis of recent developments in education policy. They examine policy relating to primary, secondary and higher education in England. The chapter argues that Labour's approach to reform has been characterised by incremental change rather than significant departures from policies introduced by the previous Conservative governments. In particular they assert that the marketisation of all levels of education has continued and change is propelled first and foremost by the needs of the global market economy. Developments in 2004 echo those in recent years in terms of a continued emphasis on employability, partnership working and selectivity. Policies designed to promote personal and parental responsibility are also discussed in the chapter along with Labour's plans to reform the school workforce.

The third chapter in Part One is by Rudolf Klein. Klein reviews the latest series of policies designed to 'transform' the National Health Service (NHS), placing them in the context of Labour's evolving approach to health service reform since 1997. Klein points out that no major health policy initiatives were introduced in 2004 and no significant shifts in government strategy were observed. However, the year was important in terms of how existing policies were implemented and how the consequences of these policies may shape the future direction of reform. Klein focuses on key themes: the central issue of expanding the capacity of the NHS; modifying the way in which the 'institutional architecture' of the NHS functions; the changing role of the centre, in particular the Department of Health; and a continued emphasis within recent health policy on population health and health improvement.

Recent developments in housing are described by Peter Malpass in Chapter Four. 2004 was an important year for housing policy with the publication of significant reports, the introduction of new initiatives and the passage of the 2004 Housing Act. Malpass examines a series of key themes including housing supply, affordability and governance. He pays particular attention to the potential implication of the final report of the review of housing supply in England and provides a critique of how New Labour's emphasis on 'choice, responsibility and opportunity' in housing has continued to exacerbate inequalities in this area of social policy.

Part One concludes with a chapter by Ann Netten examining social service reform. Netten focuses specifically on adult Personal Social Services. Within the context of growing public funding of Personal Social Services in recent years she uses the social production of welfare approach as an analytical framework to identify whether recent policies are or have the potential to be effective. The chapter describes current trends in policy and practice including the continued shift to maintain more people in their own homes and increase choice and independence through the promotion of policies initially introduced by New Labour in its first term, such as direct payments. Netten also assesses critically the continued emphasis on performance measurement and targets in social care and argues that despite recent reforms we are still some way away from demonstrating how services directly contribute to improved well-being for users and their carers.

Despite focusing on different policy areas, similar themes emerge in each of the chapters in this section. The central role of market considerations in driving reform cuts across all areas of social policy. Likewise an emphasis on measuring performance and reaching targets continues to affect most policy areas. Several of the chapters in this section argue that recent policies continue to emphasise the responsibilities of clients and citizens that accompany any rights they may have to goods and services. Perhaps most importantly, even in policy areas where important developments have occurred in 2004, the emphasis is much more on continuity with New Labour's early policies than any dramatic shifts. This is perhaps not surprising for a second-term government facing an election in 2005. It remains to be seen what changes may be introduced by a third-term Labour government, but the signs suggest that the pace of change may be slowing and the implications of earlier policy decisions are only now beginning to emerge.

The second part of *Social Policy Review 17* examines recent developments in social policy from a broader perspective, moving away from a focus on the five principal welfare services to consider a number of cross-cutting issues. Eithne McLaughlin's chapter completes the review of devolution in the UK begun in *Social Policy Review 16* with an examination of the brief period of devolution in Northern Ireland, between 1999 and 2004. She places this in the context of a much longer history of devolved government under Ulster Unionist control since the partition of Ireland in 1922. She identifies a number of distinctive features of Northern Ireland's welfare system involving 'small government', a particularly strong and influential position for middle-class welfare professionals, marked social inequality and poorly developed social citizenship relative to the rest of the UK. This in turn raises questions about the degree of commitment to guaranteeing a common social citizenship across the constituent countries of the UK. Northern Ireland developed its own distinctive systems in education and in health and social services. McLaughlin argues that the particular political circumstances in Northern Ireland and the institutions established for devolution in the most recent period (1999–2004) have resulted in policy initiatives which focus on those groups on which cross-party agreement is most easily achieved – children and older people. She identifies some important areas of policy convergence with the rest of the UK as well as areas of divergence in health, education, social security and equality legislation.

Theodore Marmor's chapter examines the significance of the re-election of George Bush for social policy in the US, through an analysis of two important legislative initiatives: changes to the Medicare system for prescription payments introduced in 2003 in the Medicare Modernisation Act; and proposed changes to social insurance pensions, which would effectively privatise and individualise the pensions system. In both cases, he argues that the changes will advantage private corporations – the pharmaceutical industry in the first case and the financial services sector in the second, at the expense of individual financial security and access to welfare. He argues that Bush's electoral success does not reflect popular support for radical neo-liberal policies in relation to tax cuts and welfare reform but was rather the result of support for the Republican position on a quite different set of issues around the family, abortion and same-sex marriages. He shows how the passage of legislation reforming the Medicare system was the result of financial scare-mongering. Marmor suggests that similar mis-information about the costs of social insurance pensions are being used to try to secure support for proposed reforms to the pension system, with the changes presented as part of a vision of creating 'an ownership society'. Marmor argues that presenting these policies as a response to new kinds of risks in the 21st century, requiring new kinds of welfare policies, is in fact an attempt to disguise an ideologically based attack on welfare policies, whose principal objective remains the provision of collective responses to the need for economic security. These policies still have broad popular support and he is sceptical about the likelihood that the pension reforms will get through Senate and Congress. His chapter is a warning to UK observers not to be unduly persuaded by partial and ideologically distorted accounts of the direction of change in US welfare policy.

Think-tanks have come to play an increasingly influential role in shaping social policy in the UK. Sally Ruane offers a review of the proposals on the health service and the role of government in providing healthcare put forward by a large number of think-tanks from across the political spectrum during the period of the New Labour governments. She shows that there is considerable consensus among right-wing and centre-left think-tanks about the desirability of an agenda of choice and competition among healthcare providers, with the role of government being limited to setting up appropriate regulatory frameworks, rather than direct provision. This involves a change in the role and responsibilities of the citizen in relation to healthcare services, towards greater individualisation, and a concomitant reduction in collective responsibility through universal institutions. Although there are differences between right-wing and centre-left think-tanks in their recommendations on how health services should be funded and in their views on the role of taxation, there is a remarkable degree of consensus on the principles of choice and marketisation. Resistance to these ideas is limited to a small number of think-tanks on the left whose position is defensive and relatively marginal to current debates on healthcare. Ruane argues that the growing significance of think-tanks in policy formation is a result of the reconstruction of the Labour Party as New Labour, and the attempts to reduce the influence of the Labour Party Conference and the trades unions in shaping policy, combined with the increasing political influence of global service corporations, seeking entry into a potentially lucrative healthcare market. Think-tanks have helped to construct a discourse which sets the framework for political debate and legitimates the move to market-based forms of provision, while not being explicitly and clearly linked to those globalised private sector interests.

The themes of choice and consumerism in public services raised in Ruane's chapter are also addressed in the chapter by John Clarke, Nick Smith and Elizabeth Vidler who argue that the rhetoric of choice intersects with different notions of inequality in the arguments of both New Labour and the Conservatives. They discuss how the construction of the service user as consumer overlooks the relative advantages that some consumers may enjoy in terms of social and symbolic capital and therefore threatens to reproduce the inequalities that the introduction of choice is intended to overcome. They point out the complex and contradictory conceptions of the consumer that underlie the notion of choice in relation to public services and the problems that are raised by using choice as the mechanism to bring about public service reform. Their chapter highlights the importance of distinguishing between voice and choice as mechanisms to bring about more responsive services.

Adriana Castelli and colleagues examine of some of the issues and problems associated with attempts to measure the outputs of the NHS. This has become an increasingly pressing political priority because of the wish to demonstrate the benefits resulting from substantial additional expenditure in areas such as health and education. Interest in measuring the outputs of public services is apparent in changes in the way in which the Office for National Statistics reports on some of the principal areas of welfare expenditure, using methodologies that are consistent with standards being recommended by Eurostat for the whole of the European Union. It is also apparent in the commissioning of a review of the measurement of government outputs by the National Statistician. Castelli and colleagues point to the problems in defining what the outputs of the health service are and the difficulty, for example, under current data systems in accessing information about individuals rather than 'treatments'. The authors draw attention to some of the problems involved in attempting to quantify multi-dimensional concepts such as quality of care, in relation to the outputs of the health service and in trying to look at change in outputs over time and relate these to changes in the quality and cost of treatments.

If citizens are increasingly seen as consumers, as Alexandra Dobrowolsky and Jane Jenson argue in Chapter Nine, then governments increasingly represent themselves as investors. Their chapter discusses New Labour's interpretation of the social investment paradigm in which state expenditure is justified in terms of the future returns on resources invested. This perspective has become an increasingly dominant one across a number of welfare states. It results in a strong future orientation for policy and a particular emphasis on children. Dobrowolsky and Jenson discuss New Labour's social investment perspective in four policy areas: child poverty; education and skills training; childcare, in terms of its benefits for children and parents; and the promotion of a culture of savings and investment through the creation of the Child Trust Fund and the Savings Gateway pilot. They point to the areas of contradiction within this perspective in New Labour's policies, for example in the continuing liberal emphasis on choice in relation to childcare and parental employment. The chapter argues that despite highly publicised personal differences within the party, New Labour is unified by its social investment perspective with implications for the identity of citizens and the governance mechanisms necessary to manage and monitor the returns on those investments.

The topic for the final part of *Social Policy Review* is an exploration of New Labour's first two terms of office. Last year we focused on the social policy impact of 1979, reflecting 25 years since Margaret Thatcher came to power. This year, we examine the impact of 1997, given a General Election in May 2005. This means that these contributions were written in the difficult context of a 'phoney war' when an election was expected, but had not been declared.

Daniel Clegg provides a continental European perspective on New Labour's welfare state. He takes up the debate in last year's *Review* by Kees van Kersbergen and Anton Hemerijck on the Christian versus Social

Democratisation of the welfare state. He reviews successes and failures of continental Europe, before turning to New Labour. He finds that social policy is more centralist and state-led under New Labour, reinforcing British exceptionalism. While Clegg points to some success, notably the lowest unemployment rate for 25 years and the highest employment rate of all time, he believes that some scepticism is admissible regarding claims that New Labour has laid the foundations for an optimal new compromise between competitiveness and solidarity, for two overlapping reasons. The first relates to the social limits of its initiatives to date. The New Deal has been a 'modest success at modest cost', and it is uncertain that 'converting the try' of the first two terms will see the necessary increased investment (and largely benign economic conditions). The second misgiving is that there may not be much structural glue holding the compromise together. Clegg concludes that the comparisons with continental European social policy brings both the most important virtues and the most serious limits of the British third way, as a progressive agenda for the reform of the welfare state, into particularly sharp focus. On the positive side, British policies seem to have been more responsive to the 'general interest', but on the negative side, a basic commitment to the reconciliation of social and economic goals still appears to be far more widely and deeply shared on the continent. This results in a 'progressive dilemma': while statism seems to be the most reactive and flexible framework for effective social policy development, policies developed within this framework will, lacking any roots in broader society, be inherently vulnerable to conflict and contestation.

Stephen Driver, in the next chapter, views New Labour as 'post-Thatcherite'. In a robust and provocative account, he argues that many of New Labour's themes are not exactly 'new' to 'old' European social democracy. In other words, contrary to some accounts, New Labour is not simply born in the US. Despite initial caution over social expenditure, New Labour has become a big spender, although this varies by sector. Public expenditure is back on the agenda for the 2005 Election, and not simply in the form of a neo-liberal 'Dutch auction'. Driver points to an impressive record on employment. He claims that while the impact of government policy on the distribution of income has been equalising, the income gap has widened. Child poverty has decreased, but poverty has increased for those of working age without children (cf Dobrowolsky and Jenson on the social investment state). He claimed that Labour has put egalitarian policy making back on the political agenda, even if it does not always trumpet its achievements (cf Robinson and Stanley, Chapter Fourteen). Turning to the 'modernisation' of public services, Driver points to differences within Labour, suggesting that Brown's Britain may be different in terms of competition, choice and diversity compared to Blair's (or Milburn's or Reid's) Britain. However, he suggests that Blairite modernisation does not necessarily undermine social democratic political economy. The Blairites, rather than being the gravediggers of social democracy, are simply acknowledging the limits of the British state first exposed in the 1970s, and are re-thinking, not undermining, collective action.

The debate on social democracy is continued by Peter Robinson and Kate Stanley who point out that social democracy can mean different things at different times even when it is the same government in office. They state that the New Labour project is not the project that might have been expected in 1997. While Labour has been keen to shed its 'tax and spend' image, Labour has taxed and spent. They focus on a number of areas: welfare spending (not admitting what you are doing), pensions (responding, or not, when circumstances change) and health policy (doing the opposite of what you said you would do). While increased expenditure is a policy target, increasing the social security budget (previously termed by Tony Blair as 'the bills of economic failure') was not. Despite this, they claim that there are disadvantaged groups who have not benefited at all as a result of the government's welfare spending, such as adults without children who are out of work. Moreover, the benefit and welfare-to-work regimes have been failing sick and disabled people. It appears that New Labour's version of New Poor Law 'less eligibility' – 'work for those who can; security for those who cannot' – still finds the division into 'can' and 'cannot' problematic. Pensions have certainly seen changes in circumstances, but the degree to which New Labour has contributed to those changed circumstances (the changing taxation of pension dividends; more 'means testing' in different guises, contrary to early statements) is unclear. Nevertheless, Robinson and Stanley consider that the early aim of changing the public–private balance in pension contributions is effectively dead. However, the question of what to do, rather than what not to do, has been kicked into touch until after the Election (along with the European constitution). Tony Blair is firmly committed to some Old Labour strategies: Harold Wilson said that Royal Commissions take minutes, and last years. Similarly, the final report of the Pensions Commission may only take months, but is likely to report after an Election. Turning to health policy, the Labour government has presided over the most fundamental changes to the structure of the NHS and over the longest period of generous increases in funding in the service's history. However, this may not link with local – and sometimes highly publicised individual – perceptions of shortcomings. Whether an Election Campaign will be based on a clear and explicit model, the challenges it implies and how it is to be paid for is doubtful, and perhaps partly contributes to – our one prediction – a large vote for the apathetic, disillusioned and 'none of the above' party.

Fiona Williams focuses on New Labour's family policy. She begins her account with the claim that the creation in 2003 of a new Ministry for Children, Young People and Families marked the emergence of an explicit, universal and child-centred family policy. This has four key features: 'hard-working families'; its child-centredness; its focus on parental responsibilities; and its acknowledgement of diversity. Williams discusses the positive and negative characteristics of these themes, along with their key tensions. She writes that there can be little doubt that the responsibility for childcare for working parents has been transformed from an individual to a public responsibility. However, the strategy has been based on a narrow cost-benefit analysis, which tends to ignore the quality of care and is based on an 'ethic of work' rather than an 'ethic of care'. This links with the 'social investment state (cf Dobrowolsky and Jenson), where the child is seen as 'the citizen-worker of the future' with an overall aim to maintain competitiveness in the global economy. Williams argues that the responsibility mantra of the 'third way', often linked in this context with a 'deficit model of family life and parenting capacity', may lead to the 'wrong sort of help' rather than the 'right sort of support'. A later point about school meals (March 2005) illustrates that *Social Policy Review* is able to be one of the most up-to-date sources on social policy available. However, school meals were introduced about a century ago after the report of the Inter-Departmental Committee on Physical Deterioration, which was set up after the Boer War, raised concerns over the efficiency of future citizen-soldiers in the Imperial army. This raises the different issue of whether it matters that the 'right' policies may be introduced for the 'wrong' reasons. Although the government's family policy recognises some diversities, it has been curiously spare in its mention of gender inequalities. It is concluded that in so far as a new normative family is emerging, this revolves around the adult couple whose relationship is based on their parenting responsibilities, and whose priorities are rooted in work, economic self-sufficiency, education and good behaviour.

While *Social Policy Review* is necessarily an analysis of the recent past, at the time of writing, much interest was focused on the expected Election, and so this section concludes with some brief thoughts summing up Labour's first two terms. Over the last eight years social policy has lived in 'interesting times'. Labour's period of office is difficult to neatly summarise, because policies have varied over time and between sectors. Moreover, the most appropriate policy yardstick is not clear: it is possible to compare Labour with the previous Conservative government, with social democratic governments in other countries, with the counterfactual of what 'Old Labour' might have achieved (assuming that 'Old Labour' would have been elected), or against the expectations that social policy commentators would have liked the government to achieve. It is important to compare against a realistic template, as idealistic expectations will necessarily be dashed. It should not be forgotten that 'Old Labour' often failed to live up to expectations and made concessions. For example, the NHS was created with pay beds and general practitioners as 'small businessmen' (perhaps unavoidably) by the icon of democratic socialism, Aneurin Bevan. Social democratic governments in other countries have worked with privately supplied public services, and have laid responsibilities on workers in conditional benefit regimes. However, all that said, New Labour still remains stubbornly resistant to evaluation for at least two main reasons.

First, the government's 'discourse' is particularly difficult to interpret, often varying over time, between speakers, and for different audiences. As Robinson and Stanley make clear, some strategy has been silent, virtually apologetic or even denied. There is no old 'tax and spend', but there appears to be new (stealth) 'tax and invest'. It may become increasingly difficult to smuggle policy in via the back door, and sooner or later, Labour may have to announce its policy intentions at the front door. When that happens, it will be easier to see whether there are genuine differences between the parties, or whether – a familiar problem for teachers and lecturers – Blair is plagiarising Howard's coursework.

Second, it is often difficult to keep an eye on exactly what is happening as money and initiatives are sometimes announced again and again. However, while the government has been legislation-heavy, it has sometimes been implementation-light. In other words, there may be a large discrepancy between what the statute book says and what is happening 'on the ground'. It is a truism that quick legislation is often bad legislation (as shown by the 1991 Dangerous Dogs Act). Similarly, moral panics do not tend to lead to quick fixes. New Labour seems to consider that problems are 'solved' when the newspaper headline appears. This sometimes leads to measures that would seem difficult to implement, such as Blair's famous brief flirtation with 'marching yobs to the cashpoint to pay fixed penalties'. Similarly, a recent headline suggests that the solution to 'binge drinking' is to fine bar staff who serve drunken customers. As far as we are aware, this has been illegal for many years, and we would guess few expect that this policy will lead to either reduced drunkenness or a large increase in fines. Any gap between promise and delivery will further fuel a downward spiral in trust in the political process.

It has been possible to add a final paragraph after the General Election of 5 May 2005. Social policy looks set to continue to live in interesting times. New Labour won a historic third term, but with a historically low proportion of the popular vote. It is not fully clear how long Tony Blair will continue as Prime Minister, but the two major parties will have new leaders at the next general election.

The Labour manifesto was regarded by Blair as the most ambitious. However, this ambition may be thwarted by (for New Labour) a majority small enough to be overturned by substantial backbench revolts.

Neither is it clear whether 'Blairism' will continue after Blair. Will a new leader change course, or will there be a new consensus (represented by the bookies' favourite, Gordon Brown)? Will the widely anticipated tax increases enter through the front door or stealthily through the back door? Will moves towards greater 'diversity' and 'pluralism' of services continue? We hope to throw some light on issues such as these in future editions of *Social Policy Review*.

Part One:
Current services

ONE

Social security and welfare reform under New Labour

Peter A. Kemp

Introduction

Since 1997, the New Labour government has been very active in reforming the social security system in Britain. As well as major changes to key benefits, there has been a succession of minor reforms, amendments and extensions to numerous aspects of social security. This almost hectic activity has been driven by a number of important factors. In part, it reflects New Labour's belief that social security needs to be modernised to reflect changes in the economy and society since the Beveridge report (DSS, 1998a). These developments include rising female labour force participation, increasing divorce and relationship breakdown, the growing number of lone-parent households, the shift from manufacturing to service employment, growth of part-time work and increasing longevity. To some extent, therefore, modernisation is about updating social security to cope with the 'new social risks' of post-industrial society (Taylor-Gooby, 2005).

The extensive reforms also reflect New Labour's desire to ensure that social security, and social policy more generally, is designed to accommodate economic policy concerns more explicitly than was previously the case (Lewis, 2004). This is believed to be necessary in order to help create and maintain a competitive economy in an increasing globalised world (Taylor-Gooby et al, 2004). This driver of reform can be seen in the central role that the Treasury has played in welfare reform. Moreover, the shift towards tax credits and away from benefits has arguably enabled the Treasury to keep a much closer grip on income maintenance than before.

The re-shaping of social security has also been influenced by New Labour's 'third way' agenda (Powell, 1999, 2000; Lewis and Surender,

2004). Among other things, the third way is a rhetorical device to reposition the Labour Party politically and distinguish it, not only from the Conservatives, but also from 'old' Labour. Thus, in his foreword to the welfare reform Green Paper, Prime Minister Tony Blair argued that the document:

> ... describes a third way: not dismantling welfare, leaving it simply as a low-grade safety net for the destitute; nor keeping it unreformed and underperforming; but reforming it on the basis of a new contract between citizen and the state, where we keep a welfare state from which we all benefit, but on terms that are fair and clear. (DSS, 1998a, p v)

As this quote also suggests, one aspect of the third way was the belief that reform of social security was required in order to create a new contract between the state and the citizen in which more emphasis needed to be placed on responsibilities and less on rights (White, 2001). Certainly, New Labour's rhetoric about welfare reform is heavily imbued with the language of personal responsibility (Hyde et al, 1999). And, as Lewis (2004) has pointed out, New Labour frequently twins the word 'responsibility' with 'opportunity'. Thus, while it is the government's task to provide people with opportunities, it is benefit claimants' responsibility to take up those opportunities:

> ... to the unemployed who can work: we will meet our responsibility to ensure that there are job opportunities and the chance to learn new skills. You must now meet your responsibility – to earn a wage. (Gordon Brown, quoted in Brewer et al, 2002, p 511)

One further driver for reform was a desire, as Tony Blair expressed it, "to cut the cost of economic failure" (DSS, 1998a, p iv) – that is, to reduce, or at least to contain the growth in, social security expenditure. In 1996/97, social security accounted for 32% of all public spending, which was more than what was being spent on health and education combined. At least initially, success in reducing spending on social security was seen as a way of enabling the government to increase spending on health and education, which the British Social Attitudes Survey showed were the public's main priorities for increased public spending (Hills, 2002). It was also important to develop the government's reputation for fiscal prudence and sound macroeconomic management.

The aim of this chapter is to examine recent developments in social security under the New Labour government. In order to place these developments in context, the chapter begins by briefly recalling some of the key themes that have dominated the welfare reform agenda since 1997. For the purpose of this chapter, 'social security' is defined to include the benefits administered by the Department for Work and Pensions (DWP) together with the income-related tax credits administered by the Inland Revenue. It does not include child maintenance or childcare.

Key themes in welfare reform since 1997

Paid work

Perhaps the most important and persistent theme running through New Labour's reform of social security has been the centrality of paid employment (Deacon, 2002). This is reflected in the government's mantra of "work for those who can, security for those who cannot" (DSS, 1998a). The government argued that it was necessary to "rebuild social security around the work ethic", and this was exemplified most of all by the introduction of the compulsory New Deals for young unemployed people and for long-term unemployed people aged 25 plus, as well as voluntary New Deals for lone parents, disabled people and others.

The emphasis on paid employment has moral undertones (Heron and Dwyer, 1999; Deacon, 2002), but it also reflects a view that work is the surest route out of poverty (DSS, 1998a). New Labour argues that, instead of passively handing out benefits, it is important to create an active welfare system in which people are helped back into work. Moving people into work reduces the cost of social security benefits. Even if they do not actually find work, the fact that unemployed people are competing for jobs will help to restrain wages and thereby enable the economy to operate at a lower level of inflation and, ultimately, create more jobs (Layard, 1997).

In return for requiring people to take steps towards work, the government has sought to ensure that those who do get a job are financially better off. The National Minimum Wage (extended to 16- and 17-year-olds in 2005) and the Working Tax Credit (and its predecessor, the Working Families' Tax Credit) are New Labour's key instruments for ensuring that people are better off in paid work than claiming benefit (Lewis, 2004). Meanwhile, a plethora of other measures has been introduced to help ease the transition into employment.

The restructuring of jobcentres and social security benefit offices to create Jobcentre Plus for claimants of working age, and the Pensions Service for those over state pension age, has also helped to reinforce the philosophy of work for those who can, security for those who cannot (Carmel and Papadopoulos, 2003). The same is true of renaming the Department of Social Security the Department for Work and Pensions. The carers and disability work of the Department for Work and Pensions has recently been made into an executive agency called the Disability and Carers Service. Significantly, its responsibilities do not include Incapacity Benefit, but instead are focused on Carer's Allowance and the extra-costs disability benefits such as Disability Living Allowance (DWP, 2005).

Security for those who cannot work

While those who could work were to be encouraged to do so, financial security was to be provided to those who could not work (DSS, 1998a). Initially, some commentators seem to have assumed that "security for those who cannot" included the unemployed. In fact, it was always much more likely that it did not include people who could work but were on the dole. Indeed, a recent government publication referred to "our commitment to provide security for those who are unable to work, whether through disability, caring responsibilities or old age" (DWP, 2005, p 5) – a list of contingencies that does not include unemployment.

Although the government has done much to tackle pensioner poverty, it has been much less active in taking steps to provide financial security for other groups of people who cannot work (Becker, 2003). Benefit levels have been increased for the most severely disabled people, but cuts have been made to Incapacity Benefit. Meanwhile, informal carers looking after frail, sick or disabled people have been relatively neglected, although important changes to their pension entitlement were made with the replacement of State Earnings Related Pensions by the Second State Pension, and the carers' premium in income-related benefits was increased in April 2001.

Tackling poverty

Since 1999, an explicit aim of government policy has been to tackle child poverty and, more recently, to address poverty among pensioners. Tony Blair's announcement in the Beveridge memorial lecture that the Labour government would seek to eradicate child poverty (Blair, 1999) came as a surprise to many people after it had gone ahead with cuts in benefits for lone parents in 1997 that had been planned by the previous,

Conservative government (Walker, 1999; Stewart and Hills, 2004). Significantly, tackling child poverty was justified by the Treasury in respect of the impact that it would have on children's life chances, including their income and employment in adulthood (Millar and Ridge, 2002).

The New Labour government has introduced substantial increases in financial support for children, which have more than outweighed the 1997 cuts in benefits for lone parents (Stewart and Hills, 2004). Financial support for children has been increased by £10.4 billion since 1997, an increase of 72% in real terms (HM Treasury, 2004, p 23). The Child Tax Credit and the new Child Trust Fund have been presented as examples of what New Labour calls the principle of 'progressive universalism'. The government has defined progressive universalism as "delivering help for all families and more help for those who need it most, when they most need it" (HM Treasury, 2004, p 23). Thus, while the great majority of families are entitled to the Child Tax Credit, low-income families are entitled to a higher amount than the better off.

The rationale behind progressive universalism is that it will build electoral support (or acquiescence) for measures that help the poor in a way that a wholly means-tested approach will not. Whatever the validity of that argument, the political limits to substantial real growth in financial support for tackling child poverty may not be far off. The Child Poverty Review, which was set up following the 2003 Budget (Bennett, 2004), contained no major new initiatives in financial support for children (HM Treasury, 2004). However, one outcome of a separate review of financial support for young people is the 2004 Child Benefit Bill, which contains provision to pay Child Benefit to 16- to 19-year-olds in unpaid work-based training and 19-year-olds completing a course of education and training.

New Labour has increased – and twice renamed - the means-tested social assistance benefits paid to low-income pensioners. The minimum income for single pensioners who claim what is now referred to as the 'guarantee credit' component of the Pension Credit has been raised from £69 per week in 1997 to £109 per week from April 2005. By contrast, the flat-rate Basic State Pension (BSP) has been raised by much less than that, despite campaigning by the pensioner and poverty lobbies. Although the government has been criticised for relying more on means testing to tackle pensioner poverty (Ginn, 2001; Falkingham and Rake, 2003), there are now 1.8 million fewer pensioners living in 'absolute poverty' (DWP, 2005). By focusing on the means-tested pension rather than the BSP, Labour has ensured that the poorest pensioners have benefited the most, the majority of whom are women (Evandrou and Falkingham, 2004).

In order to allay concerns about overreliance on means testing, the government has tried to increase take-up of the guarantee credit by reducing the hassle, and minimising the possibility of stigma, involved in claiming it (Brewer et al, 2002). For example, the application form has been greatly reduced in length, the need to report changes of circumstances has been reduced and the treatment of capital has been made more generous.

The improvements in financial support for families with children and pensioners have resulted in a significant amount of income redistribution (Sutherland et al, 2003; Sefton and Sutherland, 2004). The government has not received the recognition from Labour supporters that this might have warranted (Stewart and Hills, 2004), possibly because it has been achieved almost by stealth (Lister, 2001) and without a symbolically important increase in the top rate of Income Tax. However, although this redistribution has benefited families with children, and pensioners, relatively little has been done to raise the income of childless people living on benefits (Hills and Stewart, 2004), other than by helping them to move into work. This is perhaps not surprising, as increasing out-of-work benefits for childless single people and couples would have reduced work incentives for these claimants and gone against the whole thrust of New Labour's welfare-to-work agenda.

Tackling fraud

A further important theme of New Labour's social security reform agenda has been tackling benefit fraud (Sainsbury, 2003). This has been given a very high profile, both in terms of taking action to prevent, detect and punish fraud, and also in terms of advertising campaigns and publicity. The 1998 welfare reform Green Paper argued that:

> Fraud undermines the integrity and purpose of the social security system. Taxpayers and genuine claimants support the system on the basis that resources go to those who are entitled, not to those who are dishonest. (DSS, 1998a, p 67)

By giving anti-fraud activity a high profile, New Labour hopes to reassure the public that it is not soft on social security and that the system is not riddled with people fiddling benefits. The danger is that giving a high profile to fraud will have the opposite effect and heighten public concern about the issue. Indeed, British Social Attitudes Survey data suggest that the belief that fraud is widespread has increased rather than decreased under New Labour (Hills, 2002).

Recent developments and emerging trends

As New Labour's second term of office comes to an end, it is instructive to examine the current trajectory of the government's agenda for social security reform. It is apparent from measures introduced or announced in 2004 and early 2005 that the core themes identified earlier that have run through their reforms in the first two terms of office continue to be highly salient. However, it also seems that paid work is becoming increasingly important. This is seen most clearly in respect of changes that have been made and are planned for Incapacity Benefit. New Labour is increasingly turning its attention to economically inactive benefit claimants and people who are harder to help than jobseekers who are closer to the labour market. It is also making increasing use of financial incentives within its work-focused benefit regime.

Welfare to work

During 2004, the government announced significant changes in the New Deal, referred to as 'Building on the New Deal' (BoND), which are to be piloted in 11 'prototype' areas across the country from late 2005 (DWP, 2004a). In the BoND pilot areas, the New Deal will be more flexible than currently in order to provide a package of support more tailored to the individual needs of particular clients. Although a national framework of core elements will remain in place, Jobcentre Plus district managers will have the discretion to select different modules from a menu of provision.

The *core framework* will include 'rights and responsibilities' such as the requirement for people receiving Jobseeker's Allowance (JSA) to be actively seeking and available for work, a minimum of 13 weeks' intensive provision when claimants reach certain thresholds, and access to the Personal Advisor Service for people who are long-term unemployed. The *discretionary menu* for the New Deal will include items such as assistance with job search, the provision of employability skills, and work trials.

The rationale for this more flexible and personalised approach to the New Deal is that an increasing number of clients are people with acute or multiple barriers to work. The present client group-based approach may not be sufficiently sensitive to their individual needs and the more intensive support that they require, compared to people who are closer to the labour market (DWP, 2004a). Focusing on hard-to-help unemployed people, and those who are economically inactive, is seen as part of the wider strategy of raising the UK employment rate from 75% to 80% (DWP, 2005).

Reform of Incapacity Benefit

Since Labour came to power, Incapacity Benefit has been subject to increasing scrutiny in an attempt to reduce the very high number of people claiming it – currently over two million – and the cost of the benefit to the Exchequer. Reforms have been introduced to stem the *inflow* onto Incapacity Benefit, to reduce the total expenditure, and to increase the *outflow* from Incapacity Benefit and into work.

In 1999, the Welfare Reform and Pensions Act introduced an income taper in Incapacity Benefit in which new claimants have their benefit reduced by 50 pence for every £1 of any private pension income in excess of £85 per week. In addition, a new medical test of incapacity to work was introduced (the Personal Capability Assessment [PCA], which replaced the All Work Test), and the rules regarding eligibility for Incapacity Benefit were made more restrictive so that only people with a recent work history could qualify for it. The long-term savings from these reforms are an estimated £400 million per annum (Brewer et al, 2002).

The New Deal for disabled people was introduced in 1999, on a voluntary basis, in order help Incapacity Benefit claimants move back into the labour market. The Disabled Persons Tax Credit was also introduced in 1999, and subsequently incorporated into the new Working Tax Credit in 2003, in order to help make work pay by supplementing wages from low-paid work. The rules governing 'permitted work' for people on Incapacity Benefit were also amended. This included limiting such work to 12 months so that it would act as a stepping stone to paid employment rather than being a long-term wage subsidy. In 2003, the government introduced innovative Job Retention and Rehabilitation pilots. This scheme aims to help people at risk of losing their jobs due to illness to get back to work, thereby reducing the possibility of their moving onto Incapacity Benefit. Also in 2003, the government introduced the Pathways to Work pilot scheme, the aim of which was to encourage and help people on Incapacity Benefit to return to work. Introduced in seven pilot areas, the scheme was compulsory for new claimants and voluntary for existing ones. It includes a weekly top-up payment of £40 for 12 months for people who take up jobs of more than 16 hours per week.

Although it is early days, the government is convinced that the Pathways to Work pilots have increased the outflow from Incapacity Benefit in the seven pilot areas, and it has gradually expanded the scheme to cover an increasing number of areas in an effort to end what it refers to as the 'sick note culture' (DWP, 2004b). Thus, in February 2005, the pilots were extended to include people who had been on Incapacity Benefit for up to three years. In addition, a new £20 per week Job Preparation Premium was introduced to encourage claimants to take steps towards getting a job. The government also announced plans to extend Pathways to Work to one third of the country from October 2005. As a result, the areas covered now included the most disadvantaged areas and local authority areas with the greatest concentrations of Incapacity Benefit claimants.

Looking to the future, the government announced plans for a long-term reform of Incapacity Benefit in order to replace the alleged 'sickness culture' with a focus on paid work (DWP, 2005). Under these proposals, new claimants would initially be placed on a holding benefit paid at the same rates as JSA until they have taken the PCA, the medical test that claimants must satisfy in order to get Incapacity Benefit. The PCA would be coupled with a new test – to be called the Employment and Support Assessment – that would make a fuller assessment of the claimant's potential future work capacity. Incapacity Benefit would be abolished and replaced by two new benefits: a Rehabilitation Support Allowance for those with potentially manageable or short-term conditions, and a Disability and Sickness Allowance for people who have more severe conditions or impairments.

The Disability and Sickness Allowance would be paid at a higher level than the current long-term rate of Incapacity Benefit. As now, recipients would be required to have some work-focused interviews. They would be encouraged, but not required, to engage in return-to-work activities, and they would be able to participate in relevant work-focused programmes and benefit from the associated financial incentives.

The proposed Rehabilitation Support Allowance for people with more manageable conditions would be paid at the same rate as JSA, presumably in order to remove any financial incentive for unemployed people to claim long-term sickness benefits. However, recipients would be able to get extra financial help if they agreed to attend work-focused interviews, and more still if they signed up to take steps to get them back towards the labour market. The latter two contingent additions to Rehabilitation Support Allowance would ensure that recipients who complied with these two requirements would receive a higher level of benefit than the current long-term rate of Incapacity Benefit. Those who refused to comply would get the same amount of benefit as unemployed people on JSA.

Topping up benefits for those who comply is presumably seen as a more positive approach than sanctioning people's benefit if they fail to do so: the sanction is presented as a carrot rather than a stick, but financially the result is the same.

Lone parents

The proposed reform of Incapacity Benefit was part of a broader range of measures that was announced in the Department for Work and Pensions' new five-year strategy, set out in a paper entitled *Opportunity and security throughout life* (DWP, 2005). This strategy also described new measures to encourage lone parents back to work. The employment rate for lone parents has risen from 45% in 1997 to 56% in 2004, an increase of just over 11% in seven years, but some way below the government's target of 70% by 2010 (Millar, 2003).

An In-Work Credit (IWC) for lone parents was introduced in three pilot areas in April 2004. This is now to be extended to a further four areas from October 2005. IWC is paid at £40 per week for the first year of the job. In order to qualify for the payment, lone parents must have been in receipt of Income Support (IS) or JSA for at least 12 months and take up a job of at least 16 hours' work per week that is expected to last for a minimum of five weeks. The aim of this payment is to encourage lone parents to take up work and ensure that they are better off than on benefits.

Opportunity and security throughout life (DWP, 2005) also announced that a new Pathways to Work for lone parents pilot scheme was to be introduced in five areas. This scheme will involve a package of measures that includes 'guarantees' about the financial gain from paid work, childcare and ongoing help from advisors. Parents with children over the age of 12 will be required to attend quarterly work-focused interviews. In addition, the government announced an intention to pilot a top-up benefit for lone parents of older children. This £20 per week 'activity premium' will be paid automatically to lone parents with secondary school age children who agree to undertake work-related activity.

Pension reform

In Britain, scarcely a day goes by without the print media carrying stories about the pensions 'crisis', and recent opinion polls suggest that pensions have become a more pressing concern for the public. New Labour has in fact been very active on pension reform, although the overall coherence of their reforms has been questioned (Falkingham and Rake, 2003). As noted earlier, the means-tested pension has been substantially increased. The 'savings credit' component of the new Pension Credit aims to encourage people to save for their retirement and reward those who have done so. In addition, the government has brought in legislation introducing importance changes to pensions in 1999, 2000 and 2004. It also published no less than four Green or White Papers – in 1998, 2002, 2003 and 2004 – setting out its proposals and aspirations for pension provision. In addition, the government commissioned a succession of reviews of different aspects of pension provision. This included reports by Paul Myners on institutional investment (2001), Alan Pickering on simplification of occupational pension schemes (2002) and Ron Sandler on retail savings (2002). An Employers' Task Force has also been established to develop and promote the role of employers in pensions provision.

Finally, following the 2002 pensions Green Paper, the government set up the Pensions Commission "to keep under review the regime for UK private pensions and long-term savings, and to make recommendations to the Secretary of State for Work and Pensions on whether there is a case for moving beyond the current voluntarist approach" (Pensions Commission, 2004, p ix). The Commission is chaired by Adair Turner (Chair of the Low Pay Commission and former Director-General of the Confederation of British Industry) and the other commissioners are Jeannie Drake (Deputy General Secretary of the Communication Workers Union) and John Hills (Professor of Social Policy at the London School of Economics and Political Science). In its first report, the Pensions Commission presented its findings on the pensions and retirement savings system in the UK; a second report is due to be published in late 2005, after the General Election, and will include proposals for reform.

The Pensions Commission's analysis of what is wrong with the UK pensions and retirement savings system covered familiar ground but was comprehensive, incisive and cogently argued. Because of increasing life expectancy and a low birth rate, the population is ageing quickly and the 'dependency ratio' (of pensioners to workers) is rising. The government hopes that, over the long term, private pension provision will become more important than state pensions (DSS, 1998b), thereby using the market to achieve welfare ends (Lewis, 2004; Taylor-Gooby et al, 2004). However, private sector employer contributions to pension schemes are falling and many people are not saving enough to meet their expectations in retirement. Moreover, the pensions system in the UK is 'bewilderingly complex'; it consequently inhibits voluntary saving and increases administrative costs. Housing assets – utilised, for example, via equity release schemes – are likely to make only a modest contribution to income in retirement. Meanwhile, business assets are unequally distributed and will fund the retirement of very few people.

In the light of these problems, and faced with an increasing retirement population, the Pensions Commission argued that society as a whole and individual citizens had to choose from four options: (1) pensioners would become poorer relative to non-pensioners; (2) taxes and National Insurance contributions spent on pensions had to increase; (3) savings must rise; or (4) the age at which people retire must on average rise. The first option was viewed as unattractive, but there are significant barriers facing the other three options.

One of these barriers is public resistance, as illustrated by the trade union protests against recent government proposals to make changes to public sector pensions. The most controversial proposal is to increase the retirement age for public sector pensions by five years, in most cases from 60 to 65. This reform would affect seven million public sector workers, who account for about one in six of the workforce in the UK. In addition, the government has proposed to switch the civil service and NHS schemes from final salary to career average pensions (Inman, 2005; Mulholland, 2005).

The government has been reluctant to embrace compulsion, either on employers or employees, as a way of increasing saving for pension provision. Instead, it has emphasised education about the need to save and about pension products in order to 'empower' individuals and promote 'informed choice' (Mann, 2003). *Opportunity and security throughout life* (DWP, 2005) argued that paid work is the best way to enable people to save for their retirement, and made clear that saving for retirement is central to New Labour's vision of personal responsibility and planning over the lifecycle (cf Mann, 2003). Thus, "saving is being elevated from a private aspiration of the prudent individual to a core duty of the good citizen supported by government" (Hewitt, 2002, p 189).

Public concern about the security of occupational pensions was behind a significant reform that was introduced by the 2004 Pensions Act. Some occupational pension schemes in Britain are underfunded compared with the promises implied in their salary-related pensions. When companies with underfunded schemes go bankrupt, the employees may lose their future pensions. A number of high profile cases have resulted in the government deciding to introduce a compensation scheme based on the US experience. Thus, the 2004 Pensions Act established the Pensions Protection Fund (PPF), with effect from 6th April 2005, which is funded by a risk-based levy charged against all private sector-defined benefit or hybrid occupational pension schemes. Where a company becomes bankrupt after that date and its defined benefit scheme is underfunded, the PPF will provide 100% compensation to people who have reached the scheme's normal retirement age, young people who are already in receipt of pension on ill-health grounds and those in receipt of survivors' benefit. For people under the scheme's normal retirement age, the PPF will generally provide compensation equivalent to 90% of the pension entitlement they have already built up, subject to a cap of £25,000 per annum.

The PPF should provide a new level of security for people in occupational pension schemes, but the scheme is not retrospective. Faced with criticism that the scheme will not help those whose company became bankrupt before the PPF was introduced, the government has introduced an interim £400 million Financial Assistance Scheme (FAS). The FAS will only apply to schemes that began winding up between January 1997 and the introduction of the PPF. Ministers claim that the scheme will ensure that people who were within three years of their scheme pension age on 14 May 2004 will get 80% of their pension entitlement. There have been claims that this 'pensions lifeboat' scheme is underfunded and criticism that it will help only 15,000 of the 65,000 members of collapsed company pension schemes (Collinson, 2005).

Opportunity and security throughout life makes clear that working beyond state pension age will be encouraged and incentivised, as it could make a modest contribution to preventing poverty in retirement (DWP, 2005). The 2004 Pensions Act introduced a new option for the deferral of take-up of the BSP. People who defer their pension for up to five years will be able to opt for a taxable lump sum as an alternative to an enhanced weekly pension. The aim of this change is to further encourage people to stay in work beyond the state pension age. It could particularly benefit women for whom the state retirement age is still 60 years (it will be increased to 65 over a 10-year period from 2010).

The 2004 Civil Partnership Act gave same-sex pensioner couples who have registered a 'civil partnership' the right to receive some of the benefits normally available to married couples. First, private pension providers are now required to provide survivors' benefits to civil partners. Second, where a couple are over state retirement age and one of them dies, the surviving civil partner will be able to gain access to their deceased partner's state pension provision to boost their own entitlement. Third, civil partners under state retirement age are now entitled to bereavement benefit in the event of their partner's death. These rights have not, however, been extended to partners in a cohabiting couple.

Looking to the future, New Labour is considering the idea of a citizens' pension based on residence as a possible long-term replacement for the contributory BSP. The BSP has not been gender neutral in its effects. It has tended to benefit men far more than women, and it has especially penalised those who have worked part time or who have gaps in their employment record due to taking time out to bring up children or to care for frail, chronically sick or disabled people. The replacement of the BSP by a citizenship pension would probably be expensive and there have been hints that anticipated savings from the reform of Incapacity Benefit would help to cover the cost (Collinson, 2005; Wintour and White, 2005).

Reforming Housing Benefit

In April 2005, the government extended to a further nine local authorities the radical reform of Housing Benefit for private tenants that it introduced in nine 'pathfinder' local authority areas in 2003/04. Once the two-year pilot and its evaluation are complete, the reform will be rolled out across the country in 2008. In due course, the new scheme will also be extended to social rented housing, but probably in modified form in order to take account of the allocation and rent-setting regimes in that part of the housing market.

The essential characteristic of the Local Housing Allowance (LHA), as introduced for private tenants in the pathfinder areas, is that the maximum entitlement is no longer based on the claimant's actual rent. Instead, within each local market area there is a standard amount for all claimants, which varies only by household size and composition. However, the income taper used in the current scheme remains in place. The LHA will normally be paid to the claimant rather than the landlord. It will only be paid direct to landlords where tenants are eight or more weeks in arrears or 'vulnerable' and unable to manage their financial affairs. Landlord organisations and pressure groups representing the poor have expressed disquiet about the end of direct payments for Housing Benefit. They claim it will lead to an increase in rent arrears, and hence also in evictions, as tenants may not be trusted to pay the rent themselves.

The rationale for this radical reform is to build choice and responsibility into Housing Benefit (DWP, 2002). The government hopes that the LHA will encourage recipients to make trade-offs between quality and price when looking for accommodation in the rental housing market. It also hopes that the new allowance will empower recipients and encourage them to take responsibility for their budgeting and rent payment obligations. Thus, tenants on Housing Benefit are expected to become active and responsible consumers in the marketplace armed with their LHA, rather than being passive recipients of Housing Benefit that is paid on their behalf directly to the landlord.

The new scheme has other objectives, including most importantly a desire to improve administration. However, while this is an important objective in its own right, a major factor behind the reform is the belief that improving administration will help to remove barriers to work currently facing tenants on benefit. Tenants will be less worried that taking up a job will result in lengthy disruption to the payment of their Housing Benefit, while those who move off the benefit will be less worried about having to pay the rent themselves (DWP, 2005). Thus the work-first welfare agenda is one of the main drivers behind the reform of Housing Benefit.

Conclusion

The key themes that have characterised New Labour's welfare reforms continue to be salient as their second term comes to an end. Although social security has now largely been recast in New Labour's image, modifications and extensions in coverage to their existing reforms, as well as new initiatives, continued to be announced or introduced during 2004. Moreover, it seems that major long-term reforms are possible if New Labour is returned to office. As well as the radical changes to housing benefit, long-term reform of Incapacity Benefit and further reforms of pensions have been promised or raised as a possibility.

What is clear is that paid work has become even more central as New Labour's welfare reforms have unfolded, and it is now predominant. Over time, the social security-claiming process has been made increasingly work-focused. More and more groups of social security claimants have been encouraged, and in some cases subsequently required, to participate in work-focused interviews with personal advisors based in jobcentres. These include lone parents, partners of the unemployed, long-term sick and disabled people on Incapacity Benefit, and even carers in receipt of Carer's Allowance. New Labour seems intent on moving as many people as possible from claimant to worker status (Hewitt, 1999), thereby shifting people into the 'work for those who can' and out of the 'security for those who cannot' category.

The increasing focus on paid work is being twinned with a heightened emphasis on the need for people on benefits to act upon their 'responsibility' to take advantage of the opportunities to move into paid employment or at least to actively search for paid work. To encourage them to do so, welfare benefits are increasingly being made contingent upon work-focused behaviour and subject to sanctions on those who fail to comply or benefit enhancements for those who do. The social security system in Britain can increasingly be described as a work-focused benefit regime.

References

Becker, S. (2003) '"Security for those who cannot": Labour's neglected welfare principle', in J. Millar (ed) *Understanding social security*, Bristol: The Policy Press, pp 103-22.

Bennett, F. (2004) 'Developments in social security', in N. Ellison, L. Bauld and M. Powell (eds) *Social Policy Review 16*, Bristol: The Policy Press/Social Policy Association, pp 45-60.

Blair, T. (1999) 'Beveridge revisited: a welfare state for the 21st century', in R. Walker (ed) *Ending child poverty*, Bristol: The Policy Press, pp 7-18.

Brewer, M., Clark, T. and Wakefield, M. (2002) 'Social security in the UK under New Labour: what did the third way mean for welfare reform?', *Fiscal Studies*, vol 23, no 4, pp 505-37.

Carmel, E. and Papadopoulos, T. (2003) 'The new governance of social security in Britain', in J. Millar (ed) *Understanding social security*, Bristol: The Policy Press, pp 31-52.

Collinson, P. (2005) 'Pensions lifeboat "too small to stay afloat"', *The Guardian*, 3 March, p 22.

Deacon, A. (2002) *Perspectives on welfare*, Buckingham: Open University Press.

DSS (Department of Social Security) (1998a) *New ambitions for our country: A new contract for welfare*, London: The Stationery Office.

DSS (1998b) *Partnership in pensions*, London: The Stationery Office.

DWP (Department for Work and Pensions) (2002) *Building choice and responsibility: A radical agenda for Housing Benefit*, London: DWP.

DWP (2004a) *Building on New Deal: Local solutions meeting individual needs*, London: DWP.

DWP (2004b) '£200 million expansion of successful scheme helping people on Incapacity Benefit get back into work', DWP press release, 2 December.

DWP (2005) *Department for Work and Pensions five year strategy: Opportunity and security throughout life*, London: The Stationery Office.

Evandrou, M. and Falkingham, J. (2004) 'A secure retirement for all? Older people and New Labour', in J. Hills and K. Stewart (eds) *A more equal society? New Labour, poverty, inequality and exclusion*, Bristol: The Policy Press, pp 167-87.

Falkingham, J. and Rake, K. (2003) 'Pension choices for the 21st century: meeting the challenges of an ageing society', in C. Bochel, N. Ellison and M. Powell (eds) *Social Policy Review 15*, Bristol: The Policy Press/ Social Policy Association, pp 197-216.

Ginn, J. (2001) *From security to risk: Pension privatisation and gender inequality*, London: Catalyst.

Heron, E. and Dwyer, P. (1999) 'Doing the right thing: New Labour's attempt to forge a new welfare deal between the individual and the state', *Social Policy and Administration*, vol 33, no 1, pp 91-104.

Hewitt, M. (1999) 'New Labour and social security', in M. Powell (ed) *New Labour, new welfare state*, Bristol: The Policy Press, pp 149-70.

Hewitt, M. (2002) 'New Labour and the redefinition of social security', in M. Powell (ed) *Evaluating New Labour's welfare reforms*, Bristol: The Policy Press, pp 189-209.

Hills, J. (2002) 'Following or leading public opinion? Social security policy and public attitudes since 1997', *Fiscal Studies*, vol 23, no 4, pp 539-58.

Hills, J. and Stewart, K. (2004) 'A tide turned but mountains yet to climb?', in J. Hills and K. Stewart (eds) *A more equal society? New Labour, poverty, inequality and exclusion*, Bristol: The Policy Press, pp 325-46.

HM Treasury (2004) *Child poverty review*, London: HM Treasury.

Hyde, M., Dixon, J. and Joyner, M. (1999) '"Work for those who can, security for those who cannot": the United Kingdom's new social security reform agenda', *International Social Security Review*, vol 52, no 4, pp 69-86.

Inman, P. (2005) 'Public sector pensions cost doubles to £700bn', *Guardian Unlimited* [online], 18 March.

Layard, R. (1997) *What Labour can do?*, London: Warner Books.

Lewis, J. (2004) 'What is New Labour? Can it deliver on social policy?', in J. Lewis and R. Surender (eds) *Welfare state change: Towards a third way?*, Oxford: Oxford University Press, pp 207-27.

Lewis, J. and Surender, R. (2004) (eds) *Welfare state change: Towards a third way?*, Oxford: Oxford University Press.

Lister, R. (2001) 'New Labour: a study in ambiguity from a position of ambivalence', *Critical Social Policy*, vol 21, no 4, pp 425-47.

Mann, K. (2003) 'The schlock and the new: risk, reflexivity and retirement', in C. Bochel, N. Ellison and M. Powell (eds) *Social Policy Review 15*, Bristol: The Policy Press/Social Policy Association, pp 217-38.

75265

Millar, J. (2003) 'The art of persuasion? The British New Deal for lone parents', in R. Walker and M. Wiseman (eds) *The welfare we want? The British challenge for American reform*, Bristol: The Policy Press, pp 115-42.

Millar, J. and Ridge, T. (2002) 'Parents, children, families and New Labour: developing family policy?', in M. Powell (ed) *Evaluating New Labour's welfare reforms*, Bristol: The Policy Press, pp 85-106.

Mulholland, H. (2005) 'Toil and trouble', *Guardian Unlimited* [online], 17 February.

Pensions Commission (2004) *Pensions: Challenges and choices*, London: The Stationery Office.

Powell, M. (1999) 'Introduction', in M. Powell (ed) *New Labour, new welfare state*, Bristol: The Policy Press, pp 1-27.

Powell, M. (2000) 'New Labour and the third way in the British welfare state: a new and distinctive approach?', *Critical Social Policy*, vol 20, no 1, pp 39-60.

Sainsbury, R. (2003) 'Understanding social security fraud', in J. Millar (ed) *Understanding social security*, Bristol: The Policy Press, pp 277-95.

Sefton, T. and Sutherland, H. (2004) 'Inequality and poverty under New Labour', in J. Hills and K. Stewart (eds) *A more equal society? New Labour, poverty, inequality and exclusion*, Bristol: The Policy Press, pp 231-49.

Stewart, K. and Hills, J. (2004) 'Introduction', in J. Hills and K. Stewart (eds) *A more equal society? New Labour, poverty, inequality and exclusion*, Bristol: The Policy Press, pp 1-19.

Sutherland, H., Sefton, T. and Piachaud, D. (2003) *Poverty in Britain: The impact of government policy since 1997*, York: Joseph Rowntree Foundation.

Taylor-Gooby, P. (ed) (2005) *New risks, new welfare*, Oxford: Oxford University Press.

Taylor-Gooby, P., Larsen, T. and Kananen, J. (2004) 'Market means and welfare ends: the UK welfare state experiment', *Journal of Social Policy*, vol 33, no 4, pp 573-92.

Walker, R. (1999) *Ending child poverty: Popular welfare for the 21st century?*, Bristol: The Policy Press.

White, S. (ed) (2001) *New Labour: The progressive future*, Basingstoke: Macmillan.

Wintour, P. and White, M. (2005) 'Citizens' pension plan to lift nearly million out of poverty', *Guardian Unlimited* [online], 29 January.

TWO

New Labour's education policy: innovation or reinvention?

Rob Hulme and Moira Hulme

Introduction

Despite the much-heralded rhetoric of inclusion and social justice, New Labour's education policy since 1997 has lacked genuine innovation. Instead a process of policy development involving the recycling, redefinition and reconstitution of policy ideas and instruments has been evident throughout the government's period in office. Clear continuity with the previous Conservative government's marketisation of education is evident. In a third term, New Labour are committed to accelerating the expansion of specialist schools in the 'post-comprehensive era', including the promotion of City Academies and foundation specialist schools. There is continued focus on 'performativity' with the introduction of School Profiles, the Pupil Achievement Tracker and more tightly focused performance-related pay for an increasingly differentiated school workforce. The return to two-tier learning pathways is signalled in a 14-19 agenda that seeks to strengthen and extend vocational learning in schools and expand the Apprenticeship system.

New Labour's reconstitution of tried and tested policy responses can be partly explained by policy makers' need for instant responses in an era of increasing global policy complexity. This proclivity to present the old as 'new' can also been seen as a means of managing the tensions and contradictions evident in a platform of education reform that is couched in the language of social inclusion, yet extends the market in education and regulates this through ever more intrusive instruments of 'governmentality'. New Labour's laudable focus on interagency working, embedded in the national childcare strategy, Sure Start and Children's Trusts has a compensatory flavour redolent of Fabian concepts of social regulation. The problem of underachievement is often framed by a deficit view of children and families in 'disadvantaged' areas. In tackling social exclusion, anti-inclusive strategies aimed at 're-socialising' and 're-educating' working-class children and their families are consequently deployed (Gewirtz, 2001).

The radical centre ground approach to politics espoused by Giddens (1998) contains an uneasy mixture of market and social democratic values. The social progressivism of New Labour operates within an economic realism that reifies the market concept as an inevitable adjunct of processes of globalisation and modernisation. New Labour's politics of education has shifted during the government's period in office to accommodate a reworking of progressive possibilities that foregrounds personal responsibility and employability. Up-skilling is advanced as both a route from poverty for individuals and a prerequisite of national economic competitiveness. The incorporation of citizenship in the revised national curriculum from September 2002 provides an example of a measure with arguably 'humanistic' and 'social democratic' intent, but which offers an individualised construction of the citizen as 'worker' and 'consumer'. Our review of policy development during 2004 reveals that education policy has served to play out a more directorial conception of citizenship: one in which the 'social' aspects of education are actively suppressed and replaced by tightly defined notions of 'personal' responsibility from early parenthood to bearing the increasing costs of higher education. We argue here that both the primacy of the economic function of education and the personalisation of responsibility are the overarching themes of education policy during 2004.

Employability

The economic function of education in reproducing labour remains a key focus of policy formation. This manifests itself in vocational discourse and has produced policies that respond to identified skills shortages and target sections of the population regarded to be most in need of intervention. A particular interest has been focused on developing key skills and engaging disaffected youth, a theme that intersects with discourses emphasising economic competitiveness and social cohesion. New Labour has encouraged and further developed links with employers in framing its portfolio of policies to tackle the 'skills deficit'. In May 2004, the Chancellor of the Exchequer, Gordon Brown, and the Education and Skills Secretary, Charles Clarke, announced an expansion of the Apprenticeship programme following recommendations made by the Modern Apprenticeship Advisory Committee (Cassels) Report (DfES,

2001) and the Modern Apprenticeship Task Force. The Sector Skills Councils have given employers a much larger role in directly influencing the design, content and entry requirements of Apprenticeships. Charles Clarke commented, "Employers need to know that they will now be in the driving seat". Foundation and Modern Apprenticeships have been diversified to four types: Young Apprenticeships (14-16 years), Pre-Apprenticeships (E2E), Apprenticeships (at NVQ level 2) and Advanced Apprenticeships (at NVQ level 3). The latter two programmes replace the (Foundation and Advanced) Modern Apprenticeship (MA) scheme introduced in 1997. The MA scheme has quickly expanded its provision from 75,800 participants in 1997 to 255,000 in 2004 and, while strengthening the educational content of earlier training initiatives, demonstrates a clear lineage with the policies pursued by successive Conservative administrations (Youth Opportunities Programme [YOP], 1978; Youth Training Scheme [YTS], 1983; Youth Training, 1990).

The Young Apprenticeship scheme was launched in September 2004, and in its first year will offer 1,000 14- to 16-year-old students 50 days of work experience over two years (in Years 10 and 11). The programme offers "industry specific vocational qualifications with employers and training providers" (DfES, 2004) delivered through 40 local partnerships. 'Entry to employment' (E2E), a level 1 programme launched in August 2003, was accessed by 50,000 young people by July 2004, 11% over profile. It targets young people aged 16-18, who may be "disengaged and disenfranchised from learning", and aims to encourage participants to continue to level 2 Apprenticeships, other vocational courses or sustained employment. A training allowance of £40 per week is payable for a minimum of 16 hours' attendance.

The imperative of a strong relationship with employers was also stressed in the final report of the *Working group for 14-19 reform* (Tomlinson Report) (DfES, 2004a), published in October 2004. New Labour expressed growing concern about attainment and retention levels among young people in two key policy documents: *Success for all* (DfES, 2002a) and the government Green Paper, *Extending opportunities, raising standards* (DfES, 2002). Department for Education and Skills (DfES) statistics indicated high drop-out rates with 87% of 16-year-olds remaining in education falling to under 60% at age 17. According to the Organisation for Economic Co-operation and Development (OECD) (2004) figures, participation rates after compulsory education in the UK fall behind many other OECD countries. Seventy-seven per cent of 15- to 19-year-olds remain in full-time education. Only Italy, Luxembourg, Mexico, New Zealand, Portugal, the Slovak Republic and the US have lower participation rates for young people. To improve attendance and retention figures, an Education Maintenance Allowance (EMA) of up to £30 per week was introduced nationally to eligible 16-year-olds from September 2004. Students from households with incomes of £30,000 or less are eligible for means-tested payments of between £10 and £30 paid directly into their bank accounts. In its first year, the DfES estimates that the EMA will allow an additional 35,000 young people to participate in further education, and reduce the number not in education or employment by 9,000. At the launch event for the introduction of the EMA, Charles Clarke announced the government's intention to "replace the culture of dropping out at 16 with the culture of getting on", with the proviso that "you only earn if you learn" (DfES, 2004b). Bonuses of up to £100 are available based on successful completion of programmes of study. The EMA is only payable on evidence of satisfactory attendance with each hour of tuition being signed off by tutors.

The Green Paper consultation process identified an over-burdensome curriculum and an absence of choice as key weaknesses of the curriculum and qualification system and potential barriers to retention and attainment. The government responded by setting out plans for wide ranging reform in *Opportunity and excellence 14-19*, published in January 2003 (DfES, 2003a). From September 2004, Key Stage 4 provides opportunities for work-related learning for all students and fewer compulsory subjects. This builds on the Increased Flexibility Programme (IFP), which currently offers work-related learning opportunities for 14- to 16-year-olds, including vocational GCSEs and the opportunity to attend a college of further education or training provider for one or two days throughout Key Stage 4. The Learning and Skills Council is responsible for both the Young Apprenticeship and Increased Flexibility Programmes. The Tomlinson Report (DfES, 2004a) went on to recommend a diploma framework, encompassing A levels, GCSEs, NVQs and Apprenticeships. The diploma would accommodate four levels: entry, foundation, intermediate and advanced. A common grading system of pass, merit and distinction is suggested (except for entry-level diplomas, which would not be graded). However, radical changes to the qualifications framework are unlikely as any incorporation of the current range of qualifications into a diploma system would be likely to take a decade. The 14-19 agenda raises challenges for the Learning and Skills Sector where lecturers are asked to work with students under 16 without qualified teacher status to work in schools (Initial Teacher Training of further education lecturers is accredited by Standards Verification UK [SVUK], formerly undertaken by the Further Education National Training Organisation [FENTO]), and with significantly lower earnings than their school-based counterparts (although school equivalent salary grades were awarded to further education lecturers in Wales in 2004). The provision of vocational courses in schools raises issues of providing appropriately skilled staff and facilities on site.

Discipline or 'strengthening partnership beyond the classroom'

The government's espoused commitment to stakeholder inclusion and citizenship rights emphasises reciprocal personal responsibility and accountability. This has been a long-standing feature of home–school contracts/agreements. A raft of new legislation has been introduced to reinforce parental responsibility. In February 2004, New Labour announced an extension of its campaign to tackle anti-social behaviour by introducing a range of education-related powers claiming to both support and penalise the parents of errant pupils. Local education authorities (LEAs), youth offending teams, police and the courts are empowered to pursue parenting contracts, parenting orders and penalty notices for truancy and misbehaviour in schools. 'Fast track to prosecution' schemes, which give parents 12 weeks to cooperate or face prosecution, are currently operating in 130 LEAs. These sanctions, which were contained in the 2003 Anti Social Behaviour Act (Home Office, 2003), represent a growing incursion by government into community and family matters. The imprisonment of Oxfordshire parent, Patricia Amos, for the second time over her daughter's truancy in March 2004 received much media attention. In 2003, 5,381 parents were taken to court and 80% were subsequently found guilty. As a result of 'fast tracking' in the first six months of the scheme, 1,490 parents were threatened with prosecution and 739 cases ended in court (DfES, 2003b). Financial penalties and the prosecution process are adding further trauma to parents in crisis, who are often coping on low incomes. Voluntary parenting contracts involve the parents of children who are excluded, or who are 'serial truants', signing a contract with the LEA or school agreeing specific action points designed to improve their child's attendance or behaviour. LEAs can apply through Magistrates' Courts for civil parenting orders against the parents of excluded children (excluded permanently or for two consecutive terms) who are deemed "unwilling to engage with the school or LEA to improve their child's serious misbehaviour" (DfES, 2004c). Failure to attend a parenting course is punishable by a maximum fine of £1,000. Education welfare officers, head teachers and police are empowered to impose penalty notices of up to £100 for truancy, as an alternative to prosecution. The Education Bill (DfES, 2004d) which applies to England and Wales, contains measures to enforce excluded pupils to attend alternative education provision, and introduces additional fines of up to £100 for parents whose children do not attend this alternative provision. The National Attendance and Behaviour Strategy, announced in *Transforming secondary education* (DfES, 2004d, p 32) and funded at a cost of £470 million, also proposes "greater involvement and visibility of police officers in schools.... They organise diversionary activities, resolve conflicts and help to reduce anti-social behaviour".

Interagency working ('joined-up government')

There is a strong emphasis on intervening early in New Labour's portfolio. Key policies for the early years include Sure Start, Educare and Children's Trusts. These policies represent New Labour's espoused commitment to 'joined-up government' in tackling social exclusion. The aim is to provide a 'seamless' provision of services, specifically targeting disadvantaged groups. The Sure Start Unit integrates government policy and services on childcare, early years education, family support, health and employment services. Sure Start provides support for families from pregnancy until the children reach 14 years (or up to 16 years for those with special needs). Sure Start local programmes were launched in 1998, targeting the poorest fifth of wards in the country. There are now 542 programmes including Children's Centres offering a 'one-stop shop' for childcare, early education, family support, health services and employment advice.

A National Audit Office report in February 2004 confirmed significant expansion in childcare and early education in England. Between 1997 and September 2003, 450,000 new childcare places were created (NAO, 2004). In February 2004, 300,000 families were claiming the childcare element of the Working Tax Credit that provides up to 70% of the costs of childcare. According to OECD (2004) figures, 81% of 3- to 4-year-olds take part in education in the UK. In April 2004, the Children's Minister, Margaret Hodge, announced the introduction of free part-time early education places for 3-year-olds, in addition to the existing entitlement for 4-year-olds (introduced in September 1998). The entitlement covers a minimum of five sessions of two and a half hours' provision per week for 33 weeks per year. However, the ratio of students to teaching staff at the pre-primary level in the UK is the highest among OECD countries (27 compared to the OECD average of 15).

Attention had also been focused on availability for employment with a proposed expansion of places that offer integrated 'Educare' (childcare that has education capacity) from 8am until 6pm. The *Five year strategy for children and learners* (DfES, 2004e) has set the target of 1,000 primary schools offering wrap-around childcare by 2008. There is recognition of the need for childcare that allows parents to work – that is, wraps around the school day and is available throughout the year, including school holidays. To this end, the DfES are promoting 'extended schools' open from 8am until 6pm and at weekends, providing breakfast clubs, after-school clubs, family learning and holiday play schemes through partnerships with private providers, the voluntary or community sector and parents' groups.

The commitment to interagency working is enshrined in the *Children's Bill* (DfES, 2004f), which set out plans to create Children's Trusts in every local authority. These trusts involve local partners in education, social care and health, sharing information, assessment, planning and accountability. Collaborative working arrangements are sought between LEAs, Primary Care Trusts, Connexions, Sure Start, youth offending teams and partners in the voluntary and community sectors. Further integration of children's services is set out in the Children's Green Paper, *Every child matters: Change for children*, published in December 2004 (DfES, 2004g).

Personalised learning and performativity

There is a growing emphasis on 'personalised learning' within New Labour discourse. The Prime Minister, Tony Blair introduced the term in his speech to the Labour Party Conference on 30 September 2003: "At secondary school, personalised learning for every child in new specialist schools and City Academies". David Miliband, then School Standards Minister, launched the 'national conversation about personalised learning' (DfES, 2004h) in October 2004. This builds on earlier work emphasising the need to attend to individual learning styles, which led to the popularisation and proliferation of learning styles inventories and assessments first in schools and later in further education colleges. Personalised learning extends the focus on differentiation in teachers' planning. It makes claims to inclusion and the promotion of equal opportunities by addressing the particular needs of every student. It accords with attention to the needs of the 'gifted and talented' as well as support for the less able. Collaboratively produced individual education plans are an established feature of the special educational needs teacher's role and personalised learning draws on this model.

> Personalised learning is not new – many of our best schools and teachers
> are already pioneering this approach – but we are determined to make it
> universal. To make personalised learning the defining feature of our
> education system, a new relationship is required between the Department
> [DfES], local education authorities and schools that brings a sharper
> focus to our work at a national level and strips out clutter and duplication
> through a stronger alignment of all activity in order to release local
> initiative and energy. (David Miliband, 8 January 2004; DfES, 2004h)

This involves a reworking of equality of opportunity as an individual
right to be addressed at an interpersonal rather than social level. Anti-
discriminatory practices move from the level of curriculum reform to
the level of individual target setting and lesson planning, and are closely
tied to tracking and accountability mechanisms. Individual Learning Plans
(ILPs) are used in the Learning and Skills Sector as the basis of learning
contracts between trainees and training providers. This method of target
setting and recording progress is also a feature of Personal Development
Planning (PDP) and Progress Files in higher education. Johnson (2004)
has warned against the commodification of education that is inherent in
prioritising the profiling of attainment:

> The government must also recognise the negative impact of a further
> stress on individual academic attainment as the purpose of schools. There
> is always a need to balance this against the social purposes of schools, in
> terms both of pupils learning social skills and also of their wider aims
> such as the inculcation of values and the promotion of social cohesion.
> Talk of personalised learning increases the perception of schooling as a
> commodity, but centre-left governments should stress its vital contribution
> to society as a whole. (Johnson, 2004, p 18)

Tracking of student attainment contributes to a culture of performativity
in schools and colleges. New Labour now advocates 'intelligent
accountability' in the form of a lighter touch, but a more regular inspection
regime and the introduction of a public annual School Profile to
complement performance table data and replace the school governors'
annual report. More frequent and short notice inspections were announced
in the *Five year strategy for children and learners* (DfES, 2004e). From
September 2005, Ofsted and the Adult Learning Inspectorate will give
schools and colleges three weeks' notice of the date of their inspection.
Light touch inspections will be given to institutions that previously
achieved high grades in the areas of leadership and management and

curriculum. The new School Profile incorporates self-evaluation based on data on students' attainment and progress, Ofsted assessment and comparisons with schools in similar contexts. Through this initiative, accountability is conflated with and justifies the drive for choice and diversity:

> School performance data in raw and value added terms is here to stay.
> Parents have the right to this information, we cannot return to a world
> where Ministers, officials and teachers know the performance of schools,
> but the public do not. (David Miliband, 8 January 2004; DfES 2004i)

Reforming secondary education

New Labour have escalated the re-stratification of state schooling in the 'post-comprehensive era' (Tony Blair, Labour Party Conference, 2002). Despite David Blunkett's proclamation at the 1995 Labour Party Conference, "Let me say this very slowly indeed. In fact, you can watch my lips. No selection either by examination or interview under a Labour government", admission by selection has increased and is likely to increase further. There are no plans to seek the abolition of the 164 remaining state-funded grammar schools in England in the five-year plan (DfES, 2004e). Since Labour came to power in 1997, grammar school places have increased by 22,029 (although they are excluded from plans to allow popular schools to expand). Independent specialist schools are able to select 10% of entrants on the basis of ability. Gewirtz et al (1995) have highlighted the inequities created by 'open enrolment' within a local hierarchy of schools. Skilled choosers, who are able to demonstrate the 'right' address or faith to their advantage, present themselves appropriately at 'informal' interviews, and are better able to meet the costs of travel and the increasingly prevalent 'voluntary deed of covenant'. Middle-class parents are thus able to draw on material advantages and cultural capital in exploiting the education market.

With the promotion of independent specialist schools, New Labour is seeking to abolish the comprehensive system in its third term. In 2002, Estelle Morris, then Education Secretary, attacked the 'sameness' of comprehensives that 'confused excellence with elitism' and argued for modernising reform: "We have to get away from the perception that one-size fits all schools and of ready-to-wear, off-the-shelf comprehensives". The 'specialist schools' programme was initiated by the Conservative administration in 1994 and adopted by New Labour to extend diversity and parental preference (if not choice). It allows schools with particular areas of curriculum expertise additional resources to develop and share this expertise. In December 2004, there were 1,953 specialist schools (62% of all secondary schools). There are now 10 categories of specialist school: Technology, Language, Arts, Sports, Business and Enterprise, Engineering, Mathematics and Computing, Science, Humanities (including History, Geography, English) and Music. Schools can also combine any two specialisms. In order to help them develop their specialism, specialist schools receive additional funding of £100,000 for a capital project to enhance the facilities in the subjects related to the school' specialism, and recurrent funding of around £123 per pupil per year for four years to implement their specialist school development plan. The application process involves raising £50,000 in private sector sponsorship (less for schools with under 500 pupils) and producing a four-year school and community development plan. Continued funding is dependent on satisfying ambitious targets for improvements in attainment. The DfES has set the target of supporting at least 2,000 specialist schools by 2006. The *Five year strategy* (DfES, 2004e) indicates that by 2008 every 'performing school' will be a specialist school.

In addition to specialist schools and the residual "bog standard comprehensive" (famously dismissed by Alistair Campbell, the Prime Minister's former spokesperson, at the launch of the government's five-year plan for secondary education in February 2001), the education market accommodates the further honorific title of 'Beacon Schools' and the proposed 'Foundation Specialist Schools'. The Beacon school programme was initiated in 1998 and will be phased out in August 2005. The DfES has identified 266 Beacon schools as among the best performing schools in the country, with examples of successful practice that are deemed worth sharing. They are given additional resources to engage in work with a 'family' of schools to 'share best practice' and 'drive innovation'. The proposed 'ultra-free', 'super foundation schools' are high performing specialist schools whose governing body has voted to take full control and responsibility for decisions relating to assets, land, pay and staffing, including shedding some aspects of the national curriculum. In effect, these will be independent specialist schools within the state sector and have aroused similar criticism from unions to that levelled against foundation hospital trusts.

A new 'Leading Edge Programme' (formerly the 'Advanced Schools Programme', designed to replace Beacon schools) was announced in *Transforming secondary education* (DfES, 2004d). Independent schools are invited to participate in this programme to facilitate cross-sectoral learning. Schools that make a successful bid will be rewarded with £60,000 per year to support their work in accelerating the improvement efforts of networked schools. The sharing of best practice that was a feature of the specialist schools movement has been extended to the current advocacy of 'federations of schools'. Federations promote collaboration across clusters of schools and might involve "employing chief executives, sharing governing bodies and/or governing body committees, establishing formal or semi-formal contracts to raise standards" (DfES, 2004d, p 19). Thus federations can be funded as if they were a single institution. Collaboration is also sought through the continuation and development of the 'Networked Learning Communities' programme, launched in 2002, which supports clusters of between six and 15 schools working in partnership; and the 'Excellence in Cities' (EiC) programme, which encourages partnerships in disadvantaged areas (41 Education Action Zones will become 'Excellence' clusters by 2006 as they come to the end of their statutory lifespan). An evaluation of EiC by Ofsted (2003) found limited evidence of impact on pupil attainment in inner city schools. Partnership work is less effective in a competitive local arena.

Details of the 'Building schools for the future' programme were unveiled in February 2004. Fourteen LEA projects involving 180 schools are involved in the programme, which is supported by £2.2 billion capital investment in 2005-06. Some of this funding is allotted to the building of new City Academies, building on the previous Conservative administration's commitment to City Technology Colleges (CTCs) sponsored by business in 1988. The first three City Academies opened in 2002. The DfES aims to have 33 open by 2006 with a total of 200 planned by 2010 to replace underachieving schools or those in special measures. Only 15 CTCs were established and several of these are considering transferring to Academy status. The costs of establishing Academies is indeed high – double the costs of building a comprehensive school. So far, £425 million has been spent on 17 Academies (Smithers, 2004). Influenced by the American charter school movement, the City Academies represent a further significant erosion of a locally administered system of education.

Imperative of leadership: decentralised decision making

Pressure to achieve high stakes performance targets encourages increasing regulation, surveillance and monitoring of teachers' work – an explicit focus on the productivity dimensions of the school's role. A consequence of such commodification is that the teacher is recast as technician, accountable for delivery of productivity targets, and school leaders are re-oriented to develop skills in 'people technology' (Morgan, 1997). Managerial techniques are employed to reinforce external directives over what is taught and how it should be taught, but also to influence how teachers think about appropriate educational goals and the means to achieve them. Values and relationships are re-orientated – from the collective to the individual, public to institutional, collaboration to competition (Gewirtz et al, 1995). The dislocation of the school from its locality in terms of accountable local governance and community participation creates a reorientation of values to promote self-regulation and internal cohesion.

Leadership is seen as vital in tackling underachievement. In *Transforming secondary education* (DfES, 2004d, p 4) Charles Clarke announced that "the 1,400 secondary schools in the toughest areas will get a grant of £125,000 per year to improve leadership at all levels; we will continue action to deal with – and where necessary close – the poorest schools and replace the weakest heads". He goes on to argue, "Specialist schools have been successful first and foremost because they have provided a means for inspirational head teachers to forge a distinctive mission and ethos which is right for their school" (DfES, 2004d, p 8). The DfES (2004d, p 6) is keen to promote the view that schools can make a difference irrespective of circumstances, arguing that there is "four times as much variation in pupil attainment *within* schools as there is *between* schools". Yet those sections of the school population identified as most at risk of underachievement follow familiar patterns: cared for children, from some minority ethnic groups, and poorer backgrounds. The government continues to fuel the moral panic over boys' achievement and this can be related to the subsequent emphasis on vocational learning. The view that "Excellent schools have excellent leaders" (DfES, 2004d, p 10) is embedded in the development of the National College of School Leadership (NCSL), established following the 1998 Green Paper, *Teachers meeting the challenge of change* (DfEE, 1998). According to OECD (2004) figures, decision making in English schools has been decentralised to a far greater extent than in other OECD countries: 85% of decisions are taken at a local level compared to an OECD average of 42%.

Education workers: reform of the school workforce

The re-stratification of the state sector has been accompanied by increasing differentiation within the education workforce. In January 2003, the government, employers and unions signed an agreement signalling workforce reform. In *Transforming secondary education* (2004d, p 4), the

DfES announced its intention to "reform the way the school team works to allow teachers more time to teach and schools to use a wider range of skilled staff". This 'school workforce remodelling' is premised on a reduction in teachers' workload and bureaucracy, and an attendant recruitment of an extra 10,000 teachers and at least an extra 50,000 support staff by 2005. Schools now have the freedom to "make use of available national pay flexibilities by giving additional main scale points for excellence, or offering recruitment and retention allowances; to develop models for the most effective use of teaching assistants under current and planned regulations; to employ teachers without qualified teacher status in some circumstances" (DfES, 2004d, p 22). In other words, head teachers have substantially increased devolved powers over workforce deployment and pay (raising issues regarding their training needs in linking performance with pay). Performance-related pay was introduced in England with the introduction of the Upper Pay Scale in September 2000; since then, 259,000 teachers have passed through the 'threshold', which is now assessed at school level rather than validated externally by trained assessors. An analysis of pay scales in 2003 by the OECD (2004, p 5) revealed that primary and secondary teachers' pay scales were 'comparatively flat' with few financial incentives for experienced teachers to stay in the profession. Fast tracking of aspirant trainees was introduced in 2002 with 1,200 teachers and trainees within the scheme by September 2004. Following the recommendation of the School Teachers' Review Body (DfES, 2004j), the 'Excellent Teacher Scheme' from September 2005 was announced. Under the new pay award scheme, the Upper Pay Scale (UPS) ends at UPS3 and progression on the main scale will be even more closely tied to performance. The pay scales of Advanced Skills Teachers are reduced and aligned with the first 18 points of the leadership spine. There were 4,400 Advanced Skills Teachers in January 2004.

Increased autonomy raises issues for workers whose services are contracted out. A 'Best value code of practice' to protect school support workers in the maintained sector came into force in April 2005, following union concerns of a two-tier workforce emerging between local authority and contract workers. The DfES and the Learning and Skills Council are promoting training for school support staff. The Learning and Skills Council enrolled 10,000 support workers on recognised courses in 2004, with a target of 20,000 in subsequent years.

Higher education: the graduate contribution scheme

New Labour set the target of 50% of young people participating in higher education by 2010. The widening participation agenda was faced with a government funding system geared for much smaller recruitment figures. Unlike Canada, New Zealand and the US, UK universities cannot rely on students, donations or other non-government resources to subsidise the proposed expansion. New Labour has pushed for funding higher education by individual loans rather than taxes (DfES, 2003c). In 1998, student grants were replaced with loans and the introduction of tuition fees. The 2004 Higher Education Bill subsequently empowered universities to charge variable fees for courses within (as well as between) universities of up to £3,000 per year from September 2006. This reflects a commitment to redistribution over the course of a person's lifetime rather than at the point of entrance to higher education (Barr, 2003). Fees will be capped at this upper limit until 2010. This system of student support replaces upfront tuition fees of around £1,200 per year for full-time students. Graduates will repay government loans through the tax system when they start to earn a salary of £15,000 or more (with effect from April 2005). From 2006, parents will not have to pay fees at any time and the poorest 30% of full-time students will be supported by £3,000 non-repayable support each year. Universities wishing to charge above the standard rate are required to establish an access agreement with the Director of Fair Access to Higher Education, which spells out the universities' strategy to attract and support students from non-traditional backgrounds (groups under-represented at university). Students are expected to carry a greater proportion of the costs of higher education as it is argued that they benefit most. Announcing the scheme, Charles Clarke proclaimed, "Higher education will now be free at the point of entrance and fair at the point of repayment, a fair and affordable option for students from all backgrounds" (DfES, 2004k). Graduate earnings are 59% higher on average than those without post-compulsory education (OECD, 2004); however, this masks significant variations that reflect the complex relationships between social class, gender, age and ethnicity.

> We have taken tough decisions because it is absolutely vital for the economic success of this country that we have the best educated and highly skilled workforce, and that means expanding higher education. We can't sustain a 21st century higher education system with a 20th-century funding model. (Kim Howells, Lifelong Learning, Further and Higher Education Minister, DfES, 2004l)

Conclusion

Our review of New Labour's education policies over 2004 has revealed a plethora of initiatives in which some 'new' rhetoric has been used to promote some very enduring themes in education. Throughout the sectors, policy resonates with Tomlinson's (2001, p 271) observation that "education had become a prop for a global market economy, a competitive enterprise in which the rhetoric of 'opportunities for the many' covered the retreat of policies promoting social justice and equity".

The enduring primacy of the economic function has been evidenced in the burgeoning spread of the education market. The progressive dismantling of comprehensive education and the reinvention of grammar schools as specialist schools and the Conservatives' business-funded CTCs as City Academies represent one aspect of this process. As we have seen, the marketisation of schools as workplaces has gathered pace with the further individualisation of teachers' work. 'Economising' post-compulsory and higher education in developing the skills market has been emphasised through initiatives that promise 'success for all' and 'extended opportunity', but which in reality replicate the differentiation and specialisation established in the school sector.

The gap between the policy rhetoric and the reality of lived experience is still greater within those initiatives designed to personalise responsibility in education. It has become a policy domain in which conceptions of education as 'humanistic' have been lost in rhetorical smokescreens about parental and individual responsibility, and 'socially progressive' themes such as equality of opportunity have been reinterpreted as individual targets and measures of personal accountability based on neo-Fabian notions of socially acceptable behaviour.

References

Ball, S.J. (2004) 'Performativities and fabrications in the education economy', in S.J. Ball (ed) *The reader in sociology of education*, London: RoutledgeFalmer, pp 143-55.

Barr, N. (2003) 'Financing higher education in the UK: the 2003 White Paper', Paper presented for the House of Commons Education and Skills Committee, Session 2002-03 (www.econ.lse.ac.uk/staff/nb/ Barr_Selcom030311.pdf), accessed 20 January 2005.

Brown, P. and Lander, H. (eds) (1992) *Education for economic survival: From Fordism to post-Fordism?*, London: Routledge.

Brown, P. and Lander, H. (1997) 'Education, globalisation and economic development', in A.H. Halsey, H. Lander, P. Brown and A. Stuart Wells *Education, culture, economy and society*, Oxford: Oxford University Press.

DfEE (1998) *Teachers meeting the challenge of change*, London: The Stationery Office.

DfES (Department for Education and Skills) (2001) *Modern apprenticeships: The way to work*, Modern Apprenticeship Advisory Committee (Cassels) Report, London: The Stationery Office, 30 October.

DfES (2002a) *Success for all: Reforming further education and training*, London: DfES.

DfES (2002b) *14-19 Extending opportunities, raising standards*, Consultation Paper, Cm 5342, London: The Stationery Office.

DfES (2003a) *Opportunity and excellence 14-19*, White Paper, London: The Stationery Office.

DfES (2003b) 'Tackling truancy: effective support, efficient sanctions', DfES press release 2003/0132.

DfES (2003c) *The future of higher education*, Cm 5735, London: The Stationery Office.

DfES (2004a) *Working group for 14-19 reform*, (Tomlinson Report), London: The Stationery Office.

DfES (2004b) 'Education maintenance allowance now available nationwide', DfES press release 2004/0053.

DfES (2004c) 'Anti-social behaviour powers to offer parents support and sanction', DfES press release 2004/0031.

DfES (2004d) *Transforming secondary education*, London: The Stationery Office.

DfES (2004e) *Five year strategy for children and learners: Putting people at the heart of public services (2005-2010)*, London: The Stationery Office.

DfES (2004f) *The Children's Bill*, 3 March, London: The Stationery Office.

DfES (2004g) *Every child matters: Change for children*, Green Paper, London: The Stationery Office.

DfES (2004h) 'Personalised learning: a national conversation', DfES press release 2004/0171.

DfES (2004i) 'Personalised learning: building a relationship with schools', DfES press release 2004/0002.

DfES (2004j) *School teachers' pay and conditions and guidance on school teachers' pay and conditions*, London: The Stationery Office.

DfES (2004k) 'Future of universities secured today as Higher Education Act is approved by Parliament', DfES press release 2004/0127.

DfES (2004l) 'Student class of 2006 to receive real terms increase in maintenance support', DfES press release 2004/0205.

Gewirtz, S. (2001) 'Cloning the Blairs: New Labour's programme for the re-socialisation of working class parents', *Journal of Educational Policy*, vol 16, no 4, pp 365-78.

Gewirtz, S., Ball, S.J. and Bowe, R. (1995) *Markets choice and equity in education*, Buckingham: Open University Press.

Giddens, A. (1998) *The third way: The renewal of social democracy*, Cambridge: Polity.

Home Office (2003) *The Anti Social Behaviour Act*, London: The Stationery Office.

Johnson, M. (2004) *Personalised learning: An emperor's outfit?*, London: Institute for Public Policy Research.

Morgan, G. (1997) *Images of organization*, Thousand Oaks, CA: Sage Publications.

Morris, E. (2002) 'Why comprehensives must change: schools have to modernise and offer children specialist education tailored to individual needs', *The Observer*, 23 June.

NAO (National Audit Office) (2004) *Early years: Progress in developing high quality childcare and early education accessible to all*, HC268, Session 2003/2004, 27 February, London: The Stationery Office.

OECD (Organisation for Economic Co-operation and Development) (2004) *Education at a glance 2004*, Paris: OECD.

Ofsted (Office for Standards in Education) (2003) *Excellence in cities and Education Action Zones: Management and impact*, ref HMI 1399, London: Ofsted.

Smithers, R. (2004) 'Flagship schools attacked over cost', *The Guardian*, 31 August (http://education.guardian.co.uk/newschools/story/0,14729.1293909,00.html), accessed 20 April 2005.

Tomlinson, S. (2001) 'Education policy, 1997-2000: the effects on top, bottom and middle England', *International Studies in Sociology of Education*, vol 11, no 3, pp 261-77.

THREE

Transforming the NHS: the story in 2004

Rudolf Klein

Introduction

In a triumphalist pre-Christmas message to the National Health Service (NHS), Sir Nigel Crisp proclaimed 2004 to have been "a very good year of sustained progress" (Crisp, 2004, p 1). Not only had the dividends of investing in the NHS become apparent, the NHS' Chief Executive reported, but waiting lists had been further reduced, premature deaths from cancer, heart disease and suicide had continued to fall, and a record number of people had quit smoking. Most importantly, though, the foundations had been laid for the transformation of the NHS: "We are changing the whole way the NHS works to ensure that everything we do fits around the individual needs of our patients and public" (Crisp, 2004, p 1). New policy initiatives in 2004 included the first wave of Foundation Trusts ("local organisations to address local needs" [Crisp, 2004, p 1]), a wider range of providers ("to bring in new ideas and create flexibility" [Crisp, 2004, p 1]), new employment contracts ("enabling us to have more staff, working differently" [Crisp, 2004, p 1]) and the introduction of a new inspectorate ("which will ... drive up standards and enable patients to be assured of the quality of care they receive" [Crisp, 2004, p 1]).

The transformation has, of course, been long in the making, as last year's *Social Policy Review* noted (Allsop and Baggott, 2004). It has involved a step-by-step retreat from Labour's 1997 model of the NHS: a model which, for the first time in the history of the NHS, allowed central government to command and control instead of merely exhorting and hoping (Klein, 2001). It has meant, conversely, a move towards a pluralistic, quasi-market model driven by consumer choice and shifting power to the periphery, where the role of central government increasingly becomes regulatory rather than managerial: setting priorities and targets, but allowing local discretion in the way these are achieved. In 2004, the two models were still coexisting: the Department of Health (DH) was in effect using its command and control powers to drive through the changes meant, in theory at any rate, to make these powers largely redundant – much as Mrs Thatcher's administration centralised in the 1990s in order to introduce its mimic market. However, as 2004 ended and a General Election loomed, government rhetoric emphasised change rather than continuity: few if any linguistic nods to Bevan's legacy (the 1997 model) but an insistence that the NHS was an exemplar of how reinvented public services could satisfy public expectations in the 21st century.

There is, inevitably, something artificial about concentrating on events in one specific year: a clip from a film that is still running and where the audience are left wondering how it will end. Moreover, 2004 was not a year of major policy initiatives. True, the DH continued to suffer – as in past years and like many other government departments – from initiative incontinence, inflicting initiative fatigue on bystanders. Concern about hospital infections and MRSA (methicillin resistant staphylococcus aureus) alone produced a series of initiatives. As the Secretary of State for Health, John Reid, memorably put it, "In the battle against the superbug I leave no stone unturned" (Reid, 2004). But, as far as the direction of government's strategy was concerned, there were no changes. The story of 2004, in policy terms, is about the working through of decisions previously taken. So, all the examples of transformative action cited by Nigel Crisp – quoted earlier – represented the putting into effect of legislation or decisions taken in previous years. Policy making was of the 'darning socks' variety (Klein and Marmor, forthcoming) – that is, filling in holes in existing policies as these revealed themselves in the process of implementation. The resurrection in 2004 of general practitioner (GP) fundholding – abolished in 1997 – is a case in point: a response, as we shall see, to a problem thrown up by other policies.

What follows is an analysis of evolving policy, organised around analytic themes and selective rather than comprehensive in the issues and initiatives covered. We begin by discussing what 2004 taught us about the lynchpin of the government's strategy for the NHS: expanding capacity. Subsequent sections examine developments in changing the NHS' institutional dynamics, regulatory framework and population health policies. The focus throughout is on the NHS in England: devolution has meant that, in many ways, Scotland and Wales have gone their own way (Greer, 2004).

Expanding capacity, improving performance

If an unprecedented rise in the NHS budget could be directly translated into public satisfaction, the NHS would now be riding a wave of unprecedented enthusiasm. Central to the government's strategy has been the expansion of NHS capacity: that is, the resources required to cut waiting times, improve standards and introduce patient choice. And the government has indeed increased the NHS' ability to expand capacity by pouring in extra billions. Over the past seven years, the NHS budget has grown from £33 billion to £67.4 billion, from £680 to £1,345 per head of population – a dramatic rise even in real terms, given that inflation was low throughout this period. In 2003-04 alone, an extra £5.9 million was ploughed into the service. Yet the impact on public attitudes towards the NHS appears to have been marginal. In December 2002, MORI asked about people's expectations for the NHS over the next few years. At the end of November 2004, the same exercise was repeated. In 2002, 30% of respondents expected the NHS to get much better, 30% expected it to stay the same and 25% expected it to get worse. In 2004 the figures were respectively 26%, 35% and 26%. The proportions expecting the NHS to get much better or much worse remained the same in both years at 3% and 7% respectively (MORI, 2004). So, seemingly, all the extra spending did not produce a commensurate public opinion dividend for the government in 2004.

Not too much should be made, perhaps, of surveys asking the population at large generalised questions about the NHS. Notoriously, opinions tend to be more favourable among those who have used the NHS. National surveys asking acute hospital patients about their experiences indicated an increase of 4% between 2001 and 2004 in those rating the service as excellent. Clearly, critical views often reflect not direct experience but the picture held out by the media: a picture that tends to highlight failure rather than success (and medical moans rather than ministerial messages). However, the disparity between the overwhelmingly impressive litany of official statistics and continued public scepticism prompts a puzzle. If the unprecedented rise in the NHS budget failed to translate into anything like an equivalent leap in public satisfaction, however ambiguous an indicator this may be, was it because the increased expenditure did not fully translate into performance? Might it be that the public, while fully conscious that the NHS was indeed improving, yet felt that the improvements fell short of the expectations cranked up by ministers? These were questions which, in various forms, got a considerable airing in 2004, with some disagreement about the ways of measuring capacity, much discussion about how to measure performance, and debate about how to assess whether the nation was getting value for its money.

The Chief Executive's 2004 report to the NHS, already cited (Crisp, 2004) was indeed a litany of statistical achievements. Increasing capacity had lead to increasing activity, thereby improving accessibility (as reflected in falling waiting lists) and availability of new services (as shown, for example, in the growth of Independent Treatment Centres specialising in elective surgery). Since 1999, 56,700 more nurses, 5,400 more consultants and 1,900 more GPs had been added to the NHS workforce. Of the extra £5.9 billion flowing into the NHS in 2003-04, 45% went towards extra staff, more activity and an increasing drug budget. Another 31%, however, was accounted for by pay increases, a reminder that a substantial proportion of the extra billions has funded not extra capacity or extra activity but higher rewards for those working in it. In the case of some notoriously low-paid NHS workers (a category that does not include doctors), these may well have been necessary to attract extra recruits. However, the extent to which better pay creates higher morale, and higher morale in turn produces better performance, remains a matter of conjecture.

Further, some of the statistics of extra capacity need qualification. In the case of hospital medical manpower, the European Work Directive limiting permissible working hours has, in effect, meant that each doctor now contributes fewer hours to patient care than in the past (and that consultants have had to take over some of the responsibilities previously carried by junior doctors). Moreover, the profession successfully defeated the government's first attempt to negotiate a contract that would have given managers greater control over consultants and first call on their spare time, so increasing NHS capacity. The new consultant contract that has now been introduced is a much watered down version: it demonstrated that "temporarily at least, the demand for clinical autonomy (defined as the absence of detailed and effective local management of activity and outcomes) has triumphed" (Maynard and Bloor, 2003, p 5), which is no doubt one reason why the government continues to stress the role of the private sector. If the NHS cannot get a grip on the spare-time activities of its consultants, at least it can buy them from the same doctors working in the private sector. More important, perhaps, is the calculation that the private sector will bring in scarce medical manpower from Europe and elsewhere, as well as capital: by the end of 2005, it is expected that 34 of the 46 NHS' Independent Treatment Centres – providing diagnostic tests as well as elective surgery – will be provided by the private sector.

In the case of general practice, the fast-rising proportion of women GPs has in turn meant a rising proportion in the numbers working part time. On a straight head count, there has been a 2% fall in average list sizes in England over the past decade, from 1,763 to 1,695. But, when the figures are recalculated to allow for the hours actually committed, there has actually been a similar 2% increase in average list sizes, from 1,808 to 1,841 (RCGP, 2004a, p 4). In the same period, the real and substantial increase – of more than 10% – has been in the number of practice nurses and other staff. So, on balance, the government's claim that access to primary care has improved is sustainable, particularly if account is taken of the role of walk-in centres and NHS Direct, although possibly access to individual GPs in person may have become slightly more difficult. Further, it looks set to become more difficult still with the introduction of the new GP contract in 2004. Apart from giving GPs a large pay rise, the contract has two main characteristics (RCGP, 2004b). First, it links rewards to quality: pay will be linked to 76 indicators of quality, such as the proportion of patients whose blood pressure is recorded annually. Second, it allows GPs much more freedom to decide what services to offer and gives them the right to opt out from providing, for example, night cover – services that become the responsibility of the local Primary Care Trust. So, for patients there seems to be a trade-off: better access to primary care, on the one hand, but, on the other, access to a different kind of primary care than in the past: walk-in clinics and NHS Direct, for example. While choice of hospital is set to expand (see later), choice of GP could become more restricted.

Trade-offs of this kind compound the long-recognised and much discussed (Powell, 1997) problems of drawing up any kind of balance sheet for the NHS, whether in 2004 or over time. Given its heterogeneity and the variability within it, the NHS is an organisation where it is possible to make two contradictory statements about its achievements (or lack of them) and both will be true. As the chairman of the Healthcare Commission, Sir Ian Kennedy, pointed out in his foreword to its 2004 *State of healthcare report* (Healthcare Commission, 2004a, p 2): "It is tempting to offer some pithy, overarching assessment: that the NHS is this or that. This is a temptation that we should avoid. The NHS is very large and complex. It does not lend itself to some general judgment". In any case, any assessment of the NHS is bound to be multidimensional. It cannot be assumed, when interpreting public attitudes and survey results, that the criteria conventionally used in academic analysis – such as equity and efficiency – have general resonance. As patients, we are probably less concerned about whether doctors are following the National Institute of

Clinical Excellence's guidelines when prescribing than about the time it has taken to see them and the way in which they and their staff behave.

So, the question of whether the rate and scale of the improvements in performance – such as those listed by Nigel Crisp and ministers – match the rate and scale at which more money has been flooding into the NHS remains unanswered, because it is probably unanswerable. More amenable to analysis is the narrower (but still difficult) question of whether the extra flow of funds into the NHS has produced a commensurate increase in outputs. Here 2004 was characterised by statistical revisionism. Following the Atkinson review of measurements of government output and productivity, the Office for National Statistics (ONS, 2004) produced a set of revised statistical estimates. These suggested that the NHS rate of change in productivity (the ratio of outputs to inputs) has been falling since the mid-1990s. From being positive, it became negative at the turn of the millennium. This implies that the NHS has been getting less efficient, but two caveats need to be borne in mind. First, the output estimates do not capture quality change. Second, the pre-1995 period of rising productivity may have reflected once and for all changes in medical technology, such as new anaesthetics and minimally invasive surgery (Smee, 2005).

Given this mixed picture, it is therefore not surprising that government policy in 2004 continued to put the emphasis on changing the dynamics of the NHS, the theme of the next section. Since the Chancellor of the Exchequer's generosity to the NHS cannot be expected to continue for ever with mounting pressure on public finances, it clearly becomes all the more important to ensure that resources are used efficiently and effectively.

Changing the institutional dynamics

The emerging institutional architecture of the NHS rests on three pillars. The first is devolution from the centre and accountability to local people, a policy theme that first emerged strongly when the then Secretary of State for Health, Alan Milburn, announced his conversion to localism (Milburn, 2003). The second is patient choice, a theme that has emerged fortissimo with the approach of a General Election. The third is a new system for paying providers that began to be introduced in 2004, a low-profile technical change that has considerable long-term implications. The model represents not some immaculate conception, sprung from the heads of the policy makers at the centre in a visionary moment, but rather reflects an evolutionary process over the past seven years, building on successes and learning from failure (Stevens, 2004). The language of cooperation has given way to the language of incentives. A plurality of providers will compete, with money following patients. However, not all has changed. The result is a policy layer cake with elements from different eras – Dobsonian, Milburnian and Reidian – coexisting, not always coherently or comfortably as we shall see. In policy analysis terms, the evolution offers an example less of path dependency (Tuohy, 1999) than of social learning (Heclo, 1974).

Foundation Trusts (FTs), the first 20 of which were launched in 2004, are the children of the new enthusiasm for devolution. FT status allows providers – acute hospitals in the first instance – to transform themselves into mutuals: that is, a new form of social ownership, modelled on cooperative societies, where control passes in theory at least to the local community. Public and patients, forming self-selected constituencies, elect a majority of the Boards of Governors. Once in existence, FTs have considerable freedom and flexibility in access to capital and use of resources, although much less than the government originally intended before being forced to bow to back-bench pressure. The legislation setting them up also makes it clear that they remain part of the NHS with an obligation to provide an appropriate range of services. However, they are accountable not to the DH but to a newly created Regulator, now styled Monitor, of FTs as well as to the local community.

Tensions in the new system, reflecting perhaps a lack of coherence in the design, became apparent even before the FTs were formally launched, and continued thereafter. Implicit in their design is the assumption that there is a public demand for involvement in the running of the NHS: that public and patients want to sign up as voting members of FTs. The results of the first round of elections put a question mark against that assumption. Some FTs did indeed drum up a respectable membership of 10,000 or more (Monitor, 2004a). But, in other cases, they found it difficult to scrape up more than 2,000. Examples of uncontested elections were frequent. Public apathy may yield to public interest as FTs settle down and become more visible. But, if the public appetite for involvement is indeed limited, it may become necessary to reconsider some of the legacies of previous policy eras. So, for example, is it really necessary to have Patient Forums even in institutions with elected governors? And, with increasing choice offering an exit option to users in a pluralistic healthcare universe, is voice as important as it was in the days of hierarchic paternalism? These are questions that the DH may already privately have asked itself since, as part of its economy-driven slaughter of arm's length agencies (DH, 2004a), it abolished the Commission for Patient and Public Involvement.

The other tension may be between accountability to the local community and accountability to the Monitor. The point was illustrated by the case of Bradford Teaching Hospitals NHS Foundation Trust. In December, the Monitor removed the Bradford Board's chairperson and replaced him with a nominee of its own. The reason was that the hospital had run up a forecast deficit of £11.3 million – in place of a forecast surplus – and had failed to come up with a credible or adequate recovery plan (Monitor, 2004b). The Board of Governors had previously passed a vote of confidence in their chairperson. So, in a sense, the Monitor was overriding the local community's representatives – but, given that Bradford had managed to muster a mere 1,153 members for its elections, it may be doubted how far the Board spoke for that community. And there remains the further question of whether representativeness (however defined) can or should override competence and expertise.

Nor are relations with central government easy. On the one hand, the Secretary of State announced that he would no longer answer parliamentary questions about the day-to-day operations of FTs: an important act of distancing the centre from the coal face, given that much ministerial intervention takes place in the name of parliamentary accountability. On the other hand, however, the Foundation Trust Network managed to capture front-page headlines (Carvel, 2004) with an attack on the DH for excessive red tape and inadequate flexibility. So, one unintended consequence of the government's policies is to have created a well-funded lobby of semi-independent NHS barons with the capacity and willingness to embarrass ministers.

The second pillar of the NHS' new model, choice, has assumed ever greater prominence with the approach of a General Election. In part, this reflects political calculation. The Conservative Party (2004) made choice a central plank of its health policy manifesto with a proposal for what would, in effect, be a voucher – valued at half what it would cost to carry out the same procedure in the NHS – if they chose to be treated in a private hospital. The Labour government, in turn, is clearly determined not to be outflanked on this issue. As from December 2005, patients will be able to choose from four to five providers for planned hospital care. And, by 2008, patients will have the right to choose from any healthcare provider which meets national standards and which can provide care within the price that the NHS will pay (Secretary of State for Health, 2004a). The Conservatives have, in effect, been trumped: under the Labour commitment, there would be no half-cost voucher but, presumably, full reimbursement.

It would be a mistake, however, to see this commitment merely in terms of short-term political expediency. It is an essential part of New Labour's reinvention of its legacy, a conscious repudiation of the paternalism implicit not only in the 1948 model NHS but in other public services as well. Indeed, the government's commitment to choice is perhaps less surprising than the fact that the concept can still raise hackles among many of its supporters: that choice – like its twin, consumerism – is seen as the canker in the apple. It is a curious case of British exceptionalism. It would be difficult to find a healthcare system in Western Europe where choice is not both seen as desirable and taken for granted.

But the case for choice does not rest exclusively, or perhaps even mainly, on the argument that it is desirable in its own right. It rests on the argument that choice is a key lever for promoting efficiency and quality in healthcare: a weapon against provider dominance. Providers in the healthcare system, as the Prime Minister's policy adviser has argued (Le Grand, 2003), are not necessarily knights who can be relied upon to act in the interests of their patients or the public. They have to be offered incentives to do so. And choice is precisely such a mechanism. Given choice (and the spare capacity that makes choice possible), patients will gravitate to those providers who provide quality services efficiently – although, of course, patients will not necessarily define efficiency in the same way as economists. Conversely, inefficient or unresponsive providers will have an incentive to mend their ways.

All this involves complex and contested arguments – about how patients define the qualities they are looking for, about the availability of relevant information and about equity (6, 2003; Roche, 2004) – that cannot be explored here. Leaving these aside, however, the impact of choice in the emergent new model NHS is contingent on and reinforced by the third pillar: payment by results. The new system, which began to be introduced in 2004 starting with FTs, "involves a complete change to NHS funding" in the words of a seminal but little noticed report from the Audit Commission (2004, p 2): Money will follow patients, so that patient choices will carry financial consequences for providers.

The new system involves setting national tariffs or prices for each procedure, classified by Healthcare Resource Groups, based on an average of all hospital costs for that procedure. No local price negotiations will take place for work covered by the tariff; unavoidable regional cost differences will be funded from the centre. Each Trust will be paid for the work done. Trusts with below average costs will receive a large bonus: the Audit Commission has calculated that this will be around £500 million in total, with some Trusts getting up to £30 million extra. In these cases there will, therefore, be little or no incentive to improve efficiency or quality. Conversely, Trusts with above average costs will have to make drastic economies to bring their costs into line with the national tariff: 15 will need to make savings of £10 million or more, rising to nearly £50 million in one case. So, cases like Bradford may multiply, and it is not self-evident that fiscal crisis promotes quality any more than fiscal ease promotes efficiency.

There are other difficulties with the new system. Some are technical: like inadequacies in the data for calculating the tariffs, particularly for specialist work. Some are more fundamental. Payment by results not only provides incentives to increase efficiency but also incentives to maximise hospital activity. And, while this may be precisely the outcome desired in the case of dealing with waiting lists, it could in other cases run counter to strategies for reducing demands for expensive hospital treatment by developing alternative services. In other words, the payment by results could crank up demand and costs. Hence the risk, to cite the Audit Commission's report again, that "the historically strong financial control of the NHS may be reduced by the powerful dynamics introduced by this system" (Audit Commission, 2004, p 5).

Whether or not that risk becomes a reality will largely depend on Primary Care Trusts (PCTs). It is they who now control more than 75% of the NHS budget and who will be responsible for operating the new system. At present, they tend to negotiate block contracts – marginally adjusted for activity – with providers. Under the new system, they will have no control over prices and much reduced control over demand, for the logic of the government's commitment to unfettered choice after 2008 is that patients, not PCTs, will decide who goes where. And it is difficult to see how PCTs will be able to cap total volume. Such capping would imply telling patients at some point in the year, if the PCT was heading for an overspend, to forget all about choice and wait for the next financial year.

This is, of course, what in effect happens now. But the emergent model NHS – extra capacity + choice + payment by results – is incompatible with this traditional form of rationing. In the past, the NHS has been successful in rationing (Klein et al, 1996), largely because payers and providers had much the same incentives: that is, neither party wanted to maximise activity. In the emergent NHS model, incentives diverge, as noted earlier. Extra capacity means providers fighting for custom, rather than disguising inadequate resources as clinical decisions (Aaron and Schwartz, 1984). Choice means that waiting lists will no longer be an effective way of rationing by delay. And payment by results will amplify both effects. Yet, as in all healthcare systems, even those with more generous spending levels than those planned for the NHS, some form of rationing is the norm.

Hence the resurrection in 2004 of GP fundholding, abolished with a fanfare of ideological trumpets in 1997. Not that the new initiative (DH, 2004b) ever mentions the word. The proposal is for "practice based commissioning", and the claim is that the concept has been in the policy oven for some years. Be that as it may, it is clear that it has been given added urgency by the new model NHS. For, if patient demands are going to be constrained – in line with budgetary resources – it is GPs who seem best placed to do the job. It is they who can prioritise between the claims of different patients (whereas PCTs can only prioritise, if at all, between different categories of patients) and decide on degrees of urgency. As the DH's document delicately puts it (p 2), GPs "often have a major influence on what care a patient receives and how a patient exercises choice". In other, less delicate, words, they are best placed to ration resources. Yet at present "all this comes without any need for practices to consider how they are using healthcare resources".

Reverting to practice budgets, indicative in the first instance, will create precisely such a need to consider how healthcare resources are being used. As an incentive to volunteer for such budgets, practices will be allowed to keep 50% of any savings. And the only penalty for overshooting will be that practices will lose their commissioning status if they cannot balance their budgets over a three-year period. It is a tentative, experimental beginning. But the logic of the new model NHS suggests that this initiative may soon gather momentum and become part of the evolving institutional structure.

From management to regulation

With PCTs controlling more than 75% of the NHS budgets, an ever-increasing proportion of providers being reincarnated as FTs accountable to an independent Monitor and to local communities, and consumer choice directing the flow of funds, what is left for the DH to do? If power is indeed flowing to the periphery, if the independent Monitor may soon emerge as more important than the NHS' Chief Executive, what is to be the role of the centre? The questions may seem premature at a time when the complaints within the NHS – even from FTs, as we have seen – continue to be about excessive demands for information, the proliferation of targets and too much bureaucracy. But, there were signs in 2004 that the role of the DH was indeed being reassessed, even while it continued to be as directive as ever in pushing through the intended transformation.

Most evidently, the DH is shrinking: the government announced a 38% cut in the number of its civil servants. And, while in the past such cuts have been largely cosmetic, with the civil servants reappearing in other agencies, this does not seem to be happening this time round. There has been a massacre of hands-off bodies – as already noted – with forced dissolutions and amalgamations, bringing their number down from 38 to 20 (DH, 2004a). Responsibility for national pay negotiations was transferred to an independent organisation, NHS Employers attached to the NHS Confederation. The protests of FTs produced an almost immediate reaction, with the Department promising to cut its information requirements by half: the hope must be that the reductions will apply to information that is irrelevant as distinct from merely inconvenient for the Trusts concerned. More generally and more importantly, the Department appears to be rethinking its role in terms of moving away from a managerial model towards a standard-setting, regulatory model. The aim is "to focus on strategic direction and holding the whole system to account" (DH, 2004a, p 3).

The strategy is encapsulated in the title of the Department's planning framework for the years 2005-06 to 2007-08, *National standards, local action* (DH, 2004c). The centre will continue to develop National Service Frameworks, blueprints for the design and delivery of services for specific groups (for example, older people) or conditions (for example, cancer). It will also continue to set priorities and the delivery targets for achieving them, although on a reduced scale. The number of targets is being cut from 62 to 20. It has, for the first time, set out a performance framework incorporating a set of standards "which set out the level of quality all organisations providing NHS care will be expected to meet or aspire to" (DH, 2004c, p 21): core standards identify the minimum level of acceptable performance, while developmental standards define the direction of continuous improvement over time. The standards are organised around seven 'domains': safety, clinical and cost effectiveness, governance, patient focus, accessible and responsive care, care environment and amenities, and public health. They are set at a level of generality "that allows scope for local determination of what works best" (DH, 2004c, p 21). So, for example, the first core standard in the governance domain requires that healthcare organisations "apply the principles of sound clinical and corporate governance" (DH, 2004c, p 30). And it will be up to the government's new inspectorate, the Healthcare Commission, to assess and report on performance in the light of these standards.

The Healthcare Commission started work in April 2004, replacing the Commission for Health Improvement (CHI) and with a wider remit as well as more scope to design its own methods. The CHI's remit was restricted to the NHS; its focus was on clinical governance and it inspected all NHS Trusts on a four-year cycle against ill-defined criteria and in the absence of any national standards at the time of its creation (Day and Klein, 2004). The Healthcare Commission's remit covers the private sector as well as the NHS, includes the audit functions previously carried out by the Audit Commission and responsibility as an ultimate court of appeal for complaints. It proposes (Healthcare Commission, 2004b) to rely not on routine, timetabled inspections by large teams – the CHI model – but on self-assessment and risk-based inspections triggered by an analysis of information from a variety of sources, ranging from patient surveys to reports from other regulatory bodies. The aim is to reduce regulatory overlap and the burden of inspection. As from 2005-06, the Commission's assessments will provide the basis for a new model of performance ratings: the much criticised star ratings will be replaced by a more complex, multidimensional report incorporating judgments not only about the achievement of the national standards and targets but also about the Trust's quality of leadership and its capacity for improvement – an approach pioneered by the Audit Commission in its local government reviews.

It remains to be seen whether it is possible to reduce the regulatory burden without also blunting the regulatory edge. The effectiveness of selective, risk-based inspection will depend on the criteria used for selection and how risks are identified, and the Commission has so far described the methods that will be used only in the most general terms. The standards prescribed by the DH have been criticised, unsurprisingly, as an odd-job lot without a strong conceptual base and resistant to measurement (Shaw, 2004). Much, therefore, will depend on the criteria used by the Commission's inspectors in interpreting them. The Commission's first shot at developing such criteria – a series of prompts or questions (Healthcare Commission, 2004c) – suggests that it will be difficult to steer a course between the twin dangers of all regulatory regimes: a rigid, box-ticking approach, on the one hand, and an overreliance on inspectorial discretion on the other. The former was the approach adopted by the regulators of the independent healthcare sector; the latter was CHI's approach. Like other inspectorates before it, the Healthcare Commission's first shot is unlikely to be its last, and a cycle of experimental change over time is likely.

From healthcare to public health

The first priority in the DH's planning framework for the years ahead (DH, 2004a) is to improve the health of the population. By 2010, it is expected that life expectancy at birth in England will rise to 78.6 for men and 82.5 years for women. And, as in the past, specific targets are set for cutting smoking rates, cancer and heart disease mortality rates, halting the rise in child obesity and reducing health inequalities, among other goals. In a familiar phrase, the course is to be set towards "a health service, not a sickness service" (Secretary of State for Health, 2004a, p 45). There is a paradox here, however. To the extent that the focus switches to improving the nation's health – as distinct from dealing with illness, sickness and disability – so the role of the DH and the NHS is likely to diminish in importance. At worst, the Department is likely to be a bit player on a crowded stage; at best, it will be the impresario of a ballet performed by others. The point emerges clearly from the two major reports on public health published in 2004.

The first Wanless Report (2002), commissioned by the Chancellor of the Exchequer, not the Secretary of State for Health, provided the rationalisation for the decision to plough extra billions into the NHS, although the decision no doubt also reflected political pressures to demonstrate Labour's commitment to improve the service. But, while providing a rationale, the report also gave a warning. This was that, looking 20 years ahead, the level spending on healthcare would depend on the degree to which people were 'engaged' (to use the report's terminology) in their own health. The final Wanless Report (2004), addressed to the Prime Minister, the Secretary of State for Health and the Chancellor of the Exchequer, analysed in detail the implications of and options for moving towards 'full engagement': that is, policies required for "reducing demand by enhancing the promotion of good health and disease prevention" (p 3).

Two characteristics of the 2004 Wanless Report are relevant for the purposes of our analysis. The first is that much of the report dealt with issues outside the control of the DH: for example, smoking and alcohol policies, and the level of salt in food. The second is that the report repeatedly stressed the lack of evidence about the effectiveness of different policy options: "There is currently limited evidence about what works in terms of preventative and public health interventions, how effectively to implement them and even less evidence about their impact on inequalities and on the cost-effectiveness of these interventions", the report pointed out (p 110).

It is against this background that the government produced its response, *Choosing health* (Secretary of State for Health, 2004b). The headlines prompted by the report concentrated chiefly on what was widely seen as an over-tentative approach to smoking in pubs and bars. More interesting than specific issues such as this, however, is the overall philosophy (if that is not too grand a word) shaping the report: a sophisticated attempt to balance the spheres of state action (the nanny state) and individual responsibility, avoiding both social determinism and atomistic individualism. The argument shaping the report is that individual choices are influenced by social and economic context: hence, the role of the state becomes not so much to ban or prohibit certain activities – except when these harm others (a good Millsian argument) – but to encourage and make it easier to opt for a healthy lifestyle. Once again, individual choice is the paramount value – but there is recognition that public policy can either constrain or promote particular kinds of choice. Hence, the only clear nannyish proposal in the report is the (untried and uncosted) planned introduction of NHS-accredited health trainers to support people who want advice, first in deprived communities and then more generally.

But, if the health behaviour of individuals reflects the context in which they live, then the potential scope for policy interventions designed to affect that scope is enormous. And indeed, *Choosing health* sometimes gives the impression of being the product of a trawl through Whitehall in which departments were asked to put any policies with a possible bearing on health into the pot. So, the catalogue of interventions, actual or planned, spans a whole range of government activities and interests: education, housing, employment, workplace practices, cycle lanes and sports facilities, among others; and all this in addition to specific NHS health promotion initiatives. There is, however, one surprising omission: nothing is said about income distribution – despite the argument (Morris and Deeming, 2004) that healthy living requires a healthy income.

This is not necessarily to argue against the individual policies concerned. Most of them can probably be justified in their own terms: cycle lanes are desirable, for example, on environmental grounds even if they have no effect on health (although they probably do). Without evidence about which interventions work best or provide most value for money – to return to the Wanless Report – such a hopeful scattergun approach may make some sense. But it does not amount to a coherent strategy, despite the reiterated emphasis in *Choosing health* on coordinating policies both nationally and locally, with NHS bodies carrying a special responsibility in this respect. Further, if the different interventions do interact with a cumulative effect, in ways that we do not fully understand, it may never be possible to determine which are the most cost-effective. And accountability for outcomes may become a casualty in the process: if life expectancy does increase as prescribed in the NHS planning framework, it will be difficult if not impossible to determine how much of the credit should go to the DH as distinct from other government departments (or factors that have nothing to do with government policy).

The DH is therefore at best one player among others. The extent to which it is able to orchestrate the actions of other departments is unclear: the fact that the first Wanless Report was commissioned by the Chancellor of the Exchequer and that the final 2004 Report went to the Prime Minister as well as the Chancellor may be indicative of where the real power lies. This, in turn, may suggest that the Department should not neglect its traditional role in running the NHS. Until the day comes when successful health promotion policies (or genetic engineering miracles) ensure that everyone lives to be 101 and then drops dead without ever having suffered a day's illness or disability, most people will probably settle gratefully for an efficient, effective and accessible sickness service.

Conclusion

By the end of 2004, the NHS was heavily pregnant with the future, even though delivery was later than expected. Ministers could persuasively argue that the NHS had to be transformed in order to be saved: that, if a tax-funded, universalistic service was to survive, the dynamics of the system had to adapt. Unchanging values, in other words, required radical institutional changes. In the event, the dividends of policy change and the extra billions were slow in coming and lacking in political visibility. The coherence and compatibility of the many policy initiatives had yet to be fully tested. But perhaps the best tribute to the government's strategy was that paid, involuntarily, by the chairperson of the British Medical Association's private practice committee (cited in Stevens, 2005, p 38). The government's policies, he lamented, were blunting incentives to take out private medical insurance and cutting the private incomes of consultants. If equity is indeed the guiding value of health policy, that comment suggests that the government is getting at least some things right.

References

6, P. (2003) 'Giving consumers of British public services more choice: what can be learned from recent history', *Journal of Social Policy*, vol 32, no 3, pp 239-70.

Aaron, H.J. and Schwartz, W.B. (1984) *The painful prescription*, Washington, DC: The Brookings Institution.

Allsop, J. and Baggott, R. (2004) 'The NHS in England', in N. Ellison, L. Bauld and M. Powell (eds) *Social Policy Review 16*, Bristol: The Policy Press/Social Policy Association.

Audit Commission (2004) *Introducing payment by results*, London: Audit Commission.

Carvel, J. (2004) 'Threat to Blair plan for NHS: Foundation Trusts attack red tape', *The Guardian*, 13 December, p 1.

Conservative Party (2004) *Right to choose: Health*, London, Conservative Party.

Crisp, N. (2004) *Chief Executive's report to the NHS*, December, London: DH.

Day, P. and Klein, R. (2004) *The NHS improvers: A study of the Commission for Health Improvement*, London: King's Fund.

DH (Department of Health) (2004a) *Reconfiguring the Department of Health's arm's length bodies*, London: DH.

DH (2004b) *Practice based commissioning: Engaging practices in commissioning*, London: DH.

DH (2004c) *National standards, local action*, London: DH.

Greer, S. (2004) *Territorial politics and health policy*, Manchester: Manchester University Press.

Healthcare Commission (2004a) *State of healthcare report*, London: Healthcare Commission.

Healthcare Commission (2004b) *Assessment for improvement*, London: Healthcare Commission.

Healthcare Commission (2004c) *Assessment for improvement: Understanding the standards*, London: Healthcare Commission.

Heclo, H. (1974) *Modern social politics in Britain and Sweden*, New Haven, CT: Yale University Press.

Klein, R. (2001) *The new politics of the NHS*, Harlow: Prentice Hall.

Klein, R. and Marmor, T. (forthcoming) 'Reflections on policy analysis: putting it together again', in R. Goodin and M. Moran (eds) *Oxford handbook of public policy*, Oxford: Oxford University Press.

Klein, R., Day, P. and Redmayne, S. (1996) *Managing scarcity: Priority setting and rationing in the National Health Service*, Buckingham: Open University Press.

Le Grand, J. (2003) *Motivation, agency, and public policy*, Oxford: Oxford University Press.

Maynard, A. and Bloor, K. (2003) 'Do those who pay the piper call the tune?', *Health Policy Matters*, no 8, October, York: University of York.

Milburn, A. (2003) 'Localism: from rhetoric to reality', Speech given by the Secretary of State, 5 February (www.dh.gov.uk/speeches/milburnfeb03localism.htm).

Monitor (2004a) *NHS Foundation Trusts: Report on elections and membership*, August, London: Independent Regulator of NHS Foundation Trusts.

Monitor (2004b) 'Monitor appoints Peter Garland as interim chairman of Bradford Teaching Hospitals NHS Foundation Trust', Press release, 14 December (www.monitor-nhsft.gov.uk).

MORI (2004) *MORI Delivery Index – November* (www.mori.com/polls/2004/mdi041130.shtml).

Morris, J.N. and Deeming, C. (2004) 'Minimum incomes for healthy living (MIHL): next thrust in UK social policy?', *Policy & Politics*, vol 32, no 4, pp 441-54.

ONS (Office for National Statistics) (2004) *Public service productivity: Health*, paper 1, London: ONS.

Powell, M. (1997) *Evaluating the National Health Service*, Buckingham: Open University Press.

Reid, J. (2004) Speech to NICE conference, Birmingham, 1 December, Press release 2004/0430, London: DH.

Roche, D. (2004) 'Choice: rhetoric and reality', *New Economy*, vol 11, no 4, pp 189-94.

RCGP (Royal College of General Practitioners) (2004a) *Profile of UK practices*, RCGP information sheet no 2, London: RCGP.

RCGP (2004b) *New GMS contract*, RCGP information sheet no 6, London: RCGP.

Secretary of State for Health (2004a) *The NHS improvement plan: Putting people at the heart of public services*, Cm 6268, London: The Stationery Office.

Secretary of State for Health (2004b) *Choosing health: Making healthy choices easier*, Cm 6374, London: The Stationery Office.

Shaw, C. (2004) 'Standards for better health: fit for purpose?', *British Medical Journal*, vol 329, no 27, November, pp 1250-1.

Smee, C. (2005) *Speaking truth to power: Two decades of analysis in the Department of Health*, London: Nuffield Trust.

Stevens, S. (2004) 'Reform strategies for the English NHS', *Health Affairs*, vol 23, no 3, pp 37-44.

Stevens, S. (2005) 'The NHS works', *Prospect*, February, pp 32-8.

Tuohy, C. (1999) *Accidental logics*, New York, NY: Oxford University Press.

Wanless, D. (2002) *Securing our future health: Taking a long-term view*, Final Report, London: Treasury.

Wanless, D. (2004) *Securing good health for the whole population*, Final Report, London: The Stationery Office.

FOUR

Housing in an 'opportunity society'

Peter Malpass

Introduction

In an important speech on welfare reform on 11 October 2004, Tony Blair claimed that:

> ... we are engaged not on a set of discrete reforms, area by area, but a fundamental shift from a 20th century welfare state, with services largely collective, uniform and passive, founded on low skills for the majority, to a 21st century opportunity society with services that are personal, diverse and active, founded on high skills. (http://news.bbc.co.uk/2/hi/uk_news/politics/3733380.stm)

Blair listed seven challenges, of which housing was the last and least detailed, continuing a pattern of paying only marginal attention to this important determinant of well-being (Blair, 1998, 2002). However, the theme of this chapter is that in 2004 housing was at the leading edge of welfare reform, and that as such it provides a valuable window on the implications of an opportunity society. Twenty-five years ago, the introduction of the right to buy rapidly privatised a million council houses and led to a steep decline in the supply of accommodation to let at prices that were affordable by people on low incomes. It also led many academic commentators to the view that housing was becoming a residual service and the 'wobbly pillar' under the welfare state (Torgersen, 1987; Harloe, 1995; Lowe, 2004). But, if the assault on housing during the 1980s was exceptional by comparison with other services (Le Grand, 1991), subsequently there has been a convergence around a trend towards privatisation, provider markets, consumer choice and individual responsibility for personal and family well-being. With 80% of housing consumption in Britain mediated by the market mechanism, it provides a good arena in which to assess the implications of an opportunity society.

Existing commentaries (Cowan and Marsh, 2001; Ford, 2003) have noted the continuities in housing policy either side of the 1997 General Election, reflecting a new orthodoxy that was in place before the change of government. This is not to argue that all governments are the same, nor to deny the distinctiveness of the policies of the post-1997 Labour government. But, in the context of a review of developments within one year, it is important not to become too focused on change at the expense of continuity.

Housing supply

Although there is a crude surplus of dwellings over households, taking the country as a whole, there is a widely acknowledged need to increase supply, especially in parts of the south of England where economic growth is strongest. Meanwhile, some other parts of the country face quite different pressures. As mentioned in last year's *Social policy review* (Lund, 2004), the Deputy Prime Minister, John Prescott, had published his *Communities plan* in March 2003 (ODPM, 2003), claiming that it marked a 'step change' in housing policy, committing the government to plans to develop 200,000 new houses in four designated growth areas in the south east of England in the period to 2016. Then, at the close of 2003, the government took delivery of the interim report of the review of housing supply carried out by Kate Barker for the Treasury and the Office of the Deputy Prime Minister (ODPM) (Barker, 2003). The final report, containing 36 recommendations, was published in March 2004 (Barker, 2004). These two documents contain a wealth of fascinating information and analysis, and provide an invaluable starting point for understanding the contemporary housing market (but see also Bramley et al, 2004; Lund, 2004). They also illustrate the need to look at the way the government defines the problem. Barker's terms of reference asked her to "conduct a review of issues underlying the lack of supply and responsiveness of housing in the UK". The main focus of the report was the housing market, given that the lack of supply of social rented housing was a direct reflection of government policy, requiring no investigation or explanation. Barker's report and recommendations have to be seen in the light of the Blair government's baffled reaction to the apparent reluctance of private builders to respond to market signals (in the form of strongly rising prices) in the way that standard economic theory predicts. A very different report might have been produced if the question had been, "What needs to be done to increase the overall supply of houses?".

The main points made by Barker were, first, that over a prolonged period house prices had risen faster in real terms in Britain than in comparable countries in mainland Europe, and that this was not good for the economy, nor for people seeking to gain access to home ownership for the first time. Second, the rise in prices was linked to the failure of housing supply to expand in line with demand. Third, land supply was identified as the main constraint on the delivery of housing. Fourth, Barker argued that, while a substantial increase in supply was necessary, it was impracticable to increase the rate of new building to the point where this would eliminate the tendency for prices to rise; even if private sector output were to double, it would not remove price increases. Fifth, she took the view that it was necessary to develop a more flexible housing market in which suppliers could and would respond more effectively to price signals. This implied reform, but not abandonment, of the land use planning system.

In her final report Barker (2004) set out four objectives to achieve:

1. improvements in housing affordability;
2. a more stable housing market;
3. location of housing supply that supports patterns of economic development;
4. an adequate supply of publicly funded housing for those who need it.

Among the key recommendations aimed at achieving these objectives were several suggestions for improving the planning system, including:

- the increased use of market information as a guide to decision making;
- the allocation of more land for development;
- a stronger role for regional planning bodies, which should be merged with the recently established regional housing bodies;
- the adoption of measures to tax windfall gains from new development.

Barker rejected the idea of specific output targets for the private sector; instead she called for the establishment of a "market affordability goal" for each region. This was not defined in detail, but the concept refers to the relationship between incomes and prices, and the aim would be to improve access to the housing market over the housing market cycle (Barker, 2004, p 24). On the other hand, Barker was explicit about the need to increase output of social housing by at least 17,000 dwellings per year. This represented almost a doubling of output compared with the rates achieved in recent years (Wilcox, 2004a; Malpass, 2005).

Barker's analysis and recommendations were welcomed and broadly accepted by the government, although the spending review announced in July 2004 made it clear that funding would be provided for only 10,000 additional social rented dwellings per year, and that this increase would not be achieved until 2007. It also emerged that a substantial proportion of investment resources depended upon the achievement of efficiency savings within the social housing sector itself (Birch, 2004; HM Treasury, 2004, p 108). Any increase in the supply of affordable rented housing is to be welcomed, especially given the historically low levels to which output had sunk by 2003, and the record numbers of homeless households living in temporary accommodation by the end of 2004 (up by 123% since 1997 according to Shelter [http:// england.shelter.org.uk/home/home-624.cfm/pressreleaselisting/2/ pressrelease/132]). There is a case for saying that Barker's own evidence pointed to a need for much, much more. A more flexible and responsive housing market may be a desirable objective; a series of regional affordability targets and all the other recommendations put forward by Barker may also be welcome in themselves, but the long-run performance of the house building industry strongly suggests that they will not be sufficient.

A final point to be made with regard to housing supply concerns the high levels of investment in private renting in recent years, something welcomed by both Barker and the government. According to the Council of Mortgage Lenders, £46 billion had been invested in buy to let between 1998 and 2004 (this refers to individuals buying properties for letting, and is apparently in addition to commercial investment in private renting). The rise of buy to let is worthy of note for at least three reasons: first, it is an unplanned, market-driven phenomenon, and yet the scale of investment is in stark contrast to the success of government initiatives to boost private renting, such as the business expansion scheme and housing investment trusts (the latter, introduced in 1996, failed completely [Kemp, 2004, pp 61-2]). Second, the amount of money involved is huge, exceeding the total invested in housing associations over the whole of the period since 1979. And third, the outcome has been a scarcely measurable increase in the overall supply of private rented dwellings; the sector grew quite strongly in the early 1990s, before the launch of buy to let, but it has remained at around 2.4 million units since that time, implying that buy to let has been more or less balanced by disinvestment by other landlords.

Affordability

During 2004, there was growing anxiety about questions of affordability in the short term, and about whether/when the boom phase of the current housing market cycle would run out of energy. This in turn raised fears of whether the housing market could achieve a gradual slowdown and so avoid the trauma of the early 1990s. House prices had been on a strongly rising trend since 1997, and by 2004 the average price in the UK had more than doubled in seven years. The Bank of England's Monetary Policy Committee introduced a series of interest rate rises during the year and the effect began to show up in quieter housing market conditions by the autumn, with evidence emerging that prices were starting to fall.

In certain parts of the country, buoyant economic conditions had fuelled demand and allowed the house price-earnings ratio (based on national average male earnings [Hamnett, 1999, p 22]) to rise above five, which has hitherto been seen as unsustainable. Rising prices during most of 2004 exacerbated problems of declining affordability; it has been suggested that in 2003 half of all working households in the age range 20-39 could not afford to buy a house, even at the lowest quartile price, and that in the south west of England as many as 68% of this group could not buy (Wilcox, 2003). In the era of low nominal interest rates, there are grounds for arguing that a higher price-earnings ratio is sustainable, but, of course, low inflation means that mortgage repayments remain heavy for longer. Moreover, Wilcox (2004b) has shown that, even by calculating the price-earnings ratio on the basis of the substantially higher measure of *household* income, for people in the first-time buyer age group (20-39), in at least 40 English local authority areas, the index had risen above five by the end of 2003 (and in the least affordable areas it was above six). Not surprisingly, therefore, the statistics published by the Council of Mortgage Lenders show falling numbers of first-time buyers, down from 55% of borrowers in 1993 to under 30% in 2004.

One set of hard-hit potential first-time buyers is the group of relatively low-paid public sector employees known as 'key workers' (teachers, NHS staff, police and probation officers, fire fighters, social workers and a range of other public sector workers). The 'key worker living' scheme, launched in March 2004 (www.keyworkerliving.co.uk), replaced the starter homes initiative announced in the Green Paper of 2000, under which some 9,000 key workers had been helped into home ownership. The new scheme is to provide assistance, in the form of equity loans, shared ownership or 'intermediate renting', to people in the named occupations living in London, the south east and the east of England. Equity loans of up to £50,000 are intended to help people purchase open market properties, or to acquire a shared ownership property, which involves the beneficiary purchasing a minimum of 25% of the equity and paying rent on the remainder; intermediate renting is described as a form of provision costing 75-80% of local market rents. Housing associations are the providers of both shared ownership and intermediate renting under the scheme. Key worker living has been given a high profile but it is expected to provide help for only 12,000 key workers up to 2006, at a cost of £1 billion (ODPM, 2004, p 24). Not only is this a very expensive way of helping a small number of workers, it is economically questionable on the grounds that giving these individuals increased spending power in a market where demand is already high and supply is inelastic can only have the effect of increasing prices for everyone.

Another way of looking at key worker living is to note that the scheme scrupulously avoids the option of offering these essential public servants conventional social rented housing. However, the intended recipients of assistance are by definition unable to afford open market house purchase, which would seem to entitle them to social housing (it certainly would have done in the past). Moreover, an influx of such people into social rented housing would broaden the social mix and help to counter the deepening trend towards residualisation. The fact that this is not seen as an option is revealing, implying that, in the government's view, reversing the slide towards residualisation is not important (or desirable). It suggests that social housing is not seen as an option for people in work (nearly 80% of social rented sector tenants do not have full-time employment [Wilcox, 2004a, p 122]) and a commitment to market, or market-like, solutions wherever possible, even at enormous unit cost to the public purse.

The commitment to the market is also clearly visible in the approach to the reform of Housing Benefit. In the early weeks of 2004, the government pressed ahead with a series of local pathfinder schemes for private tenants, introducing a flat rate payment system based on type and size of household and local market conditions. This is often referred to as the introduction of 'shopping incentives' because, unlike the established system that relates benefit directly to rent, claimants are given an incentive to shop around for cheaper accommodation, at or below the flat rate. The then Work and Pensions Secretary, Andrew Smith, was quoted in February 2004 as saying:

> This new system for Housing Benefit will increase choice and responsibility for tenants. It will be much simpler and quicker to

administer. Anyone getting the new Local Housing Allowance will also have greater certainty about how much help with their housing costs they can expect if they went back to work, helping them bridge the gap between being unemployed and taking a job. (http://www.dwp.gov.uk/mediacentre/pressreleases/2004/feb/index.asp)

Achieving a system that is simpler and quicker to administer has attractions, but there are potential costs and losses from the point of view of tenants, to the extent that simplicity is often associated with rough justice. Some tenants will be able to find good quality accommodation that suits their needs and is priced at less than their flat rate benefit, but others will not be so lucky and may end up out of pocket. In any case, it is not clear how the pursuit of another government objective – namely, sustainable communities – is enhanced by encouraging people to move around in search of cheaper accommodation. Shelter's monitoring of the scheme in four areas suggested that, on the early evidence, the Local Housing Allowance was more generous than Housing Benefit, increasing the proportion of properties affordable by people on benefits. However, in three of the four areas, there had been an increase in the number of property advertisements specifying 'No DSS', suggesting perhaps that landlords are not enthusiastic about the scheme (Reynolds, 2004). So far, the Local Housing Allowance is being piloted in selected areas and only in the private sector.

In the social rented sector, it is seen to be necessary to prepare the ground for flat rate Housing Benefit by way of a 10-year process known as rent restructuring, which is designed to bring local authority and housing association rents closer together and to create a more coherent pattern of rents within each locality. Social sector rents will remain substantially lower than market rents, but within the sector individual rents should more accurately reflect the features that matter to tenants, a development that is congruent with the contemporary emphasis on choice in lettings. Rent restructuring is a complex process concerned with several objectives for, while it is about reducing the differences in the rents charged by different social landlords, it is also about *increasing* the differences in rents within the stocks of houses owned by individual landlords. In the past, reform was mainly driven by average rent levels, but rent restructuring addresses the problem of the relatively flat rent profiles of social landlords, particularly local authorities. The objective is to ensure that rents reflect both incomes and property values within localities. Each dwelling has a target rent based on a formula reflecting these two factors, and over a run of a year landlords are expected to move towards these targets (Walker and Marsh, 2003; Marsh, 2004).

Governance

Rent restructuring represents an extension of central government intervention in an area of decision making that was traditionally left to the localities. Some social housing organisations, particularly certain stock transfer associations in England that had been established to take over local authority housing on a set of business plan assumptions requiring year-on-year real term increases, were threatened with difficulty as a result of rent restructuring. However, this was not allowed to interfere with the drive to separate the ownership and/or management of council housing from the local authorities and, by the end of 2004, nearly a million dwellings had been transferred since the first authority sold its entire stock in 1988 (of these 860,000 were in England and 100,000 in Scotland). During 2004, a total of 58,000 dwellings were transferred by local authorities in England, a rate of progress well below the 200,000 per annum envisaged in the Green Paper of 2000 (DETR, 2000), but government commitment to this form of modernisation is entrenched.

A new pattern of governance of housing is emerging across Britain. At one level, this can be understood in terms of the Blairite enthusiasm for the modernisation of public services through demunicipalisation (Blair, 1998). This vision of the future sees elected local authorities handing over responsibility for day-to-day service delivery to non-municipal organisations, such as housing associations, and, in England at least, those authorities that have not already done so face intense pressure to come to terms with the government's determination to bring an end to the 20th-century model of council housing. These authorities are required to complete options appraisals by July 2005 and, in October 2004, John Prescott wrote to all council leaders to assure them that they were expected to select one of the three options set out by his department, and that there would be no fourth option providing additional funding for a continuing municipal service (although authorities can opt to retain their stock, if their business plans indicate that they have the resources to meet the decent homes standard). The options available are the sale of the stock to a new owner or owners, the creation of an arm's length management organisation (ALMO) and the Private Finance Initiative (PFI). The problem to which these options are said to be the answers is the need to raise investment finance in order to meet the government's target of all social rented housing meeting the 'decency standard' by 2010, but the key point is that each option involves loss of local democratic control of the housing service developed and partly paid for by local people over the best part of a hundred years. As in other areas (such as the creation of foundation hospitals), the need to raise money is being used as a pretext and as a lever for a shift to a new governance paradigm. In the case of the sale of council houses, the ownership and management passes to one or more registered social landlords (housing associations), typically run by a board comprised of equal proportions of tenants, councillors and others (known as independents). The same model of corporate governance applies in the case of ALMOs; the key differences here are that the stock remains in the ownership of the local authority and investment funding is provided by the Office of the Deputy Prime Minister rather than by direct borrowing from private institutions. Hitherto, the most widely adopted option has been sale, involving 154 English local authorities up to the end of 2004 and raising more than £5 billion for improvement expenditure; the ALMO option was introduced in 2001 and is only available to local authorities judged to be good or excellent by the Audit Commission Housing Inspectorate. By 2004, 20 were in receipt of funding and a further 29 were in the pipeline. The PFI allows the authority to retain ownership of its stock, but service delivery and investment are handed over to a private contractor for a specified period of years. Up to the present, this has not attracted much interest from housing authorities, partly because of its complexity, but in any case the PFI has been seen in terms of generating resources for estate refurbishment rather than as a solution applicable across the whole of a local authority's stock, and it really needs to be seen in conjunction with one of the other strategies (Garnett and Perry, 2005).

It is not possible to predict with any precision the pattern of social housing governance in five or 10 years' time, partly because of the range of options offered to local authorities, and partly because past experience in this area suggests an evolving and dynamic story (Malpass and Mullins, 2002). However, it does seem very unlikely that the general thrust of policy will be reversed, and therefore it is reasonable to predict a continuing decline in the council sector. Given that housing has traditionally been the major service provided by district councils, its gradual elimination might be expected to lead to question marks over this tier of local government. Reinforcing this point is another policy development: in 2003, the government announced the establishment of Regional Housing Boards in England. The main function of these bodies was to develop regional housing strategies, reflecting the view that many aspects of housing need to be planned on a regional or sub-regional basis because housing markets cross local authority boundaries. No sooner had the Regional Housing Boards been convened than the Barker report recommended that they should be combined with Regional Planning Bodies, and this was accepted by the government during 2004 for implementation in 2005. The growing importance of regional bodies, of course, represents a departure from the previous emphasis on the role of local authorities in the development of housing strategies at district level, and it was clear in 2004 that local housing authorities faced an uncertain future.

Another dimension of uncertainty and source of diversity arises from the devolution of housing policy to the Scottish Parliament and the Welsh Assembly. Local authorities in Scotland and Wales demonstrated much less enthusiasm for stock transfer, and the establishment of the devolved administrations opens up the possibility for continued divergence of policy and practice. In Scotland, the majority of dwellings transferred so far were accounted for by just one local authority, Glasgow District Council, but, during 2004, Edinburgh District Council moved towards transferring its stock, and the policy of the Parliament was clearly supportive of a programme of transfers (http://www.scotland.gov.uk/News/Releases/2004/06/5725). In Wales, however, a different strategy has been developed, reflecting a more sceptical view of stock transfer, and the Assembly has developed a distinctive model, known as the Community Housing Mutual Model, designed to transfer ownership to tenants(www.housing.wales.gov.uk/index.asp?task=content&a=h9).

Choice, responsibility and opportunity

Choice, responsibility and opportunity are key political watchwords of our time reflecting the wider transformation in the discourse around social policy, away from an emphasis on collective protection and provision for individuals to a new emphasis on individuals taking responsibility for their own well-being, primarily through participation in the labour force and consumption of goods and services through market-based choices. In the last 30 years, changes in the labour market and growing instability in the housing market have combined with the deregulation of capital markets and the contraction of the social security safety net to increase risk and uncertainty for home owners (Ford et al, 2001, p 44). At the same time, governments have sought to expand home ownership, which effectively means attracting more low-income purchasers, and increased the rhetoric around the idea that people must take more responsibility for themselves; New Labour's housing Green Paper listed as one of the party's key principles for housing policy, "Giving responsibility to individuals to provide their own homes where they can, providing support for those who cannot" (DETR, 2000, p 16).

Responsibility for the consequences of decisions is the price paid for choice, and every choice is accompanied by some degree of risk. The problem, of course, is that choices, opportunities and ability to bear responsibility are not evenly distributed. Exaltation of markets and the notion of choice reflect insouciance in relation to the inescapable fact that markets work best for those who have the most money and/or credit, and they work least well for those with the least of these resources. The contemporary housing market tends to sort people by income (even if, in the case of older home owners, this tends to be based on past income). Owner occupation not only reflects but also amplifies inequalities created in the labour market. As Hamnett has pointed out:

> The home ownership market in Britain has functioned as a massive, though far from random, lottery, distributing differential gains and losses to millions of owners across the country and over time. It is far from random because there is a broadly consistent pattern of gains and losses depending on type of property bought, where and when, and who bought it. (Hamnett, 1999, pp 10-11)

He goes on to demonstrate (1999, p 100) that over a lifetime professional and managerial home owners generally gain almost twice as much as owners in manual occupations. There is also a gender dimension to the role of home ownership in increasing inequality: to the extent that women still tend to earn less than men, households headed by women will tend to be disadvantaged in the housing market. But, of course, it is not just about wealth accumulation through home ownership; location not only influences the rate of house price appreciation but also access to a range of spatially distributed resources, such as schools, shops, job opportunities and leisure facilities. There is anecdotal evidence, supported by limited research (Butler and Robson, 2003, p 5; Cheshire and Sheppard, 2004), suggesting that house prices can be significantly affected by the reputations of local schools, and that houses are marketed on this basis. Housing is implicated in inequality in all sorts of ways, including intergenerational transfers of wealth and privilege, given that houses constitute the largest proportion of inherited wealth for most people. People buying houses are also buying access to the facilities and benefits of the neighbourhood, tangible and intangible, which may have a critical effect on their wider life chances or those of their children.

In the context of the contemporary housing market, therefore, choice and opportunity are slogans that serve to gloss over and to legitimise inequality. Housing highlights the point made by Bauman, (1998, pp 58-9) that consumerism and the welfare state are at cross purposes; the principles on which the welfare state was founded emphasised sameness and equality, whereas the idea of choice only makes sense where difference is apparent and where different outcomes are attainable. Choice and the opportunity society appeal to and work for people with money in their pockets, but for the rest they offer only the prospect of second-class services and second-class status, as demonstrated by the current state of social renting.

Here too, the issue of choice has been high on the agenda for some time, especially in relation to the lettings process where the emphasis on prospective tenants choosing rather than being allocated a house is seen as an advance from the old bureaucratic ethos of local government. It is about relating to service users as consumers rather than applicants. Choice-based lettings emerged as policy in 2000 and, in 2004, the government published research evaluating the early results (Marsh et al, 2004). Critics quickly pointed out that in areas of low demand tenants effectively had choice already, and in areas of high demand the key issue was that choice depended on increasing supply rather than changing the procedures for deciding who got what. But the really telling criticism is that the problem with social housing is that people with choice tend to choose other tenures, and are positively encouraged to do so by government policy. Social renting is officially a tenure for those who cannot operate in the market, and as such it has become both a site and a badge of social exclusion, concentrating in certain readily identifiable localities groups of 'flawed consumers' (Bauman, 1998, p 90).

The 2004 Housing Act

It would be wrong to conclude a review of this kind with no reference to the fact that there was a Housing Act passed during the year. Equally, it would be wrong, in this particular case, to spend too much time on it. The 2004 Housing Act reached the statute book in November, having made a slow and leisurely progression through its various parliamentary stages. The main measures in the Act amount to a number of minor amendments and additions to:

- the powers of local authorities to license private landlords;
- the powers of local authorities to tackle anti-social behaviour in social housing;

- introduce mandatory licensing of larger houses in multiple occupation;
- 'modernise' the right to buy to tackle 'profiteering';
- allow The Housing Corporation in England to allocate social housing grants direct to companies other than registered social landlords;
- introduce home information packs, to make buying and selling easier.

Each of these is worthy of legislative action, but even taken together they do not amount to an effective assault on the really big issues of the day: housing supply, especially affordable housing of all kinds, rising levels of homelessness, the deepening residualisation of social housing and the inequitable housing market.

Conclusion

The insignificance of the 2004 Housing Act is the final proof that, in housing policy terms at least, the most interesting thing about the year under review was that it marked the 25th anniversary of the election of the first Thatcher government, an event that guaranteed the introduction of the right to buy. In 1979, council housing reached a peak in numerical terms, and it has been going downhill ever since. After a generation of decline and denigration, it is arguably remarkable that the sector remains as large as it is, and that it is still a long way from the sort of utterly marginal, rundown public housing seen, for example, in the US. On the other hand, it is clear that there is no going back, and that it is necessary to come to terms with the fact that social housing in Britain faces a long-term future as a residual sector for the least well off. In 2004, there was no sign that government had a strategy for tackling residualisation, and every indication of enthusiasm for home ownership solutions and the expansion of private renting rather than investment in new social rented accommodation. No matter how convincing the critique of market-based policies, and no matter how unstable the housing market, there was also no sign of slackening enthusiasm among policy makers, nor, it must be acknowledged, the majority of the general public. Whichever party or faction is in power in Britain over the next few years, housing policy seems certain to be framed in terms of support for the market, and the risk and inequality that result from such an approach. To the extent that housing epitomises the application of opportunity society principles in social policy, it also indicates the distance travelled since the creation of the welfare state nearly 60 years ago, when risk and inequality were the targets of policy, not the desired outcomes.

References

Barker, K. (2003) *Review of housing supply: Interim report*, London: HM Treasury and ODPM.

Barker, K. (2004) *Review of housing supply: Final report*, London: HM Treasury and ODPM.

Bauman, Z. (1998) *Work, consumerism and the new poor*, Buckingham: Open University Press.

Birch, J. (2004) 'Is less more?', *Roof*, September/October, p 33.

Blair, T. (1998) *Leading the way: A new vision for local government*, London: Institute of Public Policy Research.

Blair, T. (2002) *The courage of our convictions: Why reform of public services is the route to social justice*, London: Fabian Society.

Bramley, G., Munro, M. and Pawson, H. (2004) *Key issues in housing*, Basingstoke: Palgrave.

Butler, T. and Robson, G. (2003) 'Plotting the middle classes: gentrification and circuits of education in London', *Housing Studies*, vol 18, no 1, pp 5-28.

Cheshire, P. and Sheppard, S. (2004) 'Capitalising the value of free schools: the impact of supply conditions and uncertainty', *Economic Journal*, vol 114, no 499, November, pp F397-F424.

Cowan, D. and Marsh, A. (eds) (2001) *Two steps forward: Housing policy into the new millennium*, Bristol: The Policy Press.

DETR (Department of the Environment, Transport and the Regions) (2000) *Quality and choice: A decent home for all. The Housing Green Paper*, London: The Stationery Office.

Ford, J. (2003) 'Housing policy', in N. Ellison and C. Pierson (eds) *Developments in British social policy 2*, Basingstoke: Palgrave, pp 153-9.

Ford, J., Burrows, R. and Nettleton, S. (2001) *Home ownership in a risk society*, Bristol: The Policy Press.

Garnett, D. and Perry, J. (2005) *Housing finance* (3rd edn), Coventry: Chartered Institute of Housing.

Hamnett, C. (1999) *Winners and losers*, London: UCL Press.

Harloe, M. (1995) *The people's home? Social rented housing in Europe and America*, Oxford: Blackwell.

HM Treasury (2004) *Spending review 2004*, London: The Stationery Office.

Kemp, P. (2004) *Private renting in transition*, Coventry: Chartered Institute of Housing.

Le Grand, J. (1991) 'Quasi-markets and social policy', *Economic Journal*, vol 101, pp 1256-67.

Lowe, S. (2004) *Housing policy analysis: British housing policy in cultural and comparative context*, Basingstoke: Palgrave Macmillan.

Lund, B. (2004) 'Housing policy: coming in from the cold?', in N. Ellison, L. Bauld and M. Powell (eds) *Social Policy Review 16*, Bristol: The Policy Press/Social Policy Association.

Malpass, P (2005) *Housing and the welfare state: The development of housing policy in Britain*, Basingstoke: Palgrave.

Malpass, P. and Mullins, D. (2002) 'Local authority housing stock transfer in the UK: from local initiative to national policy', *Housing Studies*, vol 17, no 4, pp 673-86.

Marsh, A. (2004) 'The inexorable rise of the rational consumer? The Blair government and the reshaping of social housing', *European Journal of Housing Policy*, vol 4, no 2, pp 185-207.

Marsh, A., Cowan, D., Cameron, A., Jones, M., Kiddle, C. and Whitehead, C. (2004) *Piloting choice based lettings: An evaluation*, London: ODPM.

ODPM (Office of the Deputy Prime Minister) (2003) *Sustainable communities: Building for the future*, London: ODPM.

ODPM (2004) *Annual Report* (www.odpm.gov.uk/stellent/groups/ odpm_about/documents/page/odpm_about_028586.hcsp).

Reynolds, L. (2004) *Housing Benefit pathfinder research: Report 2*, London: Shelter.

Torgersen, U. (1987) 'Housing: the wobbly pillar under the welfare state', in B. Turner, J. Kemeny and L. Lundqvist (eds) *Between state and market: Housing in the post-industrial era*, Stockholm: Almqvist and Wiksell.

Walker, B. and Marsh, A. (2003) 'Setting the rents of social housing: the impact and implications of rent restructuring in England', *Urban Studies*, vol 40, no 10, pp 2023-47.

Wilcox, S. (2003) *Can work – can't buy: Local measures of the ability of working households to become home owners*, York: Joseph Rowntree Foundation.

Wilcox, S. (2004a) *UK housing review 2004-2005*, Coventry/London: Chartered Institute of Housing/Council of Mortgage Lenders.

Wilcox, S. (2004b) *Affordability differences by area for working households buying their homes – 2003 update*, York: Joseph Rowntree Foundation.

FIVE

Personal Social Services

Ann Netten

Introduction

The objective of raising standards and improving the quality of publicly provided and purchased services crosses all aspects of public policy. This runs alongside continued emphasis on achieving or improving value for money. In 2004, and indeed during the past decade, there have been increased real levels of expenditure in areas such as criminal justice, health and social care, together with a plethora of performance indicators and targets associated with these objectives. To judge the success of such policies, we need to know whether these activities and expenditure are achieving benefits, both in terms of increased well-being and increased productivity of the resources used. This raises two questions – have such benefits been generated, and can we demonstrate that they have?

In the field of adult Personal Social Services (PSS), these are particularly difficult questions to answer. The overarching aims of PSS for adults are expressed in terms such as choice and independence, user-led and tailored services, and so on. Such global concepts do not lend themselves easily to measurement. Nevertheless, public funding of PSS in pursuit of these objectives continued to increase above the rate of inflation in 2004, and is planned to continue to increase at 6% above inflation until 2008 (DH, 2002a). If we are to assess the impact and improve targeting of such spend, there is a need to identify the benefits both at the macro level for evaluating progress and at the micro level to assist in service provision and performance measurement. There is increasing emphasis on using outcomes in setting targets and monitoring progress, but we need to be clear what we mean by outcomes and how they relate to other aspects of service quality that affect service users' lives.

The chapter starts by identifying what we mean by 'social care', using a theoretical framework, the social production of welfare, which draws on economic theory and puts individuals and their carers at the centre of the process. This allows us to consider what it is that we mean by outcome in social care and the implications for quality. It also allows us to identify whether trends in PSS policies and practice in recent years have the potential for delivering improved well-being and efficiency. The chapter ends by briefly speculating on the implications for performance measurement.

The consumption and production of social care

PSS for adults are concerned with improving the well-being of people or carers of people with mental, physical or emotional impairments. In the social production of welfare, our starting point is to consider how, in the absence of such impairment, we produce our own well-being. Mainstream consumer economics presents well-being as being directly derived through the consumption of goods and services. Ideas proposed by Becker (1965) and Lancaster (1966) are used in 'household' or 'home' economics to represent the household as both a unit of consumption of goods and services and a unit of production. In this approach, benefit is not gained directly from buying items such as rice and vegetables. Individuals also have to spend time and energy, and use consumer durables, in preparing and eating meals. The overall objective of the household is to produce well-being (or 'utility') for members of the household through what are termed 'commodities' such as social interaction, recreation and so on from which well-being is derived. The resources at the household's disposal in this process are primarily the time of household members, physical facilities and unearned income. These resources are used to generate income, to purchase goods and services, and to produce 'commodities' directly.

The effect of impairment of an individual will change the production process (Netten and Davies, 1990). From the individual household member perspective, it will change what they do and contribute to the household, and increase their demand for commodities. Thus, for example, if an individual breaks a hip, they may no longer be able to prepare meals and will need help getting dressed. As a result, the demand on household resources increases and the resources on which it can draw decrease. Long-term severe impairment (be it physical, mental or emotional) can mean the resources of the household can no longer produce enough for household members, so people from other households become routinely involved in helping out. Thus, the unit of production for social care becomes the informal care network.

Figure 5.1 shows the key elements of production in this framework:

- resource inputs: the time of informal care network members, physical facilities, unearned income and goods and services;
- costs: expenditure on goods and services;
- non-resource inputs: include attitudes and relationships between members of the household or informal care network;
- intermediate outcomes: include meals produced and social events;
- final outcomes: include all benefits derived from commodities including well-being of household members.

While the economic terminology reflects that used in descriptions of formal production, it is important to be clear that there are key differences between formal and informal sectors in the production of care. Litwak (1985), who drew on Weber, and Pollak (1985), who drew on transactions cost literature, arrived at very similar conclusions about the characteristics of formal and informal means of production. Both observers suggest that home production is characterised by simple technology and lack of need for technical skill. As the production of commodities becomes technologically more complex and/or more technical skill is required,

Figure 5.1: The social production of welfare

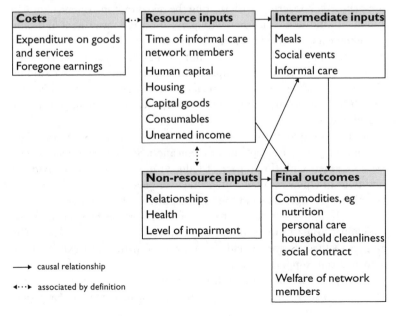

87

production is moved outside the domestic setting and becomes the responsibility of the state or the market. Thus, hospitals and schools increasingly provide health and education, historically provinces primarily of home production, as economies become more technologically advanced. The implication of this is that the commodities that are seen as the concern of social care agencies are culturally and historically specific.

Informal and formal production also differs in terms of motivation of members and structure of groups. Litwak (1985) argues that the type of task that can be undertaken by a group will depend upon the group structure. He classifies tasks by whether they require face-to-face continual contact or distance, long- or short-term commitment, large or small groups, common or different life styles and internalised or instrumental forms of motivation. He identifies a number of group structures and those tasks to which they are most suited. Thus, tasks that require long-term commitments and low division of labour, such as personal care of elderly disabled people, are best performed by a modified extended family.

In the formal sector, public expenditure in supporting production of welfare in the presence of impairment is associated with a number of different departments and agencies, each of which has different (if overlapping) objectives. PSS are concerned with the *impact* of impairment on people's lives, traditionally compensating for the impairment and more recently moving to an active promotion of well-being. Health services are primarily concerned with treating the *causes* of impairment, although public healthcare is concerned with prevention and investment in health. With respect to disabled people, housing services are primarily concerned with providing a *facilitative* environment. Public transport services are concerned with *facilitating* people with impairment in getting around. Education and employment services are concerned with *enhancing individuals' abilities*, primarily with the objective of participation in the workforce.

So, for example, for someone with severe arthritis, the NHS might provide a replacement hip and/or medication. Social care services would be concerned with the impact of reduced mobility on the individual's ability to get their meals, whether they were becoming socially isolated, whether they were safe and the sustainability of the care network. The type of housing, the degree to which transport services enabled the individual to get to the shops and so on, would affect these issues. The impact of these factors would depend on the nature and extent of the informal care support network.

Clearly, not all commodities in all circumstances have been regarded as social care issues: for example, the effect of impairment in older people on activities such as skiing has not been a matter of concern to social service agencies. Activities only become classified as care issues when the impact of their shortfall is identified as a matter of concern by the state. The question was at what point, and for which commodities, does a shortfall becomes the collective concern? In addressing the role of the state, Dasgupta, (1986) uses the concept of positive freedom, which is concerned "... among other things, with the *ability* of a person to *function*" (p 31; italics in original). This freedom is represented as dependent upon *basic* needs. Social care, therefore, could be represented as a set of basic commodities required to enable an individual and their care network to continue to function.

The commodities regarded as basic will depend to a degree on life-cycle considerations. For example, when adults with physical or mental difficulties are below retirement age, social care agencies will be concerned to ensure that they spend time on purposeful activity, be this employment or a near substitute. Traditionally, the emphasis of PSS has been very much on a compensatory approach. Changes in perceptions of the role of PSS could potentially raise questions about which commodities are regarded as 'basic', and the level of functioning at which people are seen as having positive freedom.

Quality and outcome in PSS

Government-funded PSS for adults will be expected to have a variety of effects depending on the type of service:

* aids and adaptations: improve the productivity of individuals with impairment;
* home care workers: usually substitute for household members by undertaking tasks such as personal care and meals preparation;
* meals services: supply intermediate outcomes directly to the household;
* social work interventions: can contribute to the technical efficiency of the care network in enabling individuals to access services, and through advocacy and counselling;
* respite and day care services: reduce the demand for help within the network;
* care management: increases the efficiency of service inputs by appropriate assessment, monitoring and matching of needs to resources;
* training and information services for carers: contribute to the 'human capital' or skills available to the household;

- financial contributions such as Direct Payments: add directly to the resources of the network and enable household members to purchase goods and services;
- residential care: replaces the entire production process.

The impact or outcome will be the difference between actual levels of well-being and the level expected in the absence of these interventions singly or combined in packages of care. As the list makes clear, the impact on the individual and the informal care network will depend both on the commodities produced and the process of production. The discussion earlier would suggest that the closer to the way that commodities are usually produced, the better the experience for the individual and the care network. This fits well with the normalisation literature that emphasises the importance of providing care in ways that fit with 'normal' lives (Wolfsenberger, 1972). However, how households are organised varies considerably, so ideally contributions to the process should fit in with the way that individuals and their care networks usually produce their own welfare.

On this basis, we would expect that services such as equipment and Direct Payments, which leave control of what is produced, and how it is produced, with the service user and their care network, would produce higher levels of well-being than services that substitute for household production such as meals and home care. Similarly, we would expect the widely observed resistance to residential care homes where the entire production process becomes communal rather than household-based and is ultimately under the control of professionals, however much homes may aim to foster autonomy and control among residents.

If outcome is the difference between actual and expected levels of well-being, this will be fundamentally dependent on the quality of service provision. The discussion earlier suggests that quality of service provision will be about:

- how much services actually deliver in terms of their potential to contribute to well-being;
- the mode of care – how well the intervention fits with individuals' abilities and preferred ways of producing their own well-being;
- the process – reliability, treating people with dignity and so on.

This leads to the question of the degree to which current policy and practice in PSS would be expected to foster or undermine quality of services and outcomes for service users.

Current trends in policy and practice

While New Labour promised a 'New Vision' for social care for adults, this did not materialise in 2004. Government policy continued, as in previous years, to focus on:

*   maximising independence;
*   maintaining people in their own home wherever possible;
*   increasing value for money;
*   providing and increasing choice;
*   user-led services;
*   protection of vulnerable people;
*   raising standards or improving quality;
*   prevention.

The objective of maximising independence has primarily been addressed through the second objective of maintaining people in their own homes as long as possible. Improving value for money and providing choice lay behind the encouragement and provision of incentives for councils with social service responsibilities (CSSRs) to develop and manage markets in social care in the early 1990s. These objectives remain very important but the current government has also put increased emphasis on drawing on the user perspective at all stages of service delivery, from strategic planning to evaluation of service performance, and on regulation to protect vulnerable consumers and raise standards of care. Partly in response to the effects of increased targeting of services (described later), there have been a number of grants and initiatives aimed at general prevention of deterioration. However, prevention has most clearly been reflected in central government concerns about the use of NHS resources. Inadequate levels or performance of social care services are seen to have knock-on consequences for the health service, particularly in the use of acute hospital beds either through inappropriate admissions or delayed discharges. This appears to be the most important driver of increased funding for PSS and has been the object of a number of specific grants including further funding announced during 2004 (DH, 2004a). Moreover, the move to partnerships between health and social care is most advanced in the development of intermediate care services where the aim is prevention of such admissions and discharges.

The results of these policies have been demonstrated in a substantial shift to independent rather than in-house provision of services, and a shift to people increasingly being cared for in their own homes. Figures

5.2-5.4 show the changing levels and balance of supply over recent years for residential care homes and home care respectively in England.

Figure 5.2: Residential care of older and younger disabled people

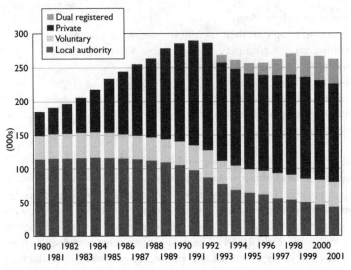

Source: DH statistics

Figure 5.3: Number of hours of home care

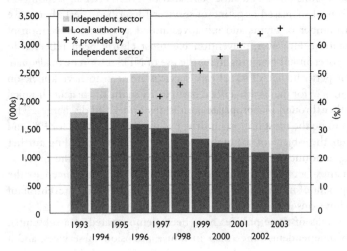

Source: DH statistics

Figure 5.4: Number of households receiving home care

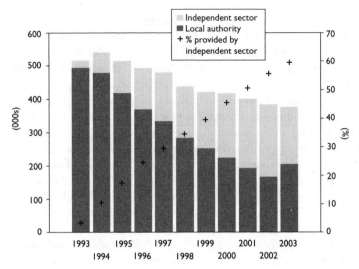

Source: DH statistics

The shift between in-house and independent provision that took place in the late 1980s and early 1990s in residential care has been mirrored in home care in the subsequent decade.

This shift has been due to the behaviour of CSSRs which, as the primary purchasers of care services, have substantial market power. They have largely used this power to keep prices down. This is not surprising as local authorities are under financial pressure, despite the increases in funding described earlier, both through competing demands on their funds and through specific government policies and efficiency targets. It was this, combined with a series of other pressures including the introduction of national care standards with their consequent cost implications, which led to a rapid rise in the rate of home closures during 1999 and 2000 (Netten et al, 2003).

The combination of maintaining people at home, who would previously have been in residential care, and increased targeting of services has led to considerable intensification of services. Figures 5.3 and 5.4 demonstrate the increase in intensity of home care provision. In recent years, the number of commissioned home care hours has been rising rapidly, but the number of households receiving home care and the number of care home places have been falling. As a result, the average number of publicly funded home care contact hours per household more than doubled from

3.5 hours per week in 1993 to 8.2 hours in 2003. Consequently, those with lower levels of need are increasingly purchasing support services independently of social services. The estimated number of older people with one problem with activities of daily living (such as bathing, dressing, feeding, washing and getting to and from the toilet) who were receiving private domestic help increased by 151% between 1995 and 1998 (Pickard et al, 2001).

Specific initiatives have been introduced in order to encourage independence and choice for older people. Extra Care Housing, a form of very sheltered accommodation where care services are available 24 hours a day, is being promoted as an alternative to traditional care home provision. The government announced plans for a 50% increase in the provision of Extra Care Housing places from 1997 (DH, 2002a) and created the Extra Care Housing for capital funding, although limits on the funds available meant a large number of proposals in the first round were not successful (DH, 2004b).

Central government is also putting considerable policy emphasis on Direct Payments where, based on an assessment of needs, the individual is allocated funds and (to a lesser or greater degree) support to organise and purchase, or commission, their own services. Direct Payments have been an option for younger disabled people for some time but became available to older people in 2000 (DH, 2000). Aside from the very significant influence of disability groups in promoting Direct Payments policies, Direct Payments have been driven forward by the government due to a number of perceived benefits:

- providing choice, control and flexibility to service users;
- providing more efficient and effective matching of resources to needs, and potentially improved outcomes as people decide on services that reflect their personal preferences;
- expanding the potential pool of caregivers with flexible arrangements appealing to personal contacts and to people who would find employment with an agency too restrictive;
- a reduction in the CSSR administrative costs associated with management of care service packages.

There have been concerns about the low take-up of Direct Payments, especially among older people. In 2004, this led the government to allocate further funding to partnerships between voluntary organisations and local authorities to provide support to those using Direct Payments (DH, 2004c).

There is increasing emphasis on interventions that represent positive contributions to well-being and in some instances this may be the reality already. For example, in *Valuing people* (DH, 2001a) the objectives for learning disabled children and adults include achieving fulfilling lives and social inclusion. Day care services for younger people have moved away from the traditional 'day centre'-type approach, still prevalent in services for older people, and towards supporting people to participate in mainstream recreational activities and employment.

Implications for quality and outcomes

Given the social production of welfare framework and the evidence available, current trends in policy and practice could be hypothesised to have both positive and negative effects on quality and outcomes for service users.

The increased use of the market in the provision of PSS fits well with the way that households and individuals produce their own welfare in our society at present: purchasing services to produce those commodities that they do not want or cannot produce themselves. However, this is an area where the impairment that leads to the use of services means the consumer is at a particular disadvantage and normal features of the market, such as businesses going out of business, can have a disproportionate effect on quality of life. This is brought into sharp relief when care homes close. Essentially, people are evicted from their homes at short notice with no rights. Moreover, it is difficult to maintain standards at a time when staff will be either leaving or looking for other jobs.

Given that people prefer to remain in their own homes, we might expect that maintaining people at home who would otherwise have moved into a care home has resulted in increased levels of well-being. On the other hand, increased targeting has resulted in reductions of numbers of people receiving low-level support, particularly domestic support, as those responsible for commissioning services have shifted away from regarding household cleanliness and tidiness as a basic commodity, a shift in perceptions that older people do not necessarily share (Clark et al, 1998). Moreover, the emphasis on keeping costs down might be expected to have a negative effect on the quality of service provision.

Although services are more intensive than in the past, are they sufficient? It is interesting to note that, while in England over 10 hours per week is regarded as intensive, in New York (admittedly an outlier even in the US) the average number of personal assistant hours (the equivalent of the home care service) is 47 per week (Simone, 2004)! Moreover, in most authorities, until recently at least there has been a task-based approach to commissioning, which has resulted in more but shorter visits of half an hour or less. This is very much a formal organisational approach to production, which contrasts with the informal household production process. It is interesting to note how more experienced care workers at the sharp end of this conflict often adopt informal procedures and use of their own time to compensate for perceived inadequacies of care (Francis and Netten, 2003). This in turn leads to inequity, as what people will get in practice will depend as much on the attitudes of the organisation and the individual care worker as on the services commissioned by the CSSR. A less formal approach might mean that the home care service would simply increase the resources of the care network and thus fit very well with the way that care is usually produced.

In the field of care homes, although the care standards are designed to improve quality, there are concerns that the long-term emphasis by local authorities on keeping prices down will have had a negative effect on service quality. Increased levels of funding were made available to local authorities to enable them to enter into long-term agreements with independent sector providers and, where necessary, to increase fees, in order to develop and improve services and to help stabilise the care home sector (DH, 2001b, 2002b). Authorities responded: Laing & Buisson reported that for care homes fee inflation exceeded wage cost inflation in 2002/03 for the first time in many years. However, they noted that increases in the fees paid varied considerably between local authorities. While we would hope that this would feed through to improved levels of quality, there is a lot of catching up to do.

The emphasis on Extra Care Housing for older people as an alternative to care homes would also be expected to have a positive effect. The household is retained as the basic unit of production, with people having their own front door, kitchen and bathroom, with the added benefit of close access to sources of help, communal facilities and other people. As identified earlier, we would also expect that the emphasis on ensuring people have access to Direct Payments should allow people to identify the way that best supports their own production of welfare. However, in both instances, it is how the policy works in practice that will ultimately affect outcomes for individuals. Under the pressure of high levels of impairment among residents, might Extra Care Housing end up delivering the worst of all worlds with isolated residents who feel they are not in their own homes and have little control over the production of their own welfare? In the case of Direct Payments, inadequate support could leave people distressed and vulnerable to exploitation.

Shifts in emphasis to the active promotion of well-being potentially could have implications for the commodities or aspects of quality of life that are seen as the concern of social services. However, it is more likely that public expenditure on PSS would continue to be limited to those commodities or aspects of well-being that are regarded as fundamentally important to individuals' abilities to function, but would put more emphasis on the individual's control and social integration through access to, and use of, mainstream facilities.

Performance measurement and targets in social care

Policy moves and changes in recent years have had the intention of raising quality and improving outcomes of PSS. However, identified earlier are a number of reasons why we might expect there to be some problems with the way policies have worked in practice. In addition, there are other factors, such as shortages in the direct care workforce (Henwood, 2001), which we might expect to have an impact on the quality of services and associated outcomes for service users.

It is clearly important that we are able to measure and monitor performance in a meaningful way. Indeed DH press notices during 2004 that relate to PSS or social care were dominated by reports of or discussions about performance measurement of one sort or another. Demand for such measurement includes:

- evaluating the effectiveness of central government policies and impact of public expenditure;
- setting Best Value targets for improving efficiency and effectiveness (DH, 1999);
- setting local public service agreements (DH, 1999);
- validating and monitoring care standards (CSCI, 2004a);
- quality assurance (CSCI, 2004a);
- measuring outputs and productivity for National Accounts (Atkinson, 2004).

Currently indicators of inputs and process dominate the measures that are used. For example, although the PSS performance assessment framework (PAF) identifies a set of indicators for adults that are intended to reflect 'effectiveness of service delivery and outcomes', in practice they represent counts of people admitted to or receiving services (CSCI, 2004b).

In each of these areas, there are moves to make measures and targets more outcomes focused – reflecting the impact on well-being rather than simply identifying levels of activity. Best Value indicators for home care of older people and community support of younger adults are now based on responses to user experience surveys (DH, 2003, 2004d). In the field of healthcare, economic evaluation outcomes are increasingly measured using quality-adjusted life years, which reflect both length of life and broad aspects of health-related quality of life weighted to reflect population views of their relative importance (Drummond et al, 1997). Moves are currently under way to build on this in the measurement of government output and productivity at a national level (Atkinson, 2004). There is a need in social care for an equivalent that reflects the objectives of PSS and can be weighted to reflect the preferences of the population most relevant for the purpose. In many instances, this will be service user views but there are also arguments that, where we are considering competing priorities for public funds, population preferences are most appropriate. This is not to suggest that such a measure would replace the need for other measures of quality – more that clarity of understanding the objectives of services and identifying the relative importance of these to service users will help us in setting targets and standards in a way that reflects the impact on people's well-being.

Taking the social production of welfare approach described earlier, we represent services as contributing to the production of commodities. One measure of outcome for PSS might be the degree to which services contribute to this process. This suggests we need to identify the 'basic' commodities with which PSS are concerned. This is focused on the 'maintenance' outcomes identified by Qureshi and colleagues (1998).

Previous work on outcomes of social care (Netten et al, 2002) identified, and has attempted to attach preference weights to, the core 'commodities' for services for older people:

- personal care;
- meals and nutrition;
- social participation and involvement;
- control over daily life;
- safety.

This study found that concerns about safety, a factor that profoundly affects the allocation of services for older people, was regarded as the least important of these by older people themselves. Measures and targets that reflect the relative importance of different dimensions of outcome build in incentives to develop services in ways that better reflect people's preferences and thus contribute to their well-being.

Other commodities that might ideally be included in order to extend
the applicability of the approach include:

* employment and occupation;
* support in caring roles (including that of parent);
* accommodation (cleanliness, order and comfort).

PSS do not have a monopoly on these commodities in terms of either
overall production (which is dominated by the informal sector) or
government spend. In many instances, and particularly as service objectives
move to active promotion of well-being, the PSS role will be more about
access to other facilities and services than delivering or facilitating the
production of the commodities directly.

Other dimensions of outcome need to be taken into consideration.
We identified earlier that where production takes place will have a
profound effect on both the process itself and how people feel about the
process and outcome. We should reflect, therefore, whether people are
living in what they regard as their own home. PSS also have an important
information and educational role, which might not be reflected in
commodity production but represents an increase in knowledge and
abilities or 'human capital' of service users and their carers. Moreover,
some services, particularly for younger disabled people, aim actively to
promote health, so we might expect improvements in health status or
prevention of unnecessary deterioration (the 'change' outcomes identified
by Qureshi and colleagues [1998]). In addition, there are process outcomes
(Qureshi et al, 1998), aspects of quality of care, such as being treated with
dignity and respect, which we would also want to reflect and which
might not be easily identified through their impact on our basic
commodities, although they would clearly influence people's sense of
control, for example.

Current work is looking at ways of bringing together these different
aspects of quality and well-being in ways that can be used to measure
performance of PSS. The work was initiated in response to concerns that
measures of government output currently do not reflect the impact of
government expenditure on the welfare of the population, or accurately
identify changes in productivity of services (Atkinson, 2004). The approach
being developed involves mapping or describing service in terms of the
commodities or domains of outcome that they affect and the degree to
which service users rely on them (Netten et al, 2005). The intention is to
link such descriptors to indicators of service quality. By enhancing our
understanding of what services are doing and for whom, the approach

offers a potentially helpful way forward in comparing and monitoring the effects of different types of intervention. Such an approach has the potential to facilitate comparability between different types of interventions both within the UK and internationally.

There is a need for a body of indicators that fulfil different functions but where we know the relationships between them. For example, increasingly people's control over their own daily lives is regarded as a key objective of PSS. For monitoring purposes or setting targets, only crude indicators of service users' sense of control over their daily lives are likely to be practical. Such indicators could potentially be weighted to reflect the relative importance of this aspect of people's quality of life. More detailed studies could explore the relationship between the indicator and more sophisticated measures of control, individual characteristics and circumstances, and service interventions. Further work that then linked such measures to judgements and reporting of care standards by regulators would enhance our understanding and the value of each of the measures or indicators.

Conclusion

Despite good intentions, the impact of prevailing policies, practice and productivity of PSS in producing well-being is uncertain. There is a need to measure the impact of PSS both to reflect macro concerns about the value of output and changes in productivity and efficiency, and to better provide feedback to providers and authorities in the management of services. In 2004, as in previous years, measures tended to be dominated by activity and process. In developing measures that better reflect outcome and quality of service provision, we need a clear understanding of how services contribute to well-being. The social production of welfare contributes to this understanding by placing the individual and their care network at the heart of the production process, and by identifying the role of service interventions. Building on this, we could envisage an approach that links services to their impact, which should enhance our understanding of the outcomes and productivity of PSS.

Acknowledgements

This chapter reflects the results of ongoing work in the Personal Social Services Unit, University of Kent, and discussions with a number of other experts in the field. I would particularly like to thank Caroline Glendinning, Eric Emerson, Raphael Wittenberg and Becky Sandhu. I am indebted to many of my colleagues but in particular Jose-Luis Fernandez and Martin Knapp for the use of figures compiled for a review undertaken for the Social Care Institute for Excellence of social care in the UK.

References

Atkinson, T. (2004) *Atkinson review: Interim report. Measurement of government output and productivity for the National Accounts*, London: The Stationery Office.

Becker, G. (1965) 'A theory of the allocation of time', *The Economic Journal*, September, vol 75, no 299, pp 493-517.

CSCI (Commission for Social Care Inspection) (2004a) *Social services performance assessment framework indicators*, London: CSCI.

CSCI (2004b) *Inspecting for better lives (modernising the regulation of social care)*, London: CSCI.

Clark, H., Dyer, S. and Horwood, L. (1998) *'That bit of help': The high value of low level preventative services for older people*, Bristol: The Policy Press.

Dasgupta, P. (1986) 'Positive freedom, markets and the welfare state', *Oxford Review of Economic Policy*, vol 2, no 2, pp 25-36.

DH (Department of Health) (1999) *A new approach to social services*, Consultation document, London: DH.

DH (2000) *Community Care (Direct Payments) Act 1996: Policy and practice guidance* (2nd edn), London: DH.

DH (2001a) *Valuing people: A new strategy for learning disability for the 21st century*, London: DH.

DH (2001b) *£300m 'cash for change' initiative to tackle 'bedblocking': Agreement with private and voluntary sectors provides foundation for radical reform programme*, Press release 2001/0464, London: DH.

DH (2002a) 'Expanded services and increased choices for older people: investment and reform for older people's social services', Press release 2002/0324, London: DH.

DH (2002b) '£200m allocated to councils to further reduce 'bedblocking': delayed discharges reduced by ten per cent since September', Press release 2002/0007, London: DH.

DH (2003) *Personal social services survey of home care users in England aged 65 or over: 2002-03*, Statistical bulletin 2003/26, London: DH.

DH (2004a) 'An extra £100 million for social services to tackle delayed discharge', Press release 2004/0502, 28 November, London: DH.

DH (2004b) "'Independence not dependence": New Extra Care Housing places for older people announced', Press release 2004/0070, London: DH.

DH (2004c) 'Successful bids to the second round', Press release 2004/0223, 14 June, London: DH.

DH (2004d) *Personal social services survey of physically disabled and sensory impaired users in England aged 18-64: 2003-04*, Statistical bulletin 2004/03, London: DH.

Drummond, M.F., O'Brien, B., Stoddart, G.L. and Torrance, G.W. (1997) *Methods for the economic evaluation of healthcare programmes* (2nd edn), Oxford: Oxford University Press.

Francis, J. and Netten, A. (2003) *Home care workers: Careers, commitments and motivations*, PSSRU discussion paper no 2053, Canterbury: Personal Social Services Research Unit, University of Kent.

Henwood, M. (2001) *Future imperfect?*, Report of the King's Fund Care and Support Inquiry, London: King's Fund.

Laing & Buisson (2004) *Care of elderly people: Market Survey 2004, 17th edn*, London: Laing & Buisson.

Lancaster, K. (1966) A new approach to consumer theory, *Journal of Political Economy*, vol 74, issue 2, pp 132-57.

Litwak, E. (1985) *Helping the elderly: The complementary roles of informal networks and formal systems*, New York, NY: Guilford Press.

Netten, A. and Davies, B. (1990) 'The social production of welfare and consumption of social services', *Journal of Public Policy*, vol 10, no 3, pp 331-47.

Netten, A., Darton, R. and Williams, J. (2003) 'Nursing home closures: effects on capacity and reasons for closure', *Age and Ageing*, vol 32, no 3, pp 332-7.

Netten, A., McDaid, D., Fernandez, J.-L., Forder, J., Knapp, M., Matosevic, T. and Shapiro, J. (2005) *Measuring and understanding social services outputs*, Discussion paper no 2132/2, Canterbury: Personal Social Services Research Unit, University of Kent.

Netten, A., Ryan, M., Smith, P., Skatun, D., Healey, A., Knapp, A. and Wykes, T. (2002) *The development of a measure of social care outcome for older people*, Discussion paper no 1690/2, Canterbury: Personal Social Services Research Unit, University of Kent (www.ukc.ac.uk/PSSRU/).

Pickard, L., Wittenberg, R., Comas-Herrera, A., Davies, B. and Darton, R. (2001) *Community care for frail older people: Analysis using the 1998/99 General Household Survey. Quality in later life: Rights, rhetoric and reality*, Proceedings of the British Society of Gerontology 30th Annual Conference, 31 August-2 September, Stirling: University of Stirling, Scotland.

Pollak, R.A. (1985) 'A transaction cost approach to families and households', *Journal of Economic Literature*, vol 23, issue 2, pp 581-608.

Qureshi, H., Patmore, C., Nicholas, E. and Bamford, C. (1998) *Outcomes in community care practice. Overview: Outcomes of social care for older people and carers*, York: Social Policy Research Unit, University of York.

Simone, B. (2004) 'Personal care services in New York', Paper given at the Gerontological Society of America 57th Annual Scientific Meeting, 19-23 November, Washington DC.

Wolfsenberger, W. (1972) *The principle of normalisation in human services*, Toronto: National Institute on Mental Retardation.

Part Two:
Current issues

Governance and social policy in Northern Ireland (1999-2004): the devolution years and postscript

Eithne McLaughlin

Introduction

The objective of this chapter is to identify the most significant developments in the governance arrangements for and the content of social policy in Northern Ireland during the period of devolution introduced by the Labour government in 1999. This period of devolution existed from 1999 to October 2002.

Protracted and difficult political negotiations in 1997 culminated in what is variously called The Belfast Agreement, the Good Friday Agreement (NIO, 1998) and the Northern Ireland Peace Agreement (Irish Government, 1998). The Agreement made provision for a form of devolved government in Northern Ireland. These provisions were subsequently legislated for in the 1998 Northern Ireland Act. The Act is not only a piece of UK legislation but an international treaty, specifically a treaty between the British and Irish governments.

The period 1999-2002 was a turbulent one politically. Four periods of short-term suspension of the devolved institutions occurred prior to the suspension, which began in October 2002 and which remained in force at the time of writing. The on and off nature of devolution was thus so great that this chapter came near to being titled 'The devolution year' rather than 'the devolution years'.

As seems always to be the case with Northern Ireland, even a short period of history such as the one under consideration here requires considerable explanation in order to render it meaningful and relevant to the external observer. A further objective of this chapter is therefore to set Northern Ireland's 21st-century experience of devolution in the context of the territory's prior experiences of devolution on the one hand, and the broader devolution experience of the UK as a whole at the turn of the 21st century on the other.

The first section of the chapter summarises key features of the history of social policy in and governance arrangements for Northern Ireland since its inception in 1922.

The second section reports on the main aspects of policy divergence and convergence in the 1999-2002 period, and describes the institutions established under devolution during that time.

The third section of the chapter notes the most significant developments that began during devolution and that have been carried forward in the post-devolution 'direct rule' period of 2002-04.

The governance and status of Northern Ireland

Northern Ireland has been a small territory within the UK since 1922, following the partition of Ireland. It includes six of the nine counties of the old Irish province of Ulster. Its population is approximately two million. For much of the period since 1922, it is and has been a jurisdiction in its own right and is therefore not properly categorised as a region of the UK. On the other hand, for many years of its existence the territory has not had autonomous government. Such ambiguities have led some to label it a 'state-let' (see, for example, Coulter, 1999).

The ambiguity of the territory is not just a matter of semantics; the ambiguity creates real methodological difficulties for comparative research involving the territory (see Rose, 1982; McLaughlin and Yeates, 1999; Rottman, 1999; McLaughlin et al, 2002; Tomlinson, 2002; McLaughlin and Kelly, 2003).

The long-standing problem of how to theorise the nature of the territory has made inclusion of it in comparative regime typologies particularly difficult. Most comparative regime analyses remain at the level of the nation state and have therefore excluded sub-national cases such as Northern Ireland, even when the institutions and systems of interest to the analysis have been very different in the sub-national unit than in the 'parent' national unit as a whole. Duncan (1995), however, provided an interesting example of a sub-national gender regime analysis. In Duncan's analysis of gender and welfare regimes within the UK, Northern Ireland is categorised as being more similar to Wales than to either Scotland or England. Northern Ireland and Wales were characterised by Duncan as remaining within 'the housewife contract' characteristic of the Bismarckian countries, while Scotland and England were characterised as being in transition from it.

As noted earlier, for much but not all of the post–1922 period, some type of subsidiary authority or government has existed at the six–county level. Four separate periods of subsidiary or devolved government have occurred. 'Direct rule' is the term used to refer to periods when elected institutions of subsidiary government have not existed within the territory. There have been 57 years of 'devolved' government of varying extent and 23 years of direct rule in the territory since 1922. The devolved arrangements agreed in 1998 in Northern Ireland were thus placed into a context weighted with expectations from previous experiences of devolution, a context very different from that pertaining in Scotland and Wales in June 1999, New Labour's 'UK devolution date'. Table 6.1 provides a summary chronology of the governance arrangements in force in Northern Ireland since 1922.

The first period of devolution in Northern Ireland ran from 1922 to 1972. During this time, a Northern Ireland Parliament was responsible for all matters except foreign policy, taxation and national security. A second period of more limited devolution ran from 1982 to 1986. During this period a locally elected Assembly existed but had very limited powers. It was boycotted by the nationalist political parties, the Social Democratic and Labour Party (SDLP) and Sinn Fein, leaving only the small Alliance Party to join Unionist party representatives. As Wilford notes, "the Assembly staggered on until 1986 but never moved beyond the first stage of scrutinising the agencies of direct rule" (Wilford, 2001, p 128). Wilford and Rose both comment on the limited powers within Westminster for scrutiny of the Northern Ireland administration and, in particular, the Northern Ireland Office under both devolved and direct rule arrangements (Rose, 1982, 1990; Wilford, 2001, p 137).

Table 6.1: An historical summary of Northern Ireland governance arrangements

1922-72	The Northern Ireland Parliament
1972-82	Direct Rule[a]
1982-86	Northern Ireland Assembly
1986-99	Direct Rule
1999-2002	Northern Ireland Assembly
2002-04	Direct Rule

Note: [a] This period of Direct Rule was interrupted in 1974 for a short period by a form of devolved government – the Power-Sharing Executive.

The 27-year period of direct rule (1972-99) was interrupted by a short period of devolution under the 1974 Power-Sharing Executive. The short-lived Executive was brought down by the Ulster Workers' Council Strike and the inability or unwillingness of the British government and military to confront the strikers. The Executive had nonetheless had time to dissolve the Community Relations Council before direct rule was re-established. Commenting on the differences between direct rule ministers in Northern Ireland and their respective parent governments in the UK over the 1972-99 period, Gaffikin and Morrissey (1990) point out that the last Labour Secretary of State for Northern Ireland had responded to civil conflict by relatively generous social policies on the one hand and a strong military posture on the other. Aspects of this stance persisted under the subsequent Conservative Secretaries of State. Nearly all Conservative Secretaries of State accepted the need for a comprehensive approach to conflict resolution, involving social and economic policies as well as the military (Wilford, 2001). It is too extreme to conclude that Northern Ireland escaped all the restrictions on public expenditure that the advent of the Thatcher administrations in Britain heralded, but it is true that the extent of restriction was less in Northern Ireland than Britain.

During the 1922-72 period of devolution, the subsequent periods of direct rule (1972-82) and limited devolution (1982-86), the content of social policy and the welfare 'state' in Northern Ireland shared a great deal of similarity with that in the rest of the UK, but it did not and still does not share all aspects or features of it. Dominated by the single party government of the Ulster Unionist Party, a majoritarian, confessional Unionist government had ruled defensively over the first 50 years of Northern Ireland's existence. Unionist administrations prioritised stability of the constitutional position over social and economic concerns. Many of the latter were delegated to local government, for which there was a restricted franchise.

Difference within the union

As a result, Northern Ireland's welfare system contrasted with that in Britain in so far as there was a stronger ethos of 'small government' and more 'arm's length' public service delivery by what today we would describe as Next Steps Agencies, quangos and/or local government.

I have argued elsewhere (McLaughlin, 1998; McLaughlin and Fahey, 1999) that, throughout most of the post-war era, these characteristics of Northern Irish welfarism coupled with the small scale of the territory inevitably resulted in a particularly influential political and cultural position for welfare professionals and the middle classes generally. Correspondingly, there was a weak culture of citizenship and social rights. These characteristics, together with significant restrictions on the civil and political rights of the population, meant that Northern Ireland in the 1922-98 period was a society with a weak social infrastructure and exaggerated hierarchies of dominance, subordination and inequality, (Darby, 1983; McGarry and O'Leary, 1995; Coulter, 1999; Ellison and Martin, 2000).

The fourth period of devolution in the territory (1999-2002) – the 'New Labour period' – involved a more restricted range of public policy domains than had the first because of the exclusion of criminal justice and policing from the devolved powers. As in the first period, the devolved government had no powers in relation to Income Tax or National Insurance. The extent of devolved powers in Northern Ireland was nonetheless more extensive in Northern Ireland than in either Scotland or Wales in the same period (see Stewart, 2004, and Chaney, 2004, for accounts of the Scottish and Welsh devolution experiences; also Tomlinson, 2002, on the Northern Ireland institutions of devolution). The Northern Ireland Assembly had responsibility for some 54% of public expenditure (Tomlinson, 2002).

The exclusion of criminal justice in this period of devolution reflected domestic and international concern that the pre-1972 history of maladministration of the justice and policing systems, and use of the latter to enforce inequalities of civil and political rights, might be repeated.

It also reflected concerns about continued paramilitary violence. The largest paramilitary organisation concerned, the provisional IRA, had ceased most but not all of its activities in 1994. Other smaller paramilitary organisations did not declare ceasefires. For example, the Ulster Defence Association (UDA), the largest loyalist paramilitary organisation, did not declare a cessation of its activities until November 2004.

Before and after 1999, public expenditure within the UK has been allocated at the sub-national level in accordance with the Barnett formula. See Tomlinson (2002) for an extended and comparative discussion of the implications of the Barnett formula for Northern Ireland compared with the rest of the UK until 2000.

The history of devolved government up to 1972, and the general denial of civil, political and social rights to the minority nationalist 'community', has been extensively documented elsewhere (see, for example, Darby, 1983; McGarry and O'Leary, 1995; Coulter, 1999). For the purposes of this chapter, what is of interest is not that history itself but rather the stance taken by successive Westminster governments to the main devolved territory it had. Westminster maintained distance from the 'internal affairs' of its devolved territory and did not proactively create or ensure a common UK citizenship – that is, a common platform of social, civil and political rights.

Some may interpret such distance as peculiar to the period, politics and territory involved, but it may also be legitimate to interpret it as a sign that Westminster, as a set of institutions and a political culture, may not be capable of creating or claiming for itself the oversight and guarantor of common standards of the citizenship role, which Jeffrey (2002) has argued is required in the re-modelled 'looser' UK brought about by New Labour devolution and consequent policy divergence between the countries of the UK. The ambiguity of the UK as a union of 'countries' rather than a unitary state (Rose, 1982) can thus be argued to both precede and postdate 'New Labour's devolution experiment' rather than originate from it.

During the various direct rule periods in Northern Ireland, policies developed in and for England and Wales, and legislation passed in Westminster, have been largely 'read across' to Northern Ireland.

Such legislation has been subject to limited consultation processes – for example, with the Northern Ireland Law Society – and minor amendment only prior to passage as 'Order(s) in Council' through the Privy Council at Westminster. The Northern Ireland Civil Service has remained largely outwith political scrutiny and oversight during these periods.

Despite considerable 'read across' of English and Welsh provisions over these lengthy periods, Northern Ireland has maintained and created distinctive structures and institutions of welfare delivery and public services. In education, a bifurcated second-level system has been maintained. In health and social services, an integrated structure of health and personal social services not involving local government was created in the 1972-74 period.

The four area Health and Social Services Boards created in 1972-74 replaced the prior Northern Ireland Hospital Trust and local council community health departments. In housing, after 1972, the Northern Ireland Housing Executive performed the social housing functions expected of local government in the rest of the UK. Official statistics and research functions have been the responsibility not of the UK's Office for National Statistics but the Northern Ireland Statistics and Research Agency. The latter, together with the academy's anglocentrism, have meant that neither UK official statistics nor most academic social policy literature have usually included Northern Ireland.

One of the least well-understood aspects of devolution in the 'New Labour' period, and a significant point of difference between Scottish and Welsh as compared with Northern Irish devolution, was that the Northern Ireland Assembly had powers in relation to social security. These powers formally permitted the Assembly to introduce social security variance between Britain and Northern Ireland. The 'small print' of the arrangements, however, made variance subject to UK Exchequer approval if it would result in an increase in public expenditure. It was understood that in such an instance approval would be conditional on the increase being met from within 'the existing Northern Ireland "block vote"' – that is, from within existing allocations to Northern Ireland for education, health services and so on.

The post-1999 Assembly did introduce one element of social security variance through the 2000 Child Support, Pensions and Social Security Act. This Act amended the Northern Ireland law relating to child support, occupational and personal pensions, and amended a number of Northern Ireland family law instruments. Specifically, the Act made provision for the removal of driving licences from parents defaulting on the child support payments required of them. This was the only major piece of social legislation introduced by the Assembly before it was suspended in 2002.

The institutions of devolution

The institutions of devolution included, as noted earlier, an Assembly that was directly elected by the population. The Assembly had committees responsible for scrutinising each of the 10 Northern Ireland spending departments.

The Northern Ireland spending departments were the Departments of Education; Employment, Education and Learning; Social Development; Culture, Arts and Leisure; Health, Personal Social Services and Public Safety; Finance and Personnel; the Environment; Enterprise, Trade and Investment; Agriculture and Rural Development; the Office of the First Minister and Deputy First Minister. The latter had a coordinating role somewhat similar to the Cabinet Office in Westminster, as well as special responsibility for equality and human rights matters. Further detail on the structure and nature of the devolved departments and the large number of non-departmental public bodies sponsored by them can be found at www.rpani.gov.uk.

The nine ministers, First Minister and Deputy First Minister were elected by the Assembly under a de Hont system. The ministers thus formed a cross-party Executive. The de Hont system has been used in UK Euro elections since 1999. Within the Northern Ireland Assembly, its use meant that ministers had to be approved by a majority of Assembly members from within each of the Nationalist and Unionist party blocs as well as a majority across them.

In addition to the Assembly, a Civic Forum was established with some members appointed to it by the Secretary of State for Northern Ireland and some elected to reserved seats on it by organisations of business and the third sector. This parallel 'Assembly of the social partners' engaged in some interesting policy development work – for example, on social inclusion (Kelly and Wilson, 2002). By the time of suspension in October 2002, the Forum had not, however, gained full acceptance of its work or role from the Assembly, the civil service or the general public. The Civic Forum mirrored some of the social partnership institutions existing in the South of Ireland (for example, the latter's National Economic and Social Council and National Economic and Social Forum).

The institutions of devolution also included a North–South Ministerial Council and joint Secretariat, the British–Irish Council and a number of North–South bodies responsible for implementing all-island policy developments in six agreed domains. These domains were transport, agriculture, education, health, environment and tourism. Tomlinson (2002, p 62) provides a list of the implementation bodies established. These bodies were accountable to the North–South Ministerial Council and thereafter to the *Oireachtas* (the Irish Parliament) and the Northern Ireland Assembly.

Divergence in the 1999-2002 period

The turbulence of 'on again'/'off again' devolution in the 1999-2002 period undoubtedly limited the capacity of the devolved institutions and elected representatives to engage in policy development and increase their policy literacy. It was also too short a period to significantly alter the culture, practices or position of strength of the Northern Ireland Civil Service. Nonetheless, in addition to the 2000 Child Support, Pensions and Social Security Act, a number of other developments and divergence with the rest of the UK occurred and are outlined later. The extent of policy divergence has been underestimated by commentators such as Keating (2002a, 2002b). Keating acknowledges that significant policy divergence did occur under Northern Irish devolution. Keating's summary of the UK's devolution experiences for the ESRC's Devolution Research

Programme, however, marginalises and misrepresents the Northern Irish experience in a number of ways.

Keating (2002b, p 8) concluded that:

> ... with the exception of Northern Ireland, devolution under 'New Labour' has been implemented and has worked extremely smoothly. There have not been any notable legal disputes about the division of competences between UK and devolved institutions, even in areas which in other decentralised states are frequently the cause of conflict, like territorial financial arrangements or devolved participation in EU affairs.

Keating proposes two main reasons why devolution in the UK occurred so smoothly under New Labour.

First, a single party has been the party of government at both central and devolved level. Second, the Home Civil Service provides a unifying force between the countries. It is true that neither of these factors pertained in Northern Ireland, which experienced anything but 'smooth' devolution. Some see the instability of devolution in Northern Ireland as rooted in the specifics of Northern Irish politics. For example, Wilson and Wilford (2000, 2001, 2003) account for it in terms of the unique nature of the devolved structures and institutions established.

Wilson and Wilford (2000, 2001, 2003) argue that the 'consociational-plus' nature of the institutions set up by the 1998 Northern Ireland Act was inherently unstable because in their view they institutionalised 'sectarianism' and sectarian political divisions. The De Hont voting system within the Assembly was argued to be especially problematic.

Others see the instability of devolution in Northern Ireland as resulting from an unwillingness on the part of the Westminster government to fully implement and support the Agreement itself – in other words, from flaws in the implementation of the Agreement rather than from flaws in the nature of the Agreement.

The first task of the cross-party Executive formed in 1999 was to develop an agreed 'Programme for Government'. The Programme for Government (2004-07) established five executive priorities. These were growing as a community, working for a healthier people, investing in education and skills, securing a competitive economy and developing North–South, East–West and international relations.

The priorities were each supported by special top-sliced executive funds: The Children's Fund, The Social Inclusion and Community Regeneration Fund, The Innovation and Modernisation Fund and The Strategic Investment Programme. The equality and human rights agenda, which had been of great prominence within the Northern Ireland Act and the political negotiations preceding it, was not explicitly reflected in either the Programme for Government priorities or the parallel special funds.

Thus, neither Targeting Social Need, the nearest Northern Ireland came to an anti-poverty or social inclusion strategy (Dignan and McLaughlin, 2002), nor equality attracted specific funds or initiatives. The imperative of cross-party agreement meant that 'the unambiguously deserving poor' – children and older people – became the population sub-groups that benefited most from divergence and devolved concern. Similarly, policy fields that did not directly embody legacies of Northern Ireland's divided past were those in which most policy development occurred. The 2000 Child Support and Social Security Act is a good example of 'cross-community' and cross-party consensus on 'family values'. The danger that under devolution a lowest common denominator of conservative social values and social policies might emerge thus appears from what was admittedly a very limited period of devolution to be a concern, with some legitimacy.

Keating's conclusions on devolution in the UK marginalise the Northern Ireland case in a further sense. In the Northern Ireland case, there has been disagreement about the competencies of the various institutions of devolution. Predictably, some of this has focused on the North–South bodies established; but further contention has also existed around the division of responsibilities between Westminster and Northern Ireland departments in the policy-making process.

The latter has been evident in relation to the policy-making processes prescribed under the 1998 Northern Ireland Act and subsequent statutory guidance. Under S75 of the Act, policy making in and about Northern Ireland is required to take a particular form wherever those policies have originated. These processes were intended to mainstream equality considerations into all policy making about and for Northern Ireland. S75 of the Northern Ireland Act was thus the first so-called 'positive equality duty' to be introduced in the UK and, along with the MacPherson Inquiry, influenced the introduction of the positive duty to promote racial equality and good relations in the UK as a whole through the 2002 Race Relations Act. The requirement under S75 of the Northern Ireland Act to act differently in relation to policy making in and for Northern Ireland was not always welcomed or followed by Westminster departments, some of whom have shown a marked preference for the less effortful practices of 'read across' (see McLaughlin, 2003; McLaughlin and Faris, 2004; and for further discussions of the Northern Ireland statutory equality duty).

Policy divergence in Northern Ireland 1999-2002

As Keating (2002a, 2002b) notes, prior to suspension, the Assembly agreed the introduction of a Commissioner for Children. The legislation setting up the Children's Commissioner Office came into effect after the suspension of devolution. The Assembly also introduced free public transport for pensioners, thus bringing Northern Ireland provisions into line with those in the Republic of Ireland. Finally, the Assembly enacted legislation to provide means-tested higher education bursaries for students from the poorest family backgrounds, a development that pre-figured similar British policy developments.

Keating's summary of policy divergence in Northern Ireland is reproduced in Box 6.1:

Box 6.1: Divergence in public policies in Northern Ireland since devolution

- abolition of school league tables;
- establishment of a commissioner for children;
- decision to provide for a Single Equality Act, considering legislation on religion, sex, race and disability with new provisions on sexual orientation and age;
- free fares for older people;
- introduction of bursaries for students;
- decision to abolish the 11+ examination.

Source: Keating (2002b, p 5)

As noted earlier, Keating's summary underestimates the extent of divergence that occurred during the devolution period. The summary excludes the 2000 Child Support, Pensions and Social Security Act and instances of divergence in the health field.

Examples of divergence in the health field include the development and adoption of a Northern Ireland public health strategy based on a strongly social model of health (DHPSS and PS, 2001). The introduction of Primary Care Trusts (PCTs) was much delayed by the refusal of Northern Ireland general practitioners (GPs) to sign up to the new UK GP contract. Following protracted negotiations and alterations to the contract, Northern Ireland GPs did eventually sign a new contract. The new Northern Ireland contract permitted the establishment of local health and social care commissioning groups (LHSCGs) in 2002. Reflecting

Northern Ireland's integrated health and social services structures, these groups commission social services as well as primary care and community health services. The formal status of the groups is that of sub-committees of the Area Health and Social Services Boards.

In the equality field, divergence involved not merely the promise of a Single Equality Act, as reported by Keating, but also the implementation of the first positive equality duty in the UK. Northern Ireland's statutory equality duty has a single equality ethos and structure covering nine dimensions of in/equality. In addition, a single equality enforcement authority was established in 1999, the Equality Commission for Northern Ireland. A single Equality and Human Rights Commission was subsequently also proposed for Britain.

In the field of education, divergence between Northern Ireland and Britain included the failure to replicate the 2001 Special Educational Needs and Disability Act (SENDA) in Northern Ireland. SENDA amended the 1995 Disability Discrimination Act and extended it to include the public educational service. SENDA was welcomed in principle by all the political parties and the children's non-governmental organisation (NGO) sector in Northern Ireland. It did, however, represent a particular challenge to the Northern Irish education systems. In Northern Ireland, mainstreamed education for children with disabilities has lagged behind that in the rest of the UK, and a strong system of special or segregated schools has continued to exist (see Monteith et al, 2002). By the time of suspension of devolution in October 2002, the challenge SENDA represented to the special school sector had not been resolved and therefore the introduction of SENDA-equivalent legislation had not occurred. A SENDO – that is, a SENDA-equivalent Order in Council – has been drafted and may be passed in 2005.

Keating's summary of divergence also includes one example of a devolved minister's attempt to reduce pre-existing policy divergence – that is, to introduce a new element of convergence between Northern Irish and British social policy. This was the decision to abolish academic selection, the 11+ examination, and consequently to reform the bifurcated second-level school system. Announcement of this decision was the last act of the Sinn Fein Education Minister prior to suspension of devolution. Implementation of the decision would bring the Northern Irish second-level education system into line with both the British and Southern Irish systems.

Post-primary education structures and transfer arrangements remain a 'live' policy issue and have been the subject of repeated public consultations and two expert reviews (DoE, 2001, 2003). 'Direct rule' ministers have stated that the decision to end academic selection stands, but they have not yet legislated for replacement methods of transferring pupils from primary to second-level schools, or determining which children may attend over-subscribed schools.

Four other developments that can broadly be described as falling under the umbrella of convergence were seeded during the devolution period and continued under post-devolution 'direct rule'. These were the review of public administration, the review of the Northern Ireland rating system, the development of a Northern Ireland Anti-Poverty Strategy and the development of a Northern Ireland Children's and Young People's Strategy. The first of these reflected political and public concern that devolution had exacerbated the existing problem of Northern Ireland being 'over governed' as a result of the multiple layers of local, Northern Ireland and UK government that existed. These layers, together with the large number of departments and non-departmental public bodies, seemed to many to be an expensive and excessive system of governance and administration for a small territory of two million people, as well as being largely impenetrable to the public.

The policy-making process is of course complex and complicated by the absence of a firm divide between policy making and policy implementation. The remoulding of policy during implementation can result in a significant gap between the outcomes experienced by those at the receiving end of services or policies and the intentions of those at the apex of the policy process, the ostensible policy makers.

In the context of outlining the structures and pathways of policy making in Northern Ireland, McLaughlin and Faris (2004) illustrated the span of multi-level governance involved in governance and public administration in Northern Ireland as including:

- ... relatively distant international bodies such as the United Nations – for example, the *Agenda 21 for Sustainable Development* from the Rio Conference on the Environment 1992;
- the institutions, procedures and law of the European Union including the directives of the European Commission and the judgements of the European Court of Justice;
- intergovernmental bodies such as the British–Irish Intergovernmental Conference;
- the government and parliament of the United Kingdom at Westminster;

- United Kingdom-wide bodies, such as [the] Inland Revenue, which are direct arms of the UK government;
- other United Kingdom-wide bodies whether statutory or publicly owned bodies such as the Post Office [and] the British Broadcasting Corporation;
- Departments of government in Northern Ireland such as the Department of Employment and Learning;
- bodies within the 'family' of each Northern Ireland department such as (in the field of education) the Area Education and Library Boards and the Catholic Council for Maintained Schools;
- local government – that is, District Councils;
- other statutory bodies in Northern Ireland such as the Equality Commission;
- other non-departmental public bodies;
- the systems of devolution – such as the Executive and the Northern Ireland Assembly as and when devolution may be restored; and
- the legal system, whether for the whole of the United Kingdom or that which is specific to Northern Ireland. (McLaughlin and Faris, 2004, pp 12-13)

The Review of Public Administration published a consultation paper in 2004 recommending removal of the Area Board structures in education, health and social services, and the merger of their functions into nine enlarged local councils (www.rpani-gov.uk).

The other development begun under devolution, which has continued prominently into the post-suspension direct rule period, is the review of the Northern Ireland rating system.

The rating system was the only element of taxation under the control of the devolved government and, as such, its structure and quantum featured in a number of policy debates in the Assembly, usually in the context of whether additional public expenditure for a particular public service or population group could or should be raised through this means to supplement the Northern Ireland allocation from Westminster.

The 'Poll Tax' and Council Tax systems were not introduced in Northern Ireland in the 1980s, nor was the water service privatised. The overall quantum of local taxation has therefore been lower in Northern Ireland than in the rest of the UK, something that has been of particular benefit to the middle and upper income strata of the population.

After the suspension of devolution, 'Direct Rule' ministers continued with a review of the rating system with a view to both raising additional revenue for investment in the historically underresourced Northern Ireland water and sewage infrastructure and to creating a more progressive local taxation system. At the same time, ministers announced proposals for the introduction of domestic charges for water. Both developments have been 'justified' or 'rationalised' politically through the argument that Northern Ireland has historically done well in terms of public expenditure on key public services such as health and education, and that it has experienced a significant 'subvention' from the British taxpayer.

However, as Tomlinson (2002) and others have shown, the apparent advantage some territories have had under the Barnett formula is more illusory than real once need and/or outputs are set against expenditure inputs. Public expenditure allocations within the UK are typically crudely analysed and compared on a simple per capita input basis. Analysis of outcomes rather than inputs of public expenditure have reached very different even opposing conclusions as to the positions of sub-national units of the UK in public expenditure 'league tables'. For example, Northern Ireland has typically been portrayed as having enjoyed high levels of social expenditure in the 1970s and 1980s (see, for example, Gaffikin and Morrissey, 1990; Coulter, 1999). However, Bernard et al (1999) carried out a comparative analysis of receipt of community health and social services among older people, which controlled for need, between Northern Ireland and Britain using the 1990s Disability Surveys in each. They showed that the probability of receiving a domiciliary service was lower not higher for equivalently disabled older people in Northern Ireland than Britain. Thus, when comparison is of the extent of social rights achieved rather than inputs of public expenditure, the view that Northern Ireland has been a significant beneficiary of union with and generous subvention from Britain becomes qualified.

The Northern Ireland Anti-Poverty and Children's Strategies have continued to be developed by the civil service led by the Office of the First Minister and Deputy First Minister's Equality and Social Need and Children's Units respectively. The European Union requires member states to have National Anti-Poverty action plans. Sub-national plans are not required, but the objective of 'mobilising' all relevant actors in the development and implementation of national plans has been assumed to require the active involvement of sub-national levels of government.

The devolved government's Programme for Government emphasised the fact that Northern Ireland has an especially young population structure. The Children's Fund and the Children's Strategy were the key means adopted to address this demographic parameter of social policy in the territory. A draft Children's Strategy has now been published (OFMDFM, 2004). Major cuts are, however, planned in both mainstream and special children's services (DFP, 2004). If implemented, the draft 2004 budget will result in reductions of 2.5% in mainstream family and social services. The former Executive Children's Fund has no provision planned for it after 2006; this will remove £1.08m out of 11 NGO-led children's services.

Conclusion

The international status of devolution in Northern Ireland, together with the territories' previous complex history of 'devolutions', means that the Northern Ireland experience of 'New Labour' devolution is not directly comparable to those of Scotland and Wales.

Northern Ireland has experienced a number of periods of devolution and direct rule since its inception in 1922. Distinctive institutions of public service delivery were created and maintained under and across both types of governance arrangement. Under direct rule arrangements, influential social institutions, professions and classes have tended to benefit disproportionately from policy divergence; in contrast in the most recent period of devolution, 'deserving social groups' and 'cross-community' conservative social values dominated the divergence from Britain that occurred.

Post-suspension, popular support for a return to devolved government remained strong, especially within the nationalist and younger populations.

References

Bernard, S., Boyle, G., McLaughlin, E., Parker, G. and Porter, S. (1999) 'The determinants of residential and nursing home care among older people in Northern Ireland', *Journal of the Statistical and Social Inquiry Society of Ireland*, vol XXVII, part IV, pp 1-41.

Chaney, P. (2004) 'The primacy of ideology: social policy and the first term of the National Assembly for Wales', in N. Ellison, L. Bauld and M. Powell (eds) *Social Policy Review 16*, Bristol: The Policy Press/Social Policy Association, pp 121-42.

Coulter, C. (1999) *Contemporary Northern Irish society*, London: Pluto Press.

Darby, J. (ed) (1983) *The background to the conflict*, Belfast: Appletree Press.

DFP (Department of Finance and Personnel) (2004) *Northern Ireland: Draft priorities and budget 2005-2008*, Belfast: DFP.

DHPSS and PS (Department of Health, Personal Social Services and Public Safety) (2001) *Investing in health*, Belfast: DHPSS and PS.

Dignan, T. and McLaughlin, E. (2002) *New TSN research: Poverty in Northern Ireland*, Belfast: OFMDFM.

DoE (Department of Education) (2001) *Education for the 21st century* (The Burns Report), Belfast: DoE.

DoE (2003) *Report of the post-primary review working party* (The Costello Report), Belfast: DoE.

Duncan, S. (1995) 'Theorising European gender systems', *Journal of European Social Policy*, vol 5, no 4, pp 82-100.

Ellison, G. and Martin, G. (2000) 'Policing, collective action and social movement theory', *British Journal of Sociology*, vol 51, no 4, pp 681-700.

Gaffikin, F. and Morrissey, M. (1990) *Northern Ireland: The Thatcher years,* London: Zed Books.

Irish Government (1998) *The Northern Ireland Peace Agreement*, Dublin: The Stationery Office.

Jeffrey, C. (2002) 'Commentary' in *Devolution: What difference has it made?*, Interim findings from the ESRC Research Programme on Devolution and Constitutional Change, pp 19-20 (www.devolution.ac.uk).

Keating, M. (2002a) 'Devolution and public policy in the UK: divergence or convergence?', in J. Adams and P. Robinson (eds) *Devolution in practice: Public policy differences within the UK*, London: IPPR.

Keating, M. (2002b) 'Devolution: what difference has it made? Interim findings from the ESRC programme on devolution and constitutional change' (www.devolution.ac.uk).

Kelly, G. and Wilson, R. (2002) *A regional strategy for social inclusion*, Belfast: The Civic Forum.

McGarry, J. and O'Leary, B. (1995) *Explaining Northern Ireland*, Oxford: Blackwell.

McLaughlin, E. (1998) 'The view from Northern Ireland', in S. McGregor and H. Jones (eds) *Party politics and social issues*, London: Routledge, pp 214-32.

McLaughlin, E. (2003) 'Equality and equity policy', in M. Hawkesworth and M. Kogan (eds) *Encyclopaedia of world government and politics* (2nd edn), London: Routledge, pp 711-23.

McLaughlin, E. and Fahey, T. (1999) 'Family and state', in A. Heath, R. Breen and C. Whelan (eds) *Ireland North and South: Perspectives from social sciences*, Oxford: British Academy/Oxford University Press, pp 141-60.

McLaughlin, E. and Faris, N. (2004) *The Northern Ireland statutory equality duty: An operational review*, A report prepared for the Northern Ireland Office, Belfast: Northern Ireland Office.

McLaughlin, E. and Kelly, G. (2003) 'Does two and two make one? A cross-border analysis of benefit entitlements in Ireland, North and South', in E. McLaughlin and G. Kelly (eds) *Edging poverty out, anti-poverty strategies in Ireland*, Proceedings of a joint seminar, vol IV, Belfast: Department for Social Development and Queen's University Belfast.

McLaughlin, E. and Yeates, N. (1999) 'The biopolitics of welfare in Ireland', *Irish Journal of Feminist Studies*, vol 3, no 2, pp 49-67.

McLaughlin, E., Kelly, G. and Yeates, N. (2002) 'Social security in Ireland, North and South', in N. Yeates and G. Kelly (eds) *Poverty and social security: Ireland North and South*, Proceedings of a joint seminar, vol III, Belfast: Department for Social Development and Queen's University Belfast, pp 1-46.

Monteith, M., McLaughlin, E., Milner, S. and Hamilton, L. (2002) *Is anyone listening? Childhood disability and public services in Northern Ireland*, Belfast: Barnardo's.

NIO (Northern Ireland Office) (1998) *The agreement reached in the multi-party negotiations*, Belfast and London: NIO.

Northern Ireland Act (1998) (c47) London: The Stationery Office.

OFMDFM (Office of the First Minister and Deputy First Minister) (2004) *Making it our world 2*, Belfast: OFMDFM.

Rose, R. (ed) (1982) *The territorial dimension in UK politics*, London: Macmillan.

Rose, R. (1990) 'Inheritance before choice in public policy', *Journal of Theoretical Politics*, vol 2, pp 263-91.

Rottman, D. (1999) 'Problems and prospects for comparing the two Irelands', in A. Heath, R. Breen and C. Whelan (eds) *Ireland North and South: Perspectives from social science*, Oxford: British Academy/Oxford University Press.

Stewart, J. (2004) 'Scottish solutions to Scottish problems? Social welfare in Scotland since devolution', in N. Ellison, L. Bauld and M. Powell (eds) *Social Policy Review 16*, Bristol: The Policy Press/Social Policy Association, pp 100-20.

Tomlinson, M. (2002) 'Reconstituting social policy: the case of Northern Ireland', in R. Sykes, C. Bochel and N. Ellison (eds) *Social Policy Review 14*, Bristol: The Policy Press/Social Policy Association, pp 57-84.

Wilford, R. (ed) (2001) *Aspects of the Belfast agreement*, Oxford: Oxford University Press.

Wilson, R. and Wilford, R. (2000) 'A bare knuckle ride: Northern Ireland', in R. Hazell (ed) *The state and the nations: The first year of devolution in the UK*, Thorverton, Essex: Imprint Academic Press, pp 35-49.

Wilson, R. and Wilford, R. (2001) 'Northern Ireland: endgames', in A. Trench (ed) *The state and the nations: The second year of devolution in the UK*, Thorverton, Essex: Imprint Academic Press, pp 33-9.

Wilson, R. and Wilford, R. (2003) 'Northern Ireland: a route to stability' (www.devolution.ac.uk).

SEVEN

At home abroad: the presidential election of 2004, the politics of American social policy and what European readers might make of these subjects

Theodore Marmor

Introduction

This chapter addresses two different, but related topics. The first is whether the US election of 2004 represents a serious mandate for social policy change. The second analyses two of the most important social policy proposals that the Bush Administration decided to promote vigorously. Fundamental change in social insurance pensions, not prominent in the election, is now the most newsworthy source of social policy debate: proposals for individual risk-bearing retirement accounts that are misleadingly termed 'privatisation'. Medicare, the health insurance programme for America's older and disabled people, was prominent in 2003-04, and remains so today. The relevant Medicare politics in 2005 are about the implementation of the fundamental and highly controversial 'reform' legislation enacted late in 2003. In both instances, the Bush Administration has used the language of imminent crisis to bolster policy reforms that in fact undermine rather than support America's two most important social programmes. This bold assertion, the core of this chapter, will require (and be given) extended argument and documentation.

In addressing these topics, one must also raise the question of whether – or in what ways – American reform programmes and proposals are relevant to European social policy discussions generally or those in the UK particularly. In connection with that issue, I will take up one strikingly conventional framing of contemporary US social policy. That is the view that a new century – the 21st – presents new challenges to social policy, throwing up such new risks that a reconceptualisation of the welfare state is warranted. The chapter closes with a largely sceptical response to that formulation.

Drawing lessons from the experience of other countries is never easy in any case (de Gier et al, 2004). This is especially problematic for Europeans when the topic is social welfare policy and the country compared is the US. For decades now, the pattern of media coverage and academic commentary has been imbalanced. The US media – television coverage, radio broadcasts, newspaper reports and magazine stories – flow northward and eastward vastly more frequently than do southward flows from Canada or westward flows from the UK or continental Europe. The result is utterly asymmetrical, with others receiving much more information (accurate or not) about the US than Americans receive about European or Canadian social policy. And, to compound matters, for most of the period after the Second World War, both European and Canadian commentators presumed that American social policy was underdeveloped, stingy and, in some formulations, nothing but mean, means-tested and humiliating programmes for the poor. This posture, comforting to the observers, was never true and that further complicates lesson drawing. To put the point another way, learning about the US with accuracy is a precondition, often not satisfied, for learning from its experience (de Gier et al, 2004).

The US election of 2004: social policy implications for those abroad?

What, given the context noted above, should other social policy observers know about recent American social policy and how the risks of the 21st century are understood? First, there is the question of what caused the electoral results in 2004 and, second, the claim of an electoral mandate to change America in the direction of what President Bush calls an 'ownership society'. There is much to learn about here, little in my view to envy and much to avoid.

A necessary condition for making sense of the role of social policy in this electoral struggle, however, is some familiarity with the rules of the American political game. US elections are almost never clear guides to the policy consequences in the following period. Partly, that is because only a third of the Senate – the second chamber – is up for election at any one time. In addition, presidential contests typically feature broad claims about the direction candidates embrace, not detailed manifestos for particular policies to be enacted with an adequate legislative majority. (So, for instance, President Bush said remarkably little in the campaign of 2004 about the policy reforms he is now advocating for social security pensions.) Furthermore, in many areas of social policy, the principles of federalism leave to the states much of the initiative in policy change. That, too, was evident in the largest healthcare programme directly affecting low-income Americans, Medicaid. Given that context, what can one conclude about the role of social policy in the 2004 election and what is foreshadowed for the Bush second term?

The election of 2004 was much more an echo of the 2000 results than a dramatic Republican triumph that will change American politics fundamentally (Martin and Nadeau, 2004). Understandably described by the White House as a 'mandate' for the future, the realities do not support this hyperbolic interpretation of a close election that, but for the outcome in Ohio, would have had a Kerry victory. For domestic politics, the likely prospects in 2005 and are – despite the President's constant appeal to a reform mandate – continued stalemate over most of the crucial social policy issues in tax, health and social security. Far from transforming the Congress, the election only marginally increased Republican majorities in the House and the Senate. Those margins are unlikely to produce anything like a Republican policy deluge. That the Bush Administration in its second term will attempt to produce a deluge is far more certain than its capacity to do so.

The clearest evidence for the 'echo' interpretation is the decisive role Ohio played in 2004, as compared with Florida's controversial result in 2000. Had Ohio – with economic conditions that were predicted to help the Democratic challenger – supported Kerry, the electoral result would have been reversed. (A change of 65,000 votes in Ohio would have made the difference, according to reports in early December. By January, the evidence was accumulating that electoral fraud was involved and lawsuits are pending.)

So, why did the line-up of blue and red states remain so close to that of 2000, but the turnout and the margin of popular approval favour Bush so clearly? The answer does not appear to be popular approval of the war, agreement with the President's position on social security pensions and medical care, or support for his persistent pursuit of tax cuts that favour wealthier Americans.

In fact, the largest margins of support for Republican views emerged in what have come to be known as 'moral disputes' about the proper form of the family, the right conception of abortion policy and, in particular, hostility to same-sex marriages. In 11 states, including 'liberal'

Oregon, citizens rejected in referenda every unorthodox challenge to the legal shape of the family. And they did so in proportions much greater than these states supported Bush over Kerry. In Ohio, for example, the ban on same-sex marriage won by overwhelming margins: 62% (3.2 million) yes votes versus 38% (2 million) no votes. In Florida, the 'moral' issue on the referendum ballot was different. There the question was whether parents should be notified about abortion decisions of their minor daughters. The yes vote was 65% and the no vote 35%, or 4.5 million Floridians agreeing with the President's views and 2.5 million against (Marmor, 2004). These results appear to have increased turnout. And that may help to explain the greater mobilisation of new voters in crucial 'swing' states towards the Republican incumbent. What they undoubtedly demonstrate is that Bush's margin on these issues greatly outdistanced his margins for the office of President.

These referenda results have little to do with the economic security issues that sharply divide the congressional parties. On social security pensions, there is no popular mandate for individual risk-bearing accounts that anyone can find. Indeed, there is public scepticism. On controlling medical care costs and Medicare reform, there is no evidence that the President made gains where previously his positions were less favourably received than those of Kerry. So, on public opinion concerning domestic politics, the picture is quite starkly opposed: support for so-called 'family' and 'wedge' issues, but not an ideological swing to the right on 'bread and butter' issues. As Democratic pollster Stanley Greenberg put it, "Very important things happened in this election to make Bush's victory possible, but support for the president's approach to domestic affairs is not one of them. The American electorate wanted change, but settled for the president" (Greenberg, 2004).

What does that foreshadow legislatively over the next four years? Stalemate is, as noted above, what I predict, with the Republican gains in the House and the Senate not enough to transform the rules of these institutions. Nor are the slight increases on the House and Senate Republican totals likely to overwhelm the capacity of a determined Democratic congressional minority to block legislation they abhor with the old tool of the conservative coalition of the 1950s: the filibuster. In the Senate, 60 votes are required to stop debate – the filibuster when used to block legislation – and the Republicans number 55, with four so-called 'liberal Republicans' likely to vote with the Democrats on issues of fundamental change in domestic policy, including changes in the make-up of the Supreme Court. What is equally important, the loss of

Democratic Senate seats included three southerners who were not party stalwarts.

Commentators from nations with parliamentary regimes, understandably used to the capacity of the majority party (or ruling coalition) to enforce voting discipline, have too easily accepted the idea of an American electoral mandate. American political institutions are designed to make it difficult to legislate, not easy. A determined minority has many means at its disposal if it has the will to use them. In the Bush first term, the President claimed a mandate when he lacked majority support in the popular vote. In the second term, Bush will surely appeal to this popular vote margin. But it is no more legitimate than Bush's remarkable capacity to convince himself of his popular approval in 2000.

The fact is that this past November's election echoed the divisions of 2000, with very few votes separating the two sides. That does not amount to saying either that social policy played no role in the election or that there are few differences between the parties on social policy. There are, but they were not decisive in this election. To matters of what Europeans would term 'social assistance', the parties paid almost no attention. That reflects most of all the concessions President Clinton made to welfare reform in 1995, cooperating with a Republican Congress' determination to "end welfare as we know it". In practice, this has meant terminating federal government guarantees of levels of social assistance that states use, effectively decentralising the crucial issues that used to separate sharply partisan attitudes towards the alleviation of poverty. As in Britain, the common ground now is connecting welfare to work, with time limits on support accepted by congressional majorities. The result in 2004 was a campaign that largely ignored America's poor.

There were two respects, however, in which the distribution of income did figure in the election and implicate federal taxes in social policy. First, the very large current federal deficit was at the core of Senator Kerry's critique of the Bush Administration's fiscal policy. That policy had from 2001 incorporated what one could call 'military Keynesianism', lower taxes and increased military outlays in connection with the wars in Afghanistan and Iraq. The Bush Administration claimed, of course, that their tax reforms were crucial to counteract the recession Bush faced. On the other hand, Kerry rightly emphasised that the bulk of the tax reductions enacted – and forecasted by Bush – were overwhelmingly concentrated on the top 1% of wealthy Americans. Whatever the merits here, the second and more crucial impact of fiscal policy on post-electoral social policy is simply this. Even if Bush's proposals for further tax reductions are *not* enacted, the fiscal realities are such that bold social policy initiatives are unlikely. The deficit is at such a level that fiscally conservative Democrats and Republicans will likely balk at any expansionary social policy reform.

Primary and secondary education is a policy topic not usually grouped under the same rubric as welfare, social security and medical care. But, because of education's crucial link to equality of opportunity, it did figure in the electoral campaign. What transpired was mostly an argument about whether the key reform of the first Bush term – the so-called 'No Child Left Behind Act' – and the ensuing programme was or was not adequately funded. The salience of that issue in the campaign was modest, while it is certain that the congressional struggle over aid to primary and secondary education will be constrained by the fiscal policy realities already discussed. Where the electorate spoke most powerfully and differently – the family issues noted earlier – it had little to do with the role of the federal government in health, education, tax and social security. An echo is, of course, a great disappointment to the Democrats. But it does not constitute a breakthrough in American domestic politics. A more accurate predictive image might be mud-wrestling for four years.

Medicare and social security: the major arenas of conflict

A snapshot of social policy – whether looking back on 2004 or forward to 2005 and beyond – almost always misleads in the sense that it understates incremental, quiet change over longer periods of time. In the case of Medicare, America's social insurance form of health financing for its citizens over 65 and its disabled workers, we have an exception. The Bush Administration's legislative reforms of late 2003 foreshadow in 2004 and beyond fundamental, non-incremental changes in the programme. Dubbed the 2003 Medicare Modernisation Act, the law provided both a complicated and controversial outpatient prescription drug benefit and, at the same time, set in motion long-term and profound changes in the terms, financing and administration of what has been largely a single health insurance plan. Understanding how that happened and what it means requires some extended political reporting and analysis.

Medicare in political flux: a story of unjustified hope, undoubted scandal, and unwarranted fear

For much of 2003, Medicare was regularly front-page news in the US. There was the initial surprising announcement in the spring that the

Bush Administration would now strongly promote the addition of outpatient prescription drugs to the Medicare programme. (This was a surprise because until then the pharmaceutical industry had typically opposed such a reform and President Bush had largely avoided Medicare in the wake of the tragedy of 9/11.) The Bush proposal, first estimated to cost $400 billion over 10 years, ignited an intense partisan fight. The question raised in that struggle was whether a Democratic or Republican version of this Medicare 'improvement' would emerge from the Congress after a decade of stalemate over the issue of whether Medicare would substantially finance outpatient drug expenses of its elderly and disabled clientele (Marmor and Hacker, 2005).

That struggle was noteworthy. Not since Medicare's enactment in 1965 had the programme generated such prominent media attention and confusion. What must be noted for a non-American audience, however, is just how much muddle there was about the problems claimed, the remedy offered and the language used. Orwellian contradiction, sheer misrepresentation and semantic sleights-of-hand best describe what passed for a debate about Medicare's historical foundations, its current realities and likely future. Why such legislation passed in 2003 is the first puzzle to address if one is to understand what this episode foreshadows for American social policy.

In 1965, Medicare's enactment was a foregone conclusion because the Democratic Party had routed the Republicans the year before and dominated the Congress by a margin of two to one (Marmor, 2000). In 2003, the serious push to legislate a drug benefit for Medicare emerged for the opposite reason. In the absence of large partisan majorities in either the Senate or the House, both parties were wary of failing to act on what was claimed to be an obvious problem for Medicare. Indeed, for almost a decade, each political party had fought to make sure the other could not take credit for introducing such an expansion of Medicare's coverage. Stalemate was the repeated result, exemplified in 1999 by the failure of the special Breaux-Thomas commission on prescription drugs to reach agreement.

In 2003, however, Republican and Democratic leaders in the Congress and the Administration judged that continued stalemate might well provide the other side with an electoral weapon for the presidential and congressional elections of 2004. Both consequently became willing to sacrifice crucial features of their traditional policy aspirations. For Democrats, that meant giving up on a generous drug benefit (with an $800 billion 10-year price tag), but insisting that whatever benefit there was included all Medicare beneficiaries. For Republicans, it meant strategic compromise, agreeing on expanding an entitlement programme they have long criticised and no longer insisting that a Medicare drug benefit be strictly restricted only to those low-income older people willing to join private plans. The $400 billion budget limit on which the Bush Administration insisted later turned out to be a ruse. But it surely constrained the complicated design of the drug benefit in ways that would prove important as Americans came to understand how limited the benefit really was.

The legislation itself, signed into law on 8 December 2003, emerged with charges of budgetary deceit and substantive distortion flying around it. Then in March of 2004 came a double headline. The cost estimates, it turned out, had not only been understated, but the media reported scandalous allegations of bribery of key members of Congress and reprehensible silencing of government actuaries in the build-up to the reform's enactment. And, as if to insist that tragedy should follow farce, the headlines in the last week of March announced, portentously, that the programme would go 'bankrupt' in 2019 if present trends were allowed to continue. Americans were and are bewildered by all this. What can anyone make of the mix of legislative drama, fiscal chicanery and distant doomsday talk? The short answer is that you should take none of the headlines seriously. The longer answer takes longer.

The reform of Medicare: unjustified hopefulness?

The passage of what came to be called the Prescription Drug Bill in December of 2003 represented Medicare's biggest legislative overhaul in 38 years. But even close observers of Washington politics wondered at the time just what exactly it was all about. On one side, congressional Republicans and the Bush Administration described the legislation – then budgeted at $400 billion over 10 years – as a moderate, commonsensical way to provide long-overdue outpatient drug insurance to both older and severely disabled Americans. On the other side, Democratic opponents decried the Bill, charging that it was an extraordinarily complex benefit as well as a monstrous giveaway to insurance companies and drug firms. Lots of commentary about a 'doughnut' hole in the insurance coverage flowed from the lips of Democratic politicians and found their way on to television news and commentary.

These conflicting characterisations are understandable when one recognises that the legislation was really two quite separable reforms. The first provides a much-needed, if modest, excessively complex, drug benefit. Because of its design and the fact that it does not include effective ways of controlling drug costs, the plan, if implemented, will likely leave most seniors little better off than they are today, and some worse off. This is the prospect of the legislative reform that has already proven most disappointing to the public. Indeed, a week after the law was passed on 8 December 2003, a national ABC poll reported a 60:40 ratio of Americans critical as opposed to pleased with the reform. And more recent polls have shown even more critical majorities.

The second, darker side of the new Medicare legislation includes changes that have little or nothing to do with drug coverage and everything to do with special-interest demands and a longstanding ideological animus toward Medicare among conservative congressional Republicans. These provisions include large new subsidies for private insurers, and requirements that ensure drug firms will be spared from their greatest fear: namely, that Medicare could use its massive buying power to demand reductions in drug prices. The law also contains provisions that favour private health insurance plans and risk further degeneration of Medicare's all-in-the-same-boat structure.

Yet, what is most striking about the 2003 legislation is not the consistency of its vision, but its deep incoherence. In the name of greater free-market competition, the law offers substantial subsidies to the pharmaceutical and insurance industries. In the name of providing greater income protection to the insured, it threatens Medicare's guarantee of universal benefits. (Indeed, it provides more than $6 billion to support individual health savings accounts outside of Medicare, risking the fragmentation of the broader insurance risk pool.) Also, in the name of greater cost containment, it encourages the expansion of private health plans that have, to date, *not* saved Medicare money. Finally, the law creates new budgetary rules that could very well make Medicare *less* equitable and affordable down the road.

All this highlights the puzzle of how such inconsistent, convoluted and far-reaching legislation could have passed in a context of the great partisan and ideological polarisation. As a product of political conflict alone, we would expect not a massive new entitlement with so many contradictions and problems. With the Congress so evenly divided in partisan terms, one would have normally expected a more modest, lowest-common-denominator agreement – for example, a Bill covering catastrophic drugs costs only. Instead, this is a law driven by a mix of high Republican ideals and low political calculations crafted almost entirely in isolation from the Democratic opposition in the Congress and then adjusted just enough to win moderate congressional votes and temporarily sidestep hostile public opinion.

This brings us to the most overlooked reason for the reform's complexity: the conservative reform agenda itself, which simultaneously reflects ideological principles that celebrate free competition and the influence of powerful industries that hope to avoid it at all costs. Private insurers and drug companies do not really want competition: they want a playing field tilted in their favour. And they have been willing to do whatever it takes to seize the advantage.

All politics, to be sure, usually requires some compromise. But what is striking about the Medicare drug law is just how deeply the compromises – or, more accurately, the concessions to private interests – undercut the stated goal of the Bill: drug coverage for seniors. The $400-$550 billion in new spending will be able to purchase only about half as much coverage as a sensibly designed bill could. This is not only because of the subsidies for private health plans and for Health Savings Accounts. It is also because of the higher overhead costs of private plans (about five to six times higher than for traditional Medicare), and the 20% to 30% higher prices for drugs that seniors will have to pay because the law forbids Medicare from using its bargaining power to negotiate better deals.

All this helps to explain why the drug benefit itself is simultaneously so convoluted and so meagre – covering, for example, only a small share of seniors' expected drug expenses overall, and reimbursing the 251st dollar of drug spending but not the 2,251st (Center for Medicare Advocacy, 2004)[1]. It also helps explain why seniors do not like the benefit the more they hear about it. And those polled are being realistic. A significant proportion of Medicare beneficiaries will almost certainly be worse, not better, off under the Act. This includes several million low-income seniors who will lose the generous coverage they now enjoy under state Medicaid programmes. It also includes millions who already have pretty good drug coverage through their former employers – coverage that may well be dropped, despite the Act's subsidies for employers that retain coverage.

The Republican hope that 'their drug benefit' would take Medicare off the political agenda has proven ill-founded. In fact, the reform was certain to cause political conflict – and has. Republicans anticipated they could transform the political parentage of Medicare, turning into an asset an issue with which they have been battered by Democrats for years. But, by pushing through such a confusing, convoluted and unwieldy Bill, they virtually ensured that the more that was known about the legislation, the more controversial it would be. Even hostile Democrats never imagined it would blow up so quickly. Nor did the Democrats turn out to be good forecasters. In 2003 they thought they 'had to go along' because, otherwise, the party would be held electorally responsible at the polls for holding up a Bill (by filibustering) and would not be able to explain their opposition. As the polls revealed just a week after enactment, this legislation never had widespread, popular support. In 2004 the disquiet increased and in 2005 there is every reason to believe that the Medicare Modernisation Act will come under increasing criticism for its confusions, disappointing benefits and sheer complexity.

Sagas, scandals and fiscal forecasts: the stories of 2004

In fact, Medicare became the biggest domestic issue of the presidential election year. But the mediagenic ingredients were not that obvious when the reform legislation passed amid all the hoopla the Bush Administration could muster. Substantive criticism of the law's provisions dominated the first phase of regret in December 2003 and early January 2004. Later attention shifted dramatically towards the alleged fiscal deception by the Bush Administration in its budget estimates for the drug reform. (In none of the episodes was clarity a feature of the reporting and discussion, which itself is part of the story.)

The tale of scandal is brief but easy to relate. The chief Medicare actuary – Richard Foster – was allegedly threatened in the summer of 2003 by his superior, Tom Scully, the director of the Center for Medical Services. The threat was that, if Foster reported budget estimates to the Congress higher than the department's early ones, Scully would fire him (Scully, 2004). In the event, Scully had left his job by late December of 2003 and was in 2004 busy doing lucrative private lobbying for a variety of health-related firms. The mix is perfect for journalistic excitement: mischievous interference by a political operative with a civil servant's obligation to report his considered opinions to the legislature, with the added spice of apparent financial greed – the former federal health executive turned richly paid lobbyist – to close out the episode.

So the story of 2004/05 was that the Bush Administration lied about what the new prescription drug coverage would cost. It said $400 billion throughout 2003, but it apparently knew it would be as much as $550 billion. (The estimates in March 2005 now reach over $700 billion.) The Congress, on this interpretation, was hoodwinked into passing the Bill, and now Washington commentators affect shock that the price was so much higher than expected. Such a story infuriates taxpayers when and if they understand it. And, in the style of he said/she said American journalism, this episode has bred its own counter interpretation. As Steve

Chapman of *The Baltimore Sun* claimed on 30 March 2004, the above account is "mostly a fairy tale". Why, according to Chapman? Because, he argues, most of the Congress knew the true budget facts all along. With this barrage of claims and counter claims, is it any wonder that making sense of the Medicare programme reforms seems nearly impossible?

To add insult to intellectual injury, the attention to Medicare turned sharply in the spring of 2004 to yet another disturbing topic: the programme's sustainability. Here, however, is quite another source of confusion, one that will take longer to explain.

Medicare trustee reports and fearful claims of 'insolvency'

The pattern of fiscal scaremongering is utterly familiar. Programme trustees report that Medicare revenues are not keeping pace with future spending obligations and, therefore, the trust fund for hospital insurance (Medicare Part A) faces a bankrupt future. Media accounts warn in these hyperbolic tones, and many politicians declare that hard choices must be made to save the programme.

Despite repeated earlier forecasts of insolvency, Medicare has never gone bankrupt. Nor will it ever. Medicare has survived four decades of such warnings with no disruption of services to its older and disabled enrolees. The practice of forecasting Medicare's future finances is intended to serve as a prudent warning. In practice, the alarmist language accompanying media reports frightens and misleads the public, and opens the door to distorted, imprudent policy debates,

Part of the problem is linguistic, and clarifying the language is essential to understanding Medicare's true condition. Terms like 'trust funds', 'solvency' and 'fiscal prudence' are taken from private and personal finance, and their meaning does not strictly apply when describing public programmes like Medicare. The concept of private bankruptcy, for instance, is simply irrelevant for Medicare, as it would be for the NHS as well.

Beginning with the New Deal programmes of the mid-1930s, the phrase 'trust fund' was an accounting term chosen to emphasise the trustworthiness of dedicated financing plans such as social security and Medicare payroll taxes, and the solidity of the government's commitment to finance benefits. Today, however, using the same term in both public and private contexts actually obscures the differences between public and private trust funds. In private firms or households, a trust fund without funds is literally insolvent, unable to finance anything. Private trusts cannot tax and have precious few other options.

Congress, on the other hand, can change the payroll tax rate for Medicare and immediately eliminate shortfalls, assuming it can muster the political will to do so. Congress can also alter benefits and reimbursement provisions of the programme's hospital or medical coverage or both, as it has done many times in different proportions since 1966 (Marmor, 2000). Thinking of the Medicare trust fund balance as the programme's crucial variable is like believing a thermometer creates the reality of a heat wave or a cold snap.

Alarmist news accounts sometimes treat Medicare's bankruptcy as a predetermined fact, which is further misleading. Trustees' reports in fact always stress that a projected date of insolvency assumes no corrective actions or policy changes. In practice, Medicare has always taken action to bring its finances into balance either by increasing taxes and premiums or reducing payments to providers of care.

In the 1980s, for example, Medicare reformed its payment system for hospitals and physicians, slowing down the growth in programme spending and pushing back the supposed date of so-called bankruptcy. More recently, the 1997 Balanced Budget Act included a series of Medicare reforms to control spending. After three years, the results of these reforms were dramatic: instead of projected insolvency by 2001, Medicare's hospital insurance trust fund was declared fiscally healthy until 2025 – the most optimistic forecast in a quarter of a century (Caplan and Brangan, 2000).

The lesson here for commentary on American social policy is straightforward. Forecasts offer only possible futures, not inevitable ones. One should focus on the problems and disappointments generated by the Medicare legislation of 2003-04 rather than wring one's hands about future decades hence. The present is pressing enough but, as the contemporary struggle over social security will illustrate, spectres of the future play a prominent role in day-to-day social politics in the US.

Social security: the politics of illusion in 2005

If Medicare figured prominently if misleadingly in the election of 2004, social security reform did not. To be sure, the presidential campaigns took predictable positions about this social insurance icon of American life: the Democrats promised to protect future benefits against Republican threats without admitting problems existed. The Republicans asserted without detail that redirecting some portion of required social insurance contributions into private, individual investment accounts would somehow solve the pension problems created by longevity and a higher ratio of retirees to workers than earlier. Neither party dealt candidly with the problems facing the programme, which are real if manageable. The result in 2004 was largely illusory political debate.

Facts, values and illusions in the current social security debate

President Bush has over the past few years dealt with social security by promising to make the retirement, survivors and disability programme secure for future generations, but claiming not to have decided on the details for doing so. This mode, successful during the election as a constraint on his opponent, gave way to any number of speculations about what kind of 'privatisation' the President will propose in 2005. The State of the Union address in late January 2005, however, revealed that the President had settled on three crucial elements (Marmor and Mashaw, 2005).

First, the President wants to permit diversion of part of workers' Federal Insurance Contribution Act (FICA) taxes into private accounts. Second, the Bush plan advocates changing the social security benefit formula from a wage-indexed to a price-indexed system. Third, it excludes all proposals for increasing social security trust fund revenues if they involve any increases, however small, in anyone's taxes.

The central reform feature, private accounts, does nothing to make social security financing secure. As a number of informed commentators have rightly noted, this part of the Bush plan makes the short-term financing problem much worse. It can make the long-term picture better only by indulging in pie-in-the-sky economic assumptions. This balloon is suspended by nothing but hot air. Unfortunately, too many press reports simply repeat the illusions in the name of journalistic 'balance'.

The benefit formula change does make a difference. Indeed, it can bring the system back into close actuarial balance while preserving the purchasing power of today's benefits. This seems helpful, but in fact it is not. Indeed, this proposal to help secure social security's future is the exact equivalent of doing nothing at all.

To see this, just remember a basic principle from high school algebra: things equal to the same thing are equal to each other. If no changes are made in taxes or benefits, social security's actuaries project that, after 2042, social security will be able to pay only about 72% of promised benefits. Changing the promise by changing the benefit formula solves this problem. But, if one does the maths, the illusion becomes obvious.

The result is possible only by making post-2042 benefits equal to the payment of 72% of currently promised benefits. This proposal, purged of its wage-index versus price-index technical jargon, is simply a 28% benefit reduction. It is precisely what the actuaries say would happen if we did nothing at all.

The issue at stake is: is this is a fair and sensible way to fix social security financing? And, to that question, the answer is clearly no. The current formula is meant to keep the standard of living of pensioners in a stable relationship to that of wage earners. With price-indexing, pensioners steadily drop behind. By 2050, actuaries predict that American wage earners will have a 40% higher standard of living than today's workers. Were the Bush proposal to be implemented, social security pensioners would be stuck at the living standard of 2005.

Creating large and increasing differentials between the standard of living of wage earners and retirees is not a trivial matter. Every 1% decrease in social security benefits increases the poverty rate of older people by roughly 1%. Loading the whole burden of fixing social security financing on to the backs of future beneficiaries would surely have disastrous social consequences.

There are in fact many sensible ways to make social security secure without putting disproportionate or unfair burdens on anyone. Why, observers might well ask, has President Bush chosen to avoid all the plans that make modest adjustments in benefits and taxes in favour of a radical dismantling of social security? Why has he ruled out all tax increases?

The President gave his answer at his December 2004 'Economic Summit'. "I love the idea of people being able to own things", he said. That was a theme of his acceptance speech at the Republican convention this past summer in New York. Privatising social security is the cornerstone of his 'ownership society'. Social security has to be dismantled because it is not about ownership. But social insurance is about social solidarity. It is built on the understanding that we run common risks that can be ameliorated only by collective action. And, by making everyone a contributor as well as a recipient, it affirms that we recognise our common fate and our obligations of both self and mutual support.

President's Bush's vision of an ownership society is starkly different. He sees citizens as 'owners' with the usual ownership right to exclude all others from sharing in their 'property'. If Americans end up poor in old age, it is because they failed to manage their property successfully. They can then throw themselves on the mercy of private charity or residual, means-tested welfare benefits.

This is an 'us'/'them' vision of society. Every ship is to float on its own bottom. According to this view, increasing taxes to finance social security benefits is not an option. In the ownership society, taxes truly are theft.

The current debate about social security reform is often mind-numbing in its complexity. Benefit formulas, price and wage indices, earnings forecasts and debt projections now fly thick and fast. But European observers should make no mistake about what the debate is about. While the devil is often in the details, the real debate is about values. It is about what kind of nation the US represents. The fundamental question is whether it should be one that recognises obligations of mutual support and collective responsibility, or one dedicated entirely to the individual pursuit of private wealth.

This question will dominate 2005's domestic American politics. But, for those interested in the likely outcome, the following can be safely argued. The claim of a mandate to insert private accounts into social security is shaky at best, an outright misrepresentation at worst. According to a *Newsweek/Wall Street Journal* poll conducted soon after the 2004 Bush re-election victory, most Americans do not support privatisation (Hickey, 2005). Thirty-five per cent of them thought Bush had a mandate to 'allow workers to invest some of their social security taxes in the stock market,' while 51% said he had no such mandate. There is nothing like a workable consensus within the public.

That is not Bush's aim in any case. He will gamble, as he did on Medicare in 2003, on persuading a majority of the Congress to pass his reform. Indeed, he has pledged to get his plan through this year, before the 2006 mid-term election year begins.

The key to the outcome is whether the President can persuade a congressional majority to take a big risk with their constituencies, which is to try to explain how risky speculation in the stock market and adding an estimated two trillion dollars to the national debt can be regarded as fiscally prudent or substantively plausible. Unlike tax cuts, which have an obvious appeal, and unlike the Medicare reform, which did have an added benefit, the Bush plan for social security is fraught with electoral danger.

In the Bush first term, his party was solidly unified and the Democrats were frequently splintered. In the social security fight, the positions are reversed. The Democrats appear united in opposition and their leaders now hope to win over at least 15 Republicans in the House of Representatives. In the Senate, not one of the 45 Democrats has defected from the party position. And this is crucial because the Democratic victory depends either on Bush's failure to have a majority in either branch of the Congress, or maintaining in the Senate at least 41 votes to defeat social security reform by a filibuster.

Bush, one must emphasise, is a radical critic of a traditional and popular programme, and that in itself presents risks to those legislators from whom he wants support. In addition, the problems of financing a transition to individual accounts without large benefit reductions is not possible without large-scale public borrowing. Such additions to the federal deficit – the estimated two trillion dollars over 10 years – is anathema to a subset of Republican fiscal conservatives in the Congress. Indeed, Tom Davis, Chair of the House Republican Campaign Committee, is reported by *The Wall Street Journal* to have said that "roughly 30 House Republicans, including himself, are already inclined to oppose Mr. Bush" on his social security plan (Hickey, 2005, p A5).

Both the Medicare and social security developments in the present period are monuments to intense controversy and the peculiarities of American political practices. We have already reported the controversy and noted the distinctiveness of American political arrangements. But, even more important to emphasise this year, these developments are fundamental challenges to two of the most durable programmes of American public life, themselves legacies of the New Deal and the social insurance ethos it exemplified. That observation raises the question of whether there is something more fundamental at issue about the merit of the American welfare state itself. Whatever one might say about the Bush vision of an ownership society, does the 21st century require a fundamental recasting of purpose and programme in social policy (Le Bourdais, 2004)?

New century/new risks: how helpful as a framing device? And how relevant is US experience?

Let's begin by asking whether the presumption of new risks for the new century is the right place to focus. What precisely are these new risks (as opposed to changing social facts) in the labour market, family circumstances and realities of social exclusion? Are these new risks ones that the parents of the modern welfare state did not realise or anticipate?

In my view, there are few such new risks, with one important exception. Unemployment was central to welfare state developments in the 20th century and remains so today. The cost of medical care has been a central concern for a century, although with a twist. In the early years of welfare state development, the major financial consideration about medicine was not the cost of care itself, but foregone wages from work. So, sickness benefits used to mean 'sick pay' not insurance payments for medical bills. Nonetheless, the common purpose of both was to deal with the risk that illness would threaten family income: in short, income protection. Indeed, providing a basis of economic security unites most of the rest of traditional social insurance programmes: disability coverage, retirement pensions and, in a limited sense, child allowances. Child allowances (whether direct or through tax concessions) reflect a concern for the adequacy of family income for a given size of family.

There are of course a whole set of familiar service programmes that are protective, but not solely of income. Child abuse efforts are illustrative, but so are programmes for people with learning disabilities, those with special chronic illnesses or injuries and those workers requiring retraining. The point here is simple: the scope of the traditional welfare state was and is very broad, and the image of a wholly new world of risk is in my view likely to mislead. The one distinctive development of the past half-century is, to be sure, changes in patterns of marriage and divorce, both of which present serious challenges to traditional social insurance cash programmes. Here is where American experience might well be interestingly illuminating.

In the US, as in most industrial democracies, the traditional retirement, old age, disability and survivors financing arrangements took for granted a model family. That family consisted of a breadwinner (male), a female spouse, with or without children, although a family with children dominated the imagery. The conception of income protection proceeded from this assumptive world. If the breadwinner were hurt at work, died prematurely or reached a retirement age, collective publicly funded (or regulated) transfer programmes were to replace the income from work. In the US, the response to the increasing prevalence of divorce has been a marriage length test: benefits for the first spouse of a marriage longer than 10 years. A second marriage, given that test, produces a second spousal benefit. But this adaptation cannot respond easily to what one could call serial marriages or partnerships: short-term marriages or long-term partnerships.

In other nations, the situation differs. In Quebec, for example, the civil code has apparently adapted more easily to the mixed realities of fewer marriages altogether and extended partnerships, whatever the gender of the partners (Le Bourdais, 2004). But nothing like this flexibility has emerged in the US, or generally elsewhere, including the rest of Canada. How to deal with same-sex marriages excites constitutional activism in the US, but with prohibitionist, not welfare state adaptation, in mind. Which children of which marriage – or partnership – are the legally entitled 'survivors' under the provisions of social security law in the US? This question, which has been both buried beneath moralistic commentary on homosexual marriage and bound by bureaucratic rules from another period, is certain to occupy more of the public agenda in the decades to come. But this prediction does not itself validate a wholesale revision of our view of the adequacy of the conception of risks the welfare state of the 20th century took on.

In fact, the most important lesson for other countries from recent American politics is that the traditional risks covered by social security are ideologically under attack in new ways. The rhetorical umbrella under which the current President Bush has placed these attacks is, as described earlier, an appeal to the idea of an 'ownership society'. Brought into prominence at the Republican convention in the summer of 2004, the ownership society is one where psychological and economic security arises largely from individual provision. So, home ownership is the key to residential security, although mortgage foreclosure amid unemployment is not mentioned. Individual savings are held out as the most reliable means of dealing with retirement, health expenses and unemployment. The role of the national government assumed by this array of wishes is that of a large charity for the unlucky, and a source of subsidies for those who can save on their own.

It is no surprise, then, that the Bush Administration has embraced health savings accounts and individual savings that are free of tax, with the added provision of catastrophic insurance as a guarantee against impoverishment. This, one perhaps does not need to add, would delight the Fraser Institute in Canada and their rightwing counterparts in the UK and Europe. The most surprising (and worrisome) instance of a revival of pre-welfare state thinking is the Bush Administration's penchant for individual investment accounts previously discussed. Not presented as an add-on with private savings, the President has since 2001 been keen to support using social insurance retirement contributions for individual risk-bearing investments. That, of course, entails transferring the risk of stock market investment to individual families. One would have thought that the rash of recent bankruptcies and loss of work-related pensions – Enron and United Airlines to name just two of the most prominent examples – would have prompted policy caution in this arena over the past three years.

The reality is that such proposals come from ideological conviction, not disciplined reflection about the risks ordinary families face. Just as most people regard their driving skills as above average, so do many citizens delude themselves into thinking the stock market must go up or that their family will somehow avoid all the risks the welfare state was designed to address. This myopia is what makes the contemporary attack on the welfare state's foundations at least possible, if not popular. In the end, the American welfare state – centred as it is on popular social security pensions, a much appreciated Medicare for older and disabled people, and modest provisions for unemployment and workers' compensation – will neither wither away nor disappear in a bold victory for its ideological enemies. But, for those observing America, it would be wise to watch out for the illusions now in play in the American social policy arena. For the next four years, these proposals will be the centre of continuing ideological conflict. The imbalanced flow of commentary from the US makes it certain that the world will learn about the claims. That makes it prudent to sort out the myths from the realities and, if the election of 2004 is any guide, that will be a substantial task.

One might close there, but for the obvious interest in what 2005 would have been like had Senator Kerry rather than President Bush won the election of 2004. On the three issues emphasised in this review, a Kerry victory would have been enormously consequential. On taxes, he would not have accepted the Bush proposals for further tax cuts disproportionately directed at the wealthy. Here the threat of a presidential veto would have been enough to count on. On the implementation of the Medicare reforms, one could confidently predict that in practice Kerry would not have accepted the statutory restraints on using Medicare's market power to bargain with the pharmaceutical industry over prices and volume. How Kerry would have proceeded here is not easy to say, but that he would either have gone back to the Congress for authorisation or used administrative means is overwhelmingly likely. And, on social security reform, nothing along the lines of the Bush plan would have been on his agenda. Had Republicans proposed and managed to pass a Bush-type plan, he would have certainly vetoed it.

The election then was important in shaping the agenda for 2005 and beyond. But while the line-up of plans and responses changed because of Bush's re-election, the fundamental partisan balance will, as I have argued, make stalemate on large-scale change the most likely scenario. The hostility to President Bush's foreign and military policies among America's allies is real. But the realities of American politics make both foreign judgements inconsequential and Bush's domestic impact less powerful than in foreign and military policy. The fears of non-Americans are great enough to make the electoral results of 2004 a matter of great interest abroad. But, for social policy, which has less of an audience outside the US, the prospects include considerable conflict and the partisan politics of efforts to change the votes of a small number of legislators.

Some observers interpret the Bush agenda with extraordinary generosity.

So, for instance, columnist Michael Barone, lauds President Bush for "fighting [over] long-term stakes, acting with an eye to what America will look like in 20, 30 even 40 years" (Barone, 2005, p 36). Understood as a justification for the programmatic reforms Bush has advanced in social policy, this is a stunning confusion of justifications offered and demonstrated merit. That Bush has his eye on long-term changes in American life is true, but that does not make either his incremental steps or his policy design defensible.

Note

[1] The structure of the drug insurance is exceedingly complex. The deductible is the first $250 of expenditures. From $251-$2,251, the plan calls for a 25% co-insurance rate for the beneficiary. From $2,251-$5,100, the patient pays 100% of the costs (the 'doughnut'), and is responsible for 5% of the drug costs above $5,101.

References

Barone, M. (2005) 'Eyes on the future', *US News and World Report*, vol 138, no 3, p 36.

Caplan, C. and Brangan, N. (2000) 'The status of Medicare Part A and Part B trust funds: the trustees' year 2000 reports (revised)', AARP Public Policy Institute, April (www.research.aarp.org/health/dd45r_funds.pdf).

Center for Medicare Advocacy (2004) 'Will the Medicare Act of 2003 really do that? Myths and realities about the new law', 1 April, Williamantic, CT: Center for Medicare Advocacy.

de Gier, E., de Swaan, A. and Ooijens, M. (eds) (2004) *Dutch welfare reform in an expanding Europe: The neighbours' view*, Amsterdam: Het Spinhuis Publishers.

Greenberg, S. (2004) 'Solving the paradox of 2004: why Americans wanted change but voted for continuity', Unpublished memorandum, 9 November, p 1.

Hickey, R. (2005) 'A battle progressives can win: Bush's privatisation splinters Republicans and unites Democrats', *The American Prospect*, 1 February, pp A4-5.

Le Bourdais, C. (2004) 'New century, new risks', Conference presentation, 'New century, new risks: challenges for social development in Canada', McGill University, 18 November.

Marmor, T.R. (2000) *The politics of Medicare* (2nd edn), New Jersey, NJ: Aldine.

Marmor, T.R. (2004) 'The presidential election, US social policy and whether Canadians should care', *Policy Options*, vol 26, no 1, pp 37-41.

Marmor, T.R. and Hacker, J.S. (2005) 'Medicare reform and social insurance: the clashes of 2003 and their potential fallout', *Yale Journal of Health Policy, Law and Ethics*, vol 5, no 1, pp 475-89.

Marmor, T.R. and Mashaw, J. (2005) 'Private ownership, collective default: the Bush proposals for social security are about dismantling the current system – and not saving it', *Newday*, 10 January, pp A31-32.

Martin, P. and Nadeau, R. (2004) 'La victoire de Bush n'annonce pas une mainmise republicaine sur la Maison-Blanche', *Policy Options*, vol 26, no 1, pp 42-7.

Scully, T. (2004) Personal interview with the author, 19 July, Washington, DC.

EIGHT

The future of healthcare in the UK: think-tanks and their policy prescriptions

Sally Ruane

Introduction

This chapter examines some of the main policy recommendations emanating from a politically diverse range of UK-based think-tanks in relation to the National Health Service (NHS). While they are by no means a new phenomenon, think-tanks have increased in prominence substantially over the past few years. The ideas and publications of think-tanks may be reported on prime-time television news, and key personnel are sometimes interviewed on pressing policy dilemmas. Moreover, the Internet now makes possible the widespread dissemination of reports, proposals and briefings, again enhancing visibility. By 1997, think-tanks were considered an 'addictive habit for politicians' (Wheen, 1997, cited by Denham and Garnett, 1999, p 54).

Think-tanks are defined as "independent bodies which provide information and ideas with the intention of assisting government decision makers" (Denham and Garnett, 1999, p 46). All the think-tanks described in this chapter seek to influence policy and are 'independent', deriving their incomes (in varying proportions) from sources such as business, trades unions, individuals, charities, government departments and others. All but one are based in London. There are also important differences among these think-tanks. Some, such as the King's Fund Institute (KFI) and the Democratic Health Network (DHN), focus exclusively on health; others, such as the Institute for Public Policy Research (IPPR) and Catalyst, develop ideas in relation to a variety of policy spheres. Some have charitable status, such as Demos and Civitas, while the Institute of Directors (IoD) is a membership body and the Centre for Public Services (CPS) describes itself as an independent, non-profit organisation. Some are very small, such as DHN with an office of two; others are substantially larger such as the IPPR and the New Economics Foundation (NEF). They vary in their philosophies and objectives. On the right, the Adam Smith Institute (ASI) describes itself as a "leading innovator of free-market policies" (www.adamsmith.org/about), while Civitas (which evolved from the Institute of Economic Affairs Health and Welfare Unit) considers its 'special domain' a new 'balance' between civil society and government. By contrast on the left of centre, Catalyst aims to promote "practical policies directed to the redistribution of power, wealth and opportunity" (www.catalystforum.org.uk), while the CPS seeks to promote the progressive modernisation of public services based upon the principles of public service, democracy and social justice. While the IPPR is closely associated with New Labour and Catalyst with Old Labour, Demos aims to "create an open resource of knowledge and learning which operates beyond traditional parties, identities and disciplines" (www.demos.co.uk/aboutus).

Warpole describes think-tanks as "intermediary institutions" (1998, p 148) which act as bridges or go-betweens, reflecting a greater ease of movement between the spaces and places of intellectual life, indispensable in networked society. It is not surprising, then, that a 'fuzziness of boundaries' among different kinds of institutions is acknowledged: for instance, by Denham and Garnett (1998). I have opted to include the non-partisan IoD and Association of Chief Executives of Voluntary Organisations (ACEVO) but to exclude Labour-affiliated Unison, although others might wish to draw the boundary elsewhere. Table 8.1 summarises the characteristics of the think-tanks whose ideas are discussed in this chapter.

The role of think-tanks during Conservative administrations has been examined in some detail (for example, Cockett, 1995; Denham, 1996). This chapter examines a number of prominent themes identifiable in think-tank proposals for the NHS under New Labour and how these can best be understood. The interest shown in the NHS reflects the political salience of public services during New Labour's period in office, and perceptions of the changing boundaries between the possible and the unthinkable. The pamphlets and reports used are identified by think-tank rather than by author.

Table 8.1: The think-tanks

Abbreviation	Name	Characteristics
ACEVO	Association of Chief Executives of Voluntary Organisations	membership organisation for chief executives of charities and not-for-profit organisations; seeks to expand role of third sector
ASI	Adam Smith Institute	non-profit organisation; seeks practical market-economic policies to reform state enterprises and roll back government
Cat	Catalyst	think-tank for labour movement and the left; challenges marketisation in public services and seeks to develop practical policies for redistribution of wealth, power and opportunity
Civ	Civitas	seeks to roll back government through better division of responsibilities between government and civil society
CPS	Centre for Public Services	non-profit organisation committed to provision and modernisation of good public services through principles of public service, democracy and social justice; challenges marketisation
Demos	Demos	charity; seeks to offer open resource of learning and knowledge across party boundaries, and to develop practical policies to redesign public services
DHN	Democratic Health Network	partner organisation to Local Government Information Unit; offers affiliates policy advice, research and training, and opportunities to exchange best practice in partnerships
IoD	Institute of Directors	membership body; seeks to enable members to fulfil leadership responsibilities, and brings its expertise to bear on major public issues
IPPR	Institute for Public Policy Research	charity; closely associated with New Labour; seeks to promote marketised, pluralist public services
KFI	King's Fund Institute	health-focused charitable foundation; offers detailed academic policy analysis and leadership courses
NEF	New Economics Foundation	seeks to challenge mainstream thinking on economic, environmental and social issues; committed to sustainable economics and mutualised public services

Think-tank prescriptions for the NHS

Excessive politicisation and the need for substantial withdrawal of government involvement in health

The KFI identifies over-politicisation as one of the major problems facing the NHS, and recommends a 'new legislative settlement' to establish distance between the government and the NHS via an arm's-length corporation responsible for monitoring standards and allocating funds locally (KFI 1). According to the KFI, the government should focus upon developing a broad strategy for health and healthcare and a broad ethical framework for healthcare services, including "how principles of equity and humanity apply to the vulnerable" (KFI 1, p 8). Withdrawal from direct regulation and allocation of resources is to be accompanied by withdrawal from delivery (KFI 2). This does not appear very different from an ASI analysis which recommends that the government should have no direct managerial role and should concentrate on policy making; ensuring a fair and efficient system; regulating purchasers and providers; establishing and enforcing minimum standards; and ensuring the poor get access (ASI 1).

These ideas bear some relation to earlier debates and organisational rearrangements within the NHS – for example, in the 1980s following the Griffiths Inquiry (DHSS, 1983). However, some right-wing think-tank reports appear to go further. While admittedly the boundary is blurred, for them the desired government roles are not policy making and strategy but regulation, ensuring access and funding. Papers from both the ASI (ASI 2) and the IoD (IoD 1) complain of the 'triple nationalisation' of funding, healthcare provision and policy making on investment and outcomes, the latter using survey evidence to back its call for depoliticisation and decentralisation (IoD 2). Civitas suggests that the primary role of the government should be to create a legal and regulatory framework; to guarantee access to a high standard of healthcare for all; and to ensure the supply of essential public health services, including accident and emergency services (Civ 1).

Greater freedoms among providers

The stripping away of government powers and involvement becomes clearer when looking at proposals for healthcare-providing organisations themselves. Healthcare is considered by some to be over-centralised, with too few powers devolved to providing units. First, there is broad advocacy of greater competition among providers, which the ASI, IPPR, KFI, Civitas, NEF and IoD all sign up to, although the KFI distinguishes elective care provision (which is suitable for market competition) from complex and integrated care (which probably is not) (KFI 3). Moreover, all of these, save the KFI, include the possibility of commercial companies participating in a competitive or 'contested' market.

For the IPPR, partnership and pragmatism are key concepts in the organisation of services, with public authorities commissioning professional, ancillary and capital development services from a range of organisations. The vision is of a dissolution of boundaries with cross-departmental service purchasing from organisations in the statutory, voluntary and commercial sectors. Public sector purchasers would face a "rich and diverse menu of partnership options". The environment would be competitive but compatible with a collaborative approach driven by trust and reputation rather than "ever more detailed legal provisions" (IPPR 1, p 255).

The ACEVO, in a pamphlet arrestingly entitled *Replacing the state* (ACEVO 1), argues for an enhanced role for voluntary sector organisations in public service delivery. The authors contend that the third sector has a strong historical pedigree and should not be marginalised in a political (and old-fashioned) debate about privatisation. Rather, it contributes to social cohesion and offers value added through closeness to customers and clients, local accountability, innovation and freedom from bureaucratic controls. The pragmatism that predominates in the IPPR can also be found in the ACEVO approach, which maintains that choice of provider should be determined by considerations of effectiveness and that long-term contracts comparable to Private Finance Initiative (PFI) deals and based on a sound financial footing should be explored.

By contrast, in a book not published under CPS' name but written by the Director of CPS with extracts available on the website, Whitfield (CPS 1) claims that job insecurity, disempowerment, weakened democratic accountability and participation, and fragmented services are direct consequences of threats to outsource on a competitive basis. The solution is for the government to reverse pro-business and pro-market policies. Instead, the government should actively pursue a 'new public service management' that promotes equity, equalities, environmental sustainability and a distinct public service ethos, all seen by Whitfield as incompatible with market models.

Substantial management freedoms are advocated. Civitas (Civ 1) advocates complete autonomy, including no restrictions on the terms and conditions for recruiting staff; moreover, providing these units renounce their right to future public funding, they should also be free to raise funds in the capital markets. According to the KFI (KFI 1), managers should be able to manage on the basis of contractual obligations (rather than central directives); to introduce new types of service; to generate and re-invest financial surpluses; and to raise additional funds on capital markets. The ASI emphasises that, although some may choose to specialise, all provider units must offer services to patients on an equal basis and on the basis of published tariffs that are equal for all patients (ASI 1).

New legal forms of ownership

Most of the think-tanks wish to see not mere devolution of decision making and market competition but dramatic changes to the structure of healthcare provision with units adopting an autonomous or semi-autonomous status. The emphasis is upon pluralism and voluntarism, rather than mere privatisation. One ASI report specifies 'managed pluralism' as the core concept for a developing NHS since this will better serve the NHS aspiration "to ensure access to high-quality healthcare for all those in need" (ASI 2, p 25) through enhancing efficiency, quality and access to more capital. The Civitas report (Civ 1) considers that *new* hospitals should be allowed to assume a commercial legal form, but that existing NHS hospitals should remain non-commercial, possibly adopting a Foundation Hospital status (at the time of the report a pre-legislative policy of New Labour). All should have the freedom to serve 'consumers' as they believe best (Civ 1). The KFI proposes an end to government-owned hospitals, suggesting they be transferred to some other legal status, such as that of universities or the 'public interest company' but, like Civitas, rules out for-profit status (KFI 1, p 13). Changes in legal form are not confined to hospitals since over 75% of the NHS budget is controlled by Primary Care Trusts (PCTs). The KFI (KFI 4) explores the potential application of the principle of changed social ownership to PCTs that, they suggest, would be untenable in the immediate future but might prove essential in the medium term.

Where the ASI emphasises the economic benefits of pluralism, for the KFI the great advantages of these developments would be the depoliticisation of the NHS and the enhancement of accountability to healthcare purchasers and the local community through new, differently constituted types of organisation with substantial involvement at board level from the local community. This, coupled with contract-driven performance and greater patient choice, would serve to hold chief executives more immediately to account, to allow local needs to be prioritised and to facilitate long-term planning that is more feasible where control over the future is exercised by the unit and not by central government (KFI 1).

A recurring theme is the concept of the public interest company. The IPPR defines this very broadly as an organisation that does not usually have shareholders, is legally independent from the state and delivers a public service, and the Institute has devoted a whole report (IPPR 2) to evaluating its benefits and drawbacks. Characteristically, the position adopted by the IPPR report is that the use of different legal forms of ownership should be governed by considerations of pragmatism and practicality rather than by ideology or prior assumptions. In the sphere of health, these ideas have been exemplified in Foundation Trusts.

By contrast, left of centre organisations such as Catalyst and the DHN have expressed doubt about the desirability of changes in legal forms of ownership, especially the version of public interest companies found in Foundation Trusts, towards which Catalyst has directed substantial hostility. With an interest in questions of redistribution and equity, Catalyst has argued that Foundation Trusts threaten equity of access to healthcare (Cat 1) and present further openings for private sector involvement with its consequent distortion of public service priorities (Cat 2). The DHN (DHN 1) rejects Foundation Trusts since their institutional arrangements are seen as wholly inadequate for holding service providers to account by local people.

Mutuality

A complementary approach to questions of legal ownership has been pursued by those who have explored mutuality as an organising principle for public services and have arrived at an end point similar to that of advocates of the public interest company. Mutuality can be understood as a system of organisations run with the close cooperation or control of their key stakeholders and, in 2000, the IoD (IoD 1, 3) was developing this idea in relation to the NHS. The IoD concedes that turning the NHS over to mutuality 'all at once' is not feasible; instead one report (IoD 3) proposes piloting with PCTs, which individuals in the local community could be encouraged to 'join' and to which they could contribute some share capital. The idea would not be to exclude others from access but to harness local spirit and resources (IoD 3, p 39). This is not far from the Civitas (Civ 1) proposal that patients be given choice of PCT (thereby extending their choice over GPs and hospitals), and that PCTs be converted either into consumer mutuals with membership control over resource use decision making or evolved into Health Maintenance Organisations (HMOs) run by doctors. HMOs developed in the US on a for-profit and not-for-profit basis to contain healthcare costs. HMOs agree to cover the costs of healthcare to enrolled members while exercising control over how these services are funded and provided.

Shortly after the IoD reports in 2001, the NEF produced *The mutual state* (NEF 1) and went so far as to establish a 'virtual' think-tank, with Mutuo (www.mutuo.org) to carry and propagate new ideas. The report advocates decentralised managerial decision making and the devolution of power (including over budgets) to users, and discusses diverse models of participation in the NHS and existing barriers to participation (NEF 2).

Recognising their overlapping visions, the IoD and the NEF joined forces in 2002 to produce collaboratively *The mutual health service: How to decentralise the NHS* (IoD/NEF 1), co-authored by Ruth Lea and Ed Mayo. Mutuality here is understood as "an institutionalised, value-based model of reciprocity" (IoD/NEF 1, p 8). The NHS, the authors argue, should cease to be a monolithic provider of care; rather, NHS Trusts should become independent, non-profit making, multi-stakeholder mutuals, which combine the entrepreneurialism of the private sector with the ethos and values of the public, and function within a cooperative network of healthcare and related public services. These would be opened up to 'comprehensive citizen participation' to enable people to take responsibility for their own healthcare: they would be owned by and accountable to their members (local people, staff, partner organisations, NHS commissioners) who would have rights to control. The IoD/NEF publication offers a step-by-step guide to achieving this.

To bring this about, a distinct legal form would have to be created (again, the public interest company) since, despite a long history of mutualism, there is no legal definition of a mutual in the UK and existing legal forms do not provide all desirable features. The report advocates that the (then) planned Foundation Trusts be established on the basis of this proposed legal form (IoD/NEF 1).

Mutuality is considered meaningless without participation and two forms of participation receive particular attention within the report. The first is the notion of practical mutual support organised via time banks that could be utilised by health centres – for example, to facilitate the return of older patients home from hospital and the care of those recovering from treatment. This form of participation makes cost savings to the NHS possible, allows those stigmatised as users of services (for example, mental health service users) to become givers and simultaneously addresses causes of ill-health that lie in atomisation, loneliness and stress. A second form of participation is found in greater individual responsibility for one's own health. The report's (IoD/NEF 1) authors conjecture that, as health budgets rise, so will the emphasis on preventative healthcare, making a new relationship between professional and patient essential.

There are somewhat different conceptualisations of the problems behind these moves towards mutualism. The NEF's preoccupation is with what it describes as a breakdown in the social contract between the individual and the state resulting from poor performing, top-down, one-size-fits-all public services; there is a need to reinvigorate civil society and democracy and this is best achieved through mutualism (NEF 1). For the IoD (IoD 1), the main problem of the NHS is that it is a vast Leviathan, virtually impossible to manage, in which patients have almost no control over the services they receive. The NHS needs to be broken up into units that can be managed properly, are open to competition and responsive to users. Mutuality is considered 'an approach to decentralisation', particularly suited where communities as well as individuals benefit from services.

Patient involvement

The left of centre think-tanks, however, remain deeply sceptical about these *approaches* to increasing local involvement in health services, although the *aim* is one they share. The notion of mutualism based upon self-selecting participants with ownership rights is considered by the DHN not only no guarantee of democratic accountability but potentially an obstacle to it since it could foster a sense of exclusion and detachment among non-members (DHN 1). Instead, the DHN, whose starting point is not to decentralise the NHS but to democratise it, retains a strong role for the state and offers a more complex model of democracy, the underpinning principles of which would include a commitment to equitable access, devolved decision making, employee and public participation, and diverse forms of accountability (DHN 1).

The notion of greater citizen engagement with, and responsibility for, healthcare is to be found in Charles Leadbeater's pamphlet on 'personalisation' (Demos 1). Personalisation is claimed to supersede the shortcomings of both paternalism and consumerism in professionally provided services. What is envisaged is a reworking of services so that they meet more exactly the needs of the individual. A five-step hierarchy of personalisation is outlined. 'Shallow' personalisation involves more customer-friendly services (for example, seven day a week call centres, booked appointments). 'Deep' personalisation involves consumers as 'co-designers and co-producers' of services, actively participating in defining problems and designing solutions that do not create dependency upon the state. Even beyond this, personalisation entails mass social innovation arising from self-organisation: the public good emerging from the myriad individual decisions about how to live and behave shaped by public policy (Demos 1). In between shallow and deep are opportunities for individuals to have some say in referral pathways and how money allocated for their healthcare (for example) is spent on them. Inevitably, this vision entails very different roles for professionals.

While the concept of personalisation overcomes the passivity evident in some models of user-choice, its emphasis is upon the role and satisfactions of the individual and is at odds with the more collective notions of citizenship found in the left of centre think-tanks. Personalisation places an enormous burden upon the individual to get it right for themselves. They must sift through information and understand it, make judgements not only about the timeliness and accessibility of a service but also its character and design, and articulate preferences and complaints. Although Leadbeater (Demos 1) claims personalisation overcomes the problems of consumerism, it reinforces the self-regarding and the onus upon the individual to participate further threatens the prospect of 'DIY welfare', Catalyst warns (Cat 3, p 37). The model of mutuality proposed by the NEF and IoD may be vulnerable to this last charge since it echoes Demos' desire for greater responsibility for one's own health. The interest of the member is limited to that of the local mutual and not more broadly to the public or common good. These significantly different philosophies between right/centre and left think-tanks unfold further when these discussions of public involvement are tied to broader debates about choice, consumerism and citizenship.

The DHN 'Green Paper' on democracy in the NHS (DHN 1) refers to a Catalyst pamphlet (Cat 3) to draw a clear distinction between the consumer and the citizen and to identify the fatal shortcomings in the former as a model for the latter. Consumers are defined only in relation to their own interests whereas the citizen considers the public good. Catalyst (Cat 3, p 14) argues that the key features of the consumer are found in the way choices are made (as self-regarding individuals), goods and services are received (through a series of temporary, instrumental and bilateral relationships with suppliers) and power is exercised (passively through aggregate signalling). By contrast, citizens *deliberate*, have regard to the interests of the whole political community and engage in an ongoing, not temporary, relationship with the state. Civic republican models of citizenship note that citizens have meaningful existence only in the context of social networks and ties of membership, loyalty and mutual obligation. Thus, extending personal choice in services cannot serve as a basis for democratic decision making. It disregards informational imperfections and asymmetries, citizens' obligation to secure the public good and the impracticality of testing or experimenting with policies or services in the way one can with consumer goods.

The KFI also advises caution. While Catalyst identifies largely philosophical and value-based objections to the use of consumer choice as a mechanism for enhanced patient control, the KFI adopts a more technical approach and warns that some forms of patient choice may make other government objectives, including equity, more difficult to achieve, particularly in a professionally dominated service (KFI 5).

Funding healthcare and limits to access

Concerned to promote individual responsibility for healthcare, some right of centre think-tanks take the discussion of extended choice into the realms of healthcare funding. Civitas (Civ 1, 2) explores three different funding systems. The first is a taxation-funded 'core' of services, which can be accessed free of charge from non-NHS providers via a treatment voucher scheme. Top-up cover could be purchased on a fee-for-service or individual insurance basis. The second, borrowing from the Swiss system, is a social insurance approach but with *no employer payment*. The third draws upon a US scheme and entails a system of healthcare purchasing cooperatives to which individuals could (but would not have to) subscribe as members. The cooperatives would make available to members a range of insurance policies offered by competing private insurance providers. The government could define a standard insurance plan (in other words, what is covered) and would pay a percentage of the cost of that plan.

In its Partnerships for Better Health Project, the ASI considers most of the NHS's failings are tied to funding. In one report (ASI 3), rebate financing would involve allowing those who wish to make arrangements for their own health to 'opt out' of the NHS by receiving back from the state a National Insurance or tax repayment to reflect the NHS care foregone. The level of rebate would reflect expenditure on healthcare for a person of the same sex and age in *normal* health with no pre-existing medical conditions. Thus, the level of rebate would be conservative, leaving sufficient funds in the NHS to guarantee treatment to those in poor health. Those who opt out can determine precisely what healthcare they wish to pay for.

Another ASI report (ASI 1) proposes a system of competing social insurance schemes in which all must participate and in which individuals pay premiums proportionate to (all) income (the state paying for the poorest); insurers must accept everyone. All services would be free at the point of access *unless* people choose to pay fees for services in order to reduce monthly premiums or to buy extra services – that is, some schemes may not cover all healthcare needs. The ASI's *Funding UK health care* (ASI 4) advocates compulsory social insurance, multiple competing funds and guaranteed access to a 'comprehensive' healthcare package.

The IoD (IoD 1) rejects social insurance schemes in favour of an 'NHS passport' – that is, an economic voucher scheme. Everyone would have an NHS passport, which would give entitlement to a universal and free-at-the-point-of-use 'core' of health services – strictly defined and concentrating on serious and long-term illness and packages of care for certain groups (notably babies, children, pregnant women and older people). NHS trusts would offer core services free; but a voucher or 'credit note' could be taken to a non-NHS unit with the difference paid for by the individual either directly or via an insurance scheme. Anything outside the core paid for would have to be settled by the individual in full. Lea believes there should be a debate about what is in the 'core' but warns that it would not include much preventative work.

Healthcare funding features more subtly in the work of other think-tanks. The concept of the public interest company, much admired by the IPPR (IPPR 2) and the IoD and NEF (IoD/NEF 1), incorporates access to private finance for the purpose of developing and expanding health services. The latter makes a passing reference to participatory budgeting and it is this which is shared more broadly across the political spectrum. Although not challenging the collective origins of service funding, two think-tanks have published papers recommending some devolution of budgets to users. The concept of personalisation includes user control over some part of the budget allocated to their care (Demos 1) with the consequent reforms necessary to financial flows. A Catalyst paper (Cat 4) advocates experiments in participatory budgeting as a means to deepen democratic involvement in policy and the administration of services.

Discussion

Looking over the analyses, some degree of overlap in think-tank conceptualisations of the NHS's problems is evident. The IoD and ASI both identify as the fundamental problem the triple nationalisation of funding, provision and decision making about resource use. This poses a threat to the future resource base of the NHS and gives rise to unmanageability and a lack of transparency, choice and responsiveness. Civitas and the KFI share this concern with excessive state involvement, the latter identifying three immediate and interrelated problems: over-politicisation, excessive centralisation and lack of responsiveness to individuals and local communities. The NEF offers a more organic diagnosis of the problem as arising from the absence of a consistent philosophy and vision by government in the face of an unravelling of the social contract between state and citizen. ACEVO and the IPPR are principally concerned with the role of ideology as a barrier to the rational and pragmatic use of multiple providers, sustaining boundaries between sectors when a more integrated approach would achieve greater efficiency and effectiveness, accountability to users and innovation.

By contrast, on the left of centre, Catalyst and the CPS identify business models, an enhanced role for the private sector and greater consumer choice not as the solutions but as the *problems* that public services, including the NHS, are forced to grapple with. Certainly a deficit in democratic engagement and accountability through insufficient participation by citizens is specified as a central problem (and by the DHN, too), but it is the inappropriate application of markets and use of individualised consumer models of service development that threaten universalism, equity and a commitment to the collective good. The CPS goes beyond Catalyst's social democratic stance and develops a Marxist conception of the problem of the conflictual and contradictory nature of the state in a global capitalist economy. For the CPS, it is the state's neo-liberal surrender to business and markets that is the danger, not the solution.

What we see in the work of these think-tanks is the apparent mainstreaming of ideas, which, only 15 years ago, would have been inconceivable or confined to the extreme edges of the political landscape. The IPPR, despite its self-definition as centre-left, has not hesitated to advocate an extension of the principles of marketisation (understood as the selection of service providers by independent commissioners on the basis of competition) and privatisation (understood as a transfer of activities away from the state to the informal and commercial spheres), traditionally associated with right of centre thinking. The right and the centre now share similar ideas in relation to diversity of provision and competition among providers; increased choice for users; a reduction in the role of government in health with a shift towards establishing regulatory frameworks; the development of public interest companies in hospitals and PCTs, with an associated levering in of private finance; and a changed relationship between citizen and service. There is *not* yet such a sharing of ideas between centre and right on matters of overall funding where the centre remains sceptical about significant moves away from taxation. As government involvement in the management and provision of healthcare is exhorted to diminish, we see a new relationship between patient and service proposed. On the one hand, individuals are to take greater responsibility for their own health and, through *individual* action, that of others. Greater engagement of individual for self and neighbour is advocated as producing both better health outcomes and significant reductions in the cost of healthcare in the foreseeable future. On the other, the *collective* responsibility for each other's health via universal institutions is attacked through proposals for mutuals, insurance-funded healthcare packages and the more generalised individualisation of healthcare encounters via notions of personal choice. Individuals are encouraged to dwell upon what they can get out of the service for themselves and how the service can be altered to suit them as individuals, rather than how it can be developed to meet adequately the needs of all. Proposals for radical changes in funding construe very individualised relationships that shift the discourse from patient and health service to user and healthcare package.

This partial sharing of positions is reflected in mainstream politics, where Foundation Hospitals, a degree of market competition and inclusion of the commercial sector have been embraced by the government but where a clear divide remains between the main political parties over funding, with Conservative Party leader, Michael Howard, taking up the NHS passport idea and New Labour, so far at least, committed in the main to funding through taxation. Both parties vie for popular support around notions of extended patient choice in the run up to the 2005 General Election.

The bold proposals emanating from the right and centre are not matched by audacious 'blue skies' visions of the NHS coming from the left. Left of centre think-tanks such as Catalyst and the CPS instead often appear reactive – understandably and perhaps inevitably: for example, in the otherwise valuable and highly technically competent critiques of proposals emanating from other think-tanks, such as the IPPR (for example, Cat 5) or from the Department of Health itself (for example, CPS 2; Cat 1, 2). The CPS has produced an account of the principles upon which a 'new public service management' could be built (CPS 1), but overall there is a paucity of work on the NHS from left of centre think-tanks, although the DHN does explore more collective mechanisms of public involvement in its Green Paper on democratisation (DHN 1). As a result, the trade union voice that would be heard via these organisations has limited expression. (Instead, Unison, for example, has commissioned high-quality research published under its own name [for example, Unison, 2003] and this constitutes by far the most left, easily accessible, mainstream critique of current health policy, although it may lack the clout of an 'independent' think-tank.) Both Catalyst and the CPS have been working to forge, through seminars, a left stance for developing public services, but as yet these have not materialised into service-specific visions or blueprints for action. Even here, we should remember that Catalyst is not 'left', as traditionally understood, but is derived from the formerly right-wing element of old Labour social democracy. The upshot of this is that in the circulation of ideas during a critical period in the evolution of New Labour's 'third way', in the discourse that surrounds health, there has been little in the way of left values, left imagination and left initiative.

One possible explanation for the proliferation of think-tank output around public services lies in Colin Crouch's analysis of post-democracy (Crouch, 2000). Crouch argues that a dilemma faces a social democratic party, such as the UK Labour Party, because its traditional base has largely crumbled through changes in the class structure of society. The leadership of such a party becomes much more dependent upon the broader electorate for office and seeks ways to appeal to it. It needs to connect with and develop policies that appeal to non-traditional interests. To achieve these aims, the leadership will have to bypass both the activists, who hitherto have served to link it to the traditional base, and the party policy-making machinery that has hitherto broadly been composed of and produced for that traditional base. In short, Crouch claims, such a party leadership needs to free itself from its party machinery and its trade union dependency. In this, New Labour has succeeded through its elimination of Conference policy-making powers and establishment of policy fora regarded by many as a mere rubber-stamping exercise. The vacuum thus created has been filled by corporate lobbyists keen to influence government policy. As a result of globalisation, these businesses increasingly find their interests lie in the service sector rather than manufacturing or heavy industry, a sector that in recent UK history has been largely publicly owned. At the same time as these businesses seek access to public services, the party leadership requires large donations to reduce its financial dependency upon trade unions and to fund the professionalised mass marketing of the party necessary to connect with the wider electorate.

Think-tanks serve a number of useful functions in this context. First, they offer a source of policy ideas and innovation that is external to the party and which can appeal across former class divides. Moreover, think-tanks are funded to do this by a range of donors and commissioners outside the party. Second, by bringing together at seminars and conferences business, public sector, academic and political personnel, they can collect ideas and test out the acceptability and attractiveness to different interest groups of proposals or potential proposals: the 'intermissaries' or 'research-brokers' Warpole (1998) speaks of.

However, perhaps the most critical contribution of think-tanks is ideological since they can help create an intellectual and political environment that serves to delimit the range of conceivable policy choices. Denham and Garnett (1999) have suggested that new right think-tanks provided policy reinforcement and conferred the impression of intellectual rigour as Thatcher sought to convert the country to economic liberalism. For New Labour, the task is not so much to convert to neo-liberalism as to facilitate a policy evolution that moves substantially in its direction while appearing not to do so. Put most crudely, think-tanks can help legitimise pro-business policies by construing them as in the public interest. This is done most effectively not by advocating a pro-business approach but by advocating innovative and imaginatively distinct policy options that are not immediately identifiable with business interests, and that gradually relax and loosen the affective grip of the public on its publicly provided services. Although conferences and seminars serve to familiarise different interests with the shifting policy agenda and precepts, these interests do not exercise equal influence on outcome as Catalyst's critique (Cat 5) of the IPPR's commission on public–private partnerships (IPPR 1) vividly illustrates.

Think-tanks can present narrative accounts, which de-couple the values underpinning a service from the structural mechanisms that allow that service to embody those values. Thus, the ASI can argue that ensuring access to good healthcare, regardless of income, is a laudable aspiration but does not require hitherto integral features of the NHS such as 'triple nationalisation' to achieve this (ASI 1). Similarly, think-tanks can serve an ideological function by discrediting core features of public services, such as professional judgements on behalf of clients, now dismissed as 'paternalistic' (for example, Demos 1), or the non-profit prerequisite of the public sector ethos, now discarded as irrelevant since there is "no simple distinction between the motivations of for-profit, not-for-profit and public providers" (IPPR 1, p 137). Apparently right-wing proposals from supposedly centre-left think-tanks are justified by appeals to pragmatism. Thus, provision for profit becomes morally equivalent to public provision, the choice between them to be determined by the specificities of the case, not by broader principles. The advocacy of the third sector is particularly useful here since it gives the impression of even-handedness among multi-sector provision and serves to weaken further the association of public services with public provision. The role of left of centre think-tanks in this is to contest the terrain mapped out by other think-tanks – to compete to define those values and assumptions that shape the way elites think, since think-tank efforts need not imply a change in the broader climate of opinion, where the electorate is acquiescent (Denham and Garnett, 1998). Ironically, the IPPR, set up in 1988 to challenge the dominance of the pro-free-market think-tanks, now contributes to the strategy to open up public services to market models and business penetration.

There are significant methodological difficulties in establishing evidence of influence, but the marked overlap between think-tank ideas and government policy suggests a certain permeability in the boundary separating decision makers from the propagators of policy innovation. Most of these think-tanks take seriously the effective dissemination of their ideas, evidenced in the presence of journalists on advisory councils and boards. Seminars, conferences and business breakfasts are all used for 'brokering' purposes. A London location is essential for this participation in and fashioning of a metropolitan elite with a view to creating an ideological climate within which government must operate. Only the Sheffield-based CPS bucks the trend. The apparent openness to these circulating ideas by New Labour, searching for a replacement for 'old Labour' values, perhaps explains the emergence of several new think-tanks over the past couple of decades and the rapid growth of some such as the IPPR, Demos and the NEF.

This notion of an intellectual climate forged through interlinked networks is visible in a degree of overlapping membership among think-tank contributors. For example, Stephen Pollard, described by one political commentator as 'New Labour-ish' (White, 2004), a senior fellow at Civitas and member of Civitas' consensus group, also directs the health policy programme at the Centre for the New Europe, is former head of research at the Social Market Foundation and former director of research at the Fabian Society. Ed Mayo is a former director of the NEF, co-published the ACEVO pamphlet on *Replacing the state* (ACEVO 1) and now works as Chief Executive of the National Consumer Council, which in part seeks to promote a consumer approach to welfare policy. Equally significant is the passage of some IPPR researchers, such as Matthew Taylor (former director) and David Miliband, and Geoff Mulgan of Demos, to the No. 10 Policy Unit.

Understood in this context, we can see that some apparent differences among think-tanks become less significant. For instance, we might distinguish the work of the KFI from that of, say, Civitas, the NEF or the IPPR. The former is strictly not political but offers a cogent academic and *technical* analysis of policies in relation to goals specified by politicians. However, by taking seriously the goals of government and by examining various policy options in relation to those goals, it not only offers ways of making those goals and policies practicable, it also confers a certain legitimacy on them. It reinforces the place of those goals and policies in the discourse, as it were. Thus, by being neutral, the KFI serves a very political and ideological function.

Ironically, despite the efforts of think-tanks to mould a policy agenda fit for the modern age, there is something decidedly old-fashioned about the current output on health and this comes back to the context Crouch (2000) depicts. Governments operate in a global context and yet there is no mention of the role of supranational institutions and supranational processes in shaping think-tank ideas and visions. Although some think-tanks have units that deal with, for instance, the European Union (EU) (for example, the IoD), this is not joined up to ideas about healthcare. Thus, the implications of EU single market provisions and competition rules for UK healthcare go unexamined. If authors are developing ideas they know to be compatible with supranational constraints (for example, in concepts of pluralism and partnership), they are certainly not making this explicit.

An analysis of think-tank prescriptions for the NHS allows us to reflect upon the role and function of think-tanks in the contemporary UK political landscape. The problems identified by some are the solutions proffered by others. The dominance of pro-market, pro-business solutions challenges the left to produce and circulate more clearly drawn, NHS-specific proposals. Whether this can be achieved via existing left of centre think-tanks, or whether others emerge to complement their work, remains to be seen.

References

ACEVO 1 (Association of Chief Executives of Voluntary Organisations) (2004) *Replacing the state*, London: ACEVO.
ASI 1 (Adam Smith Institute) Browne, A. and Young, M. (2002) *NHS reform: Towards consensus*, London: ASI.
ASI 2 Bosanquet, N. (1999) *A successful National Health Service: From aspiration to delivery*, London: ASI.

ASI 3 Booth, P. (2002) *Getting your health back: Rebate financing for medical care*, London: ASI.

ASI 4 Adam Smith Institute (nd) *Funding UK health care*, London: ASI.

Cat 1 (Catalyst) Mohan, J. (2003) *Reconciling choice and equity: Foundation Hospitals and the future of the NHS*, London: Catalyst.

Cat 2 Pollock, A. and Price, D. (2003) *In place of Bevan? Briefing on the Health and Social Care (Community Health standards) Bill*, London: Catalyst.

Cat 3 Needham, C. (2003) *Citizen-consumers: New Labour's market democracy*, London: Catalyst.

Cat 4 Eagle, A. (2004) *Deepening democracy*, London: Catalyst.

Cat 5 Pollock, A., Shaoul, J., Rowland, D. and Player, S. (2001) *Public services and the private sector: A response to the IPPR*, London: Catalyst.

Civ 1 Civitas (2003a) *The final report of the Health Policy Consensus Group: A new consensus for NHS reform*, London: Civitas, the Institute for the Study of Civil Society.

Civ 2 Civitas (2003b) *Step by step reform: Interim report of the Consensus Group*, London: Civitas.

Cockett, R. (1995) *Thinking the unthinkable: Think-tanks and the economic counter-revolution, 1931-1983*, London: Fontana Press.

CPS 1 (Centre for Public Services) Whitfield, D. (2001) *Public services or corporate welfare: Rethinking the nation state in the global economy*, London: Pluto Press.

CPS 2 Centre for Public Services (2001) *Private Finance Initiative and Public Private Partnerships: What future for public services?*, Sheffield: CPS.

Crouch, C. (2000) *Coping with post-democracy*, Fabian Ideas no 598, London: Fabian Society.

Demos 1 Leadbeater, C. (2004) *Personalisation through participation*, London: Demos.

Denham, A. (1996) *Think-tanks and the New Right*, Aldershot: Dartmouth.

Denham, A. and Garnett, M. (1998) *British think-tanks and the climate of opinion*, London: UCL Press.

Denham, A. and Garnett, M. (1999) 'Influence without responsibility? Think-tanks in Britain', in *Parliamentary Affairs*, vol 52, no 1, pp 46-57.

DHSS (Department of Health and Social Security) (1983) *NHS Management Inquiry* (The Griffiths Management Report), London: DHSS.

DHN 1 (Democratic Health Network) Morley, A. and Campbell, F. (2003) *People power and health: A Green Paper for democratising the NHS*, London: Local Government Information Unit.

IoD 1 (Institute of Directors) Lea, R. (2000) *Healthcare in the UK: The need for reform*, London: IoD.

IoD 2 Day, G. (2001) *Healthcare Provision Policy Group: Report of a survey of views on healthcare provision*, London: IoD.

IoD 3 Day, G. (2000) *Management, mutuality and risk: Better ways to run the National Health Service*, London: IoD.

IoD/NEF (New Economics Foundation) 1 Lea, R. and Mayo, E. (2002) *The mutual health service: How to decentralise the NHS*, London: IoD/NEF.

IPPR 1 (Institute of Public Policy Research) Commission on Public Private Partnerships (2001) *Building better partnerships: The final report of the Commission on Public Private Partnerships*, London: IPPR.

IPPR 2 Maltby, P. (2003) *In the public interest? Assessing the potential for public interest companies*, London: IPPR.

KFI 1 (King's Fund Institute) (2002) *The future of the NHS: A framework for debate*, London: KFI.

KFI 2 Dewar, S. (2003) *Shaping the new NHS: Government and the NHS – time for a new relationship?*, London: KFI.

KFI 3 Dixon, J., Le Grand, J. and Smith, P. (2003) *Shaping the new NHS: Can market forces be used for good?* London: KFI.

KFI 4 Lewis, R., Dixon, J. and Gillam, S. (2003) *Shaping the new NHS: Future directions for Primary Care Trusts*, London: KFI.

KFI 5 Appleby, J., Harrison, A. and Devlin, N. (2003) *Shaping the new NHS: What is the real cost of more patient Choice?*, London: KFI.

NEF 1 (New Economics Foundation) Mayo, E. and Moore, H. (2001) *The mutual state: How local communities can run public services*, London: NEF.

NEF 2 Burns, S., Boyle, D. and Krogh, K. (2002) *Putting the life back into our health services: Public involvement and health*, London: NEF.

Warpole, K. (1998) 'Think-tanks, consultancies and urban policy in the UK', in *International Journal of Urban and Regional Research*, vol 22, no 1, pp 147-55.

Unison (2003) *Seven reasons why Unison is opposed to Foundation Trusts*, London: Unison.

White, M. (2004) 'Blind passion', *Guardian Review*, 11 December, p 11.

NINE

Consumerism and the reform of public services: inequalities and instabilities

John Clarke, Nick Smith and Elizabeth Vidler[1]

In reality, I believe people do want choice, in public services as in other services. But anyway, choice isn't an end in itself. It is one important mechanism to ensure that citizens can indeed secure good schools and health services in their communities. Choice puts the levers in the hands of parents and patients so that they as citizens and consumers can be a driving force for improvement in their public services. We are proposing to put an entirely different dynamic in place to drive our public services; one where the service will be driven not by the government or by the manager but by the user – the patient, the parent, the pupil and the law-abiding citizen. (Tony Blair, quoted in *The Guardian*, 24 June 2004, p 1)

Introduction

This extract from a speech made by Tony Blair in the summer of 2004 captures something of the centrality of the idea of citizens as consumers to New Labour's approach to public service reform. This conception of citizens as consumers registers how significant the 'choice' issue has become for current debates about the future of healthcare – and public services more generally. Its importance in current policy debates is further illustrated when we consider that, despite it being New Labour's 'meta-value' (Bunting, 2003), the Conservative Party has also claimed choice as their 'big idea'. Unsurprisingly, this focus upon choice/consumerism in policy debate raises a whole range of issues[2]. These include different proposals for means of institutionalising choice; different views about the problems of choice; arguments about whether choice can, or should, be the main coordinating mechanism for health and other services; implications about the relationships between resources and service provision; different views of the relationships between the public, patients, professionals and political representatives; and differing conceptions of the relationship between choice and inequality (see, for example, Needham, 2003; Leadbeater, 2004; NCC, 2004). In this chapter, we want to take up two clusters of issues arising from this consumerist focus:

1. the relationship between consumerism and inequalities; and
2. the unstable consequences of consumerism in the reform of public services.

We end with some reflections on the implications of these two issues for the politics and policies of choice in public services.

Choice: reproducing or redressing inequalities?

The collective provision of services 'in the public interest' has historically been justified as a response to the limitations or inadequacies of markets. During the 19th and 20th centuries, the turbulence and unpredictability dimensions of market exchange were seen as creating a need for forms of collective security – a role increasingly taken on by the state in western capitalist societies. But markets were also seen as a setting in which forms of social or economic inequality were reproduced or even intensified. The 'cash nexus' required cash for participation (thus effectively excluding the poorest), and its commodities were stratified – with greater expenditure being rewarded with greater perceived value. De-commodification (in Esping-Andersen's terms, 1990) was therefore a central effect of the collective provision of welfare and public services. Collective provision, as opposed to individual purchase, has the potential to reduce, break or even redress the relationship between individual (or household) income and levels of welfare/well-being.

This overarching distinction between state and market (or between public and private; or between collective and individual) overshadows contemporary political debates about reforming public services[3]. For critics of New Labour's 'consumerist turn', it marks the shift from social democratic politics to neo-liberalism – where the market is elevated over the public realm (Needham, 2003; Marquand, 2004). Marquand, for example, while arguing that New Labour is not simply a continuation of Thatcherite conservatism, nevertheless points to the centrality of marketisation and privatisation as central strands in their remaking of public and private realms:

New Labour has pushed marketisation and privatisation forward, at least as zealously as the Conservatives did, narrowing the frontiers of the public domain in the process.... Ministerial rhetoric is saturated with the language of consumerism. The public services are to be 'customer focussed'; schools and colleges are to ensure that 'what is on offer responds to the needs of consumers; the 'progressive project' is to be subjected to 'rebranding'. (Marquand, 2004, p 118)

More significantly, the transformation of citizens into consumers diminishes the collective ethos and practices of the public domain (embodied in the figure of the citizen), and both privatises and individualises them (in the figure of the consumer). For Needham (2003), this corrodes the public domain as the site of both collective solidarity and political choice and mobilisation. The shift from citizen to consumer individualises relationships to collective services and depoliticises 'choice' by subjecting the public domain to the logics of markets and management that constitute 'choice' in the private/market domain:

Consumers are therefore distinctive in the way that they make choices (as self-regarding individuals), receive goods and services (through a series of instrumental, temporary and bilateral relationships with suppliers), and exercise power (passively, through aggregate signalling). To claim that the citizen is being treated as a consumer is to argue that citizens are being encouraged to behave on the basis of the same principles. It takes the private sector consumer as the model for citizenship, and the private firm as the model for the government–citizen relationship. (Needham, 2003, p 14)

The consumer thus embodies the private (rather than the public); the market (rather than the state); and the individual (rather than the collective). The power that these distinctions command in political discourse is reflected in the ways in which the political elaboration of choice (in both Labour and Conservative discourse) explicitly engages with the question of *inequality*. This elaboration of choice summons up inequality in a number of different ways. For example, it is argued that the state – in its public services – has created inequality (Le Grand, 1982). Alternatively, it is claimed that choice can be a means of producing equality:

To those on the left who defend the status quo on public services defend a model that is one of entrenched inequality, I repeat: the system we inherited was inequitable. It was a two-tier system. Our supposedly uniform public services were deeply unequal as league and performance tables in the NHS and schools have graphically exposed.... The affluent and well educated ... had the choice to buy their way out of failing or inadequate provision – a situation the Tories' 'opting out' reforms of the 1980s encouraged. It was a choice for the few, not for the many. (Blair, 2003)

The idea of 'two tier' systems in public services has, of course, been a critique from the Labour left of New Labour's marketising/privatising reforms. Here the choice discourse is elaborated through an historical inversion: New Labour inherited a 'two tier' system, and generalising choice – creating choice for the many – will overcome these inequalities. It is worth noting the echoes of 'two tierism' in Michael Howard's comments on choice and the NHS:

> Our policy will eradicate the inequalities that exist in our two tier health service where the rich get what they pay for and the poor have to shut up and take what they are given.... We utterly reject the idea that political dogma or ideology should stand in the way of what works. If the private sector can help drive up standards, let's use it.... We are confident that our policies to give patients choice, free up hospitals from bureaucracy and give incentives to increase capacity and activity will bring on stream the extra capacity to treat those on the waiting lists. (Michael Howard, quoted in *The Guardian*, 24 June 2004, pp 1-2)

Extending choice to the many has emerged as an anchoring point for both political parties – although the means of institutionalising choice clearly differ (as do their conceptions of the boundaries of 'systems' and the relationship between sectors). New Labour proponents of choice have taken this view further, arguing that extending choice to active consumers of public services will actively enhance equality (and public services will be preserved):

> Now there is concern that by moving away from the monolithic, one size fits all approach, inequity is created in the system. That it is unfair not to treat all in the same way. By providing choice you introduce an element of competition, of difference, which is corrosive of public services. I reject these criticisms. To deny choice would lead to the break up of public service provision as we know it today. It would create real two tierism, as those who could afford it would flee to the private sector in order to be able to exercise choice. If this were to happen it would put at

risk universal provision funded through general taxation. We cannot allow this to happen. Offering choice is one way in which we can bind into the public sector those that can afford to go private. (Byers, 2003)

'Choice' is glossed in two different political ways here. First, the extension of choices previously only available to the affluent (those able to buy themselves out of the public system) to all is an extension of equality. But, second, choice is a necessity to bind the affluent into the public system – and prevent the emergence (or extension, the tenses make it unclear) of 'two tierism' as a split between private and public provision. There is a further, recurrent, version of inequality that is deployed in New Labour's conception of consumer choice and public services – the spatial inequalities of access and provision identified in the phrase 'postcode lottery':

> Local autonomy without national standards may lead to increased inequality between people and regions and the return of the post code lotteries. And the view we take on the appropriate balance between efficiency, diversity and equity will be shaped by the values we hold. The modern challenge is to move beyond old assumptions under which equity was seen to go hand in hand with uniformity; or diversity appeared to lead inevitably to inequality. Instead we should seek the maximum amount of diversity consistent with equity. (Brown, 2003)

Like other New Labour 'keywords' (including 'one size fits all', mentioned earlier), the image of a postcode lottery involves a complex representation of social processes. Here, patterns of geographically distributed inequality are reworked into a popular spatial representation (the postcode) and rendered as matters of chance – the idea of inequalities resulting from a 'lottery'. Despite the attempt to articulate consumer choice and inequality in a positive direction, a number of questions remain unresolved about New Labour's adoption of consumerism. New Labour policy statements involve a claim that a consumerist strategy can address forms of inequality in the context of public services. To some extent, it is argued that economic inequalities can be overcome by making choice available to all, rather than being based on the capacity to pay. At the same time, unequal treatment or access may be overcome by valuing diversity (and giving consumers the opportunity to articulate their demands/needs/wants). There remain, however, some continuing problems about public services and inequalities. In brief, we might suggest that the relationship between public services and inequality has three aspects:

1. whether public services reproduce or remedy forms of social inequality;
2. whether access to forms of service depends on economic capacity; and
3. whether access to, and treatment within, forms of public provision is shaped by other social inequalities.

At the same time, new organisational modes for providing public services pose a double question about their relationship to inequality. Do they reproduce or redress existing inequalities? Do they create new forms of inequality?

Economic inequalities have persisted (and in some accounts deepened) in the New Labour period, and their reduction has not been a political priority (see Goodman and Oldfield, 2004; Jackson and Segal, 2004). The capacity to use financial power remains a distinctive form of social inequality – and one that has a particular potential application to public services, given that they are not 'closed systems'. The boundaries between public and private (commercial/commodified) provision have become more permeable, increasing the possibilities for privately purchasing privately provided versions of services (for example, private health treatments, private residential or domiciliary care, or private security). In the conception of 'two tierism', there are different images of how public service systems may produce or reproduce inequality. 'Two tierism' may result from the capacity of some to buy themselves out of public services. Alternatively, financial capacity may create the possibility of gaining advantage within the system of publicly provided services (for example, it makes possible geographical mobility to access 'better' services – most notably in terms of school catchment areas).

But consumerism raises the question of other forms of inequality that might be made more significant in service provision. In particular, the exercise of choice as an active consumer implies non-economic forms of 'capital' (in Bourdieu's sense, cf Greener, 2002). It is possible that the effective or successful exercise of choice involves skills or capacities that are unevenly distributed (information gathering, assessment, calculation and articulation). In Bourdieu's terms, these may be forms of 'cultural capital' that will privilege their possessors in encounters with service providers. At the same time, some consumers may be privileged in their encounters because they are marked by forms of 'symbolic capital' (manner, style, mode of speech, articulacy and so on) that providers find acceptable or desirable.

At the same time, the policy landscape has been significantly remade by movements that have articulated 'user perspectives' as sources of expert knowledge and authority, thus disrupting the dominance of professional knowledge and power. Much policy and professional discourse emphasises the multiple ways in which 'users' are finding their 'voice'. Such movements have disrupted the taken-for-granted alignments of cultural and symbolic capital and authority – bringing more 'voices' into play around services. However, voices remain both unequally distributed and unequally listened to: not all voices may carry the same weight. Indeed, there are forms of professional or provider nervousness about differential capacities to articulate wants and needs. Such concerns focus on variations in articulacy, organisation and what might be called 'volume' (the capacity to shout loudest). Service organisations struggle to manage their relationships with multiple users and their representatives (claims about representation and representativeness are a constant focus of boundary management practices by organisations). There are persistent instabilities about 'voice' – about forms of consultation, participation and involvement in the provision of services (see, for example, Barnes et al, 2003; SCIE, 2004).

The consumerist model has an odd relationship to older controversies about public services – especially those concerned with the unequal relationship between demand and resources that underpins forms of service rationing (Langan, 1998). Where 'choice' fits into the persistent discrepancy between demand and supply in public services is not clear. Throughout public sector organisations there is an awareness that the range of potential needs/wants continues to outstrip what the service can deliver. In the process, rationing persists in some form or another – usually through the medium of 'professional judgement' or other forms of collective priority-setting (preceding the evaluation of individual needs/wants). In the absence of conventional market information (price signals) and the associated forms of 'consumer power' (capacity to pay, and ability to exit), the consumer of public services exists in a more ambiguous relationship to 'producers' (see Smith and Clarke, 2004). Articulating choices or wants as an individual consumer is not the same as enforcing them, unless they are statutory entitlements. Being able to voice one's needs or wants to service providers carries no guarantee that they will be met. They are subject to organisational and occupational filtering (administrative criteria or professional evaluation). Where such needs are formalised as enforceable rights or entitlements, they may be perceived organisationally as pre-empting the space for either professional judgement or collective deliberation.

Choice and unstable systems

Our second cluster of issues concerns instabilities rather than inequalities. It is clear that 'choice' is the means through which attempts to resolve a range of political and policy problems are being expressed. Choice – and the associated construction of the figure of the citizen-consumer as an active choice-maker – provides a way of reconstructing the troubled relationship between the public, the government and public services (Clarke, 2004a, 2004b). Whether this model of organising services can indeed reconcile and resolve the multiple problems and pressures that beset public services is, of course, much debated. In this section, we explore whether the 'consumer' can provide a stabilising locus around which to organise service provision and service relationships.

The political commitment to choice may create some new instabilities in public services. There are substantial arguments that 'choice' is not the primary value in relation to public services – but is seen as 'second best' to the provision of high-quality, accessible and responsive services (for example, NCC, 2003; Schwartz, 2004a, 2004b). At the same time, the capacities to make and enforce choices may not be universally distributed (see, for example, the concept of health literacy [Sihota and Lennard, 2004]). In such circumstances, encounters between service providers and service users may become more unpredictable. In the ideal scenario, a consumer-responsive organisation encounters a model consumer (self-directing, knowledgeable and assertive). Here the 'expert patient' meets the 'enabling' health service, which provides the support, services and commodities identified by the expert patient as the means for managing their own condition. This model encounter rests on a conception of the redistribution of knowledge/expertise and authority away from the professional ownership of knowledge and power. However, it is also possible that the ideal consumer – ready and able to exercise choice – meets a non-responsive organisation (constrained, for example, by resource limitations, or by an assumption that it knows best). Alternatively, the ready-to-be-responsive organisation hopes to meet a self-directing consumer, but in practice encounters someone else – possibly the traumatised, ready-to-be-dependent and trusting patient. These are likely to be uncomfortable encounters – leaving both parties feeling disoriented, puzzled or aggrieved.

It is also possible that the experience of cash-nexus consumption is less than adequate preparation for the conditions of choice in public services – that is, behaving 'like a consumer' may not match service provider expectations of how a consumer should behave. The skills and styles acquired in the marketplace (and embedded in the capacity to pay for what you want) may not be the best repertoire for asserting rights, needs or wants in encounters with public services. Indeed, many surveys of public expectations of public services recognise that such services 'are different' in complicated ways. There are uneasy and uncertain oscillations around how people would like to be treated, their understanding of the 'public-ness' of public services and the means through which they can make themselves 'assertive' about their needs, wants and interests.

This suggests that we might want to think about the other expectations and identities that might be in play alongside those of the consumer. This is not the place to explore this point in detail, but the possibilities might include:

- the deferential supplicant;
- the assertive rights claimant;
- the willing-to-be-patient member of the public;
- the anxious or distressed vulnerable person;
- the reluctant recipient; or
- the outraged citizen-curmudgeon.

There is no reason why people should remain tied to one identity. On the contrary, moving between different sorts of identifications and their implied relationships may well be a feature of the public's relationship with public services. In our study, people talk of their relationship to the NHS being a multiple one (being in receipt of treatment, being an 'expert on their own condition', being a taxpayer and so on). In practice, public services encounter a wide range of identities and expectations, and expend a lot of emotional labour on managing these complex encounters with members of the public. And, despite the temptation to talk of public services in general, service-specific identities – such as patient, client, victim, villain – linger on (and there may be good reasons why they linger):

> There is nothing like a short spell in hospital to concentrate the mind and put to one side all the market-led, consumerist nonsense implicit in endless reform. I was – and, to some extent, still am – a patient. I wanted treatment at the nearest hospital. It responded promptly. The staff were dedicated, caring and compassionate to those much less fortunate than me, uncomplaining and very supportive. I do not take them for granted. Attending an acute hospital, with all the sophisticated equipment that it offers, is a great leveller. You are injured. You need help fast. And only

the NHS can provide. Everyone, regardless of income and background,
is rightly equal. No one can jump the queue. (Hetherington, 2004, p 7)

This persistence of other identities points to some analytical and political
problems about consumerism. In the quotation from Tony Blair that
opened this chapter, we can hear some of those persistent identities: *the
patient, the parent, the pupil and the law-abiding citizen*. This is an interestingly
formulated list – the patient is apparently straightforward (unless we think
that there are consumers of health services who are not patients – in the
post-SARS [Severe Acute Respiratory Syndrome] world of public health,
perhaps?). But then we encounter both parents (the consumers who make
school choices) *and* pupils (who do not make school choices). And, last
but not least, who is the 'law-abiding citizen' and what do they consume
– police services, community safety, public order, the absence of a fear of
crime? On what basis is the non-law-abiding citizen excluded from being
a consumer of public services – even the ones that involve their arrest,
detention, judgement or imprisonment?

The enforced or involuntary consumption of public services is a
reminder that this is not simply a benevolent field of choice. There is a
danger of talking of public services as though their receipt is an unalloyed
blessing, actively sought by its recipients. However, children are statutorily
required to attend school (or its equivalent) and many of them go to
considerable lengths to avoid receiving the service. 'Problem' families are
required to receive the attentions of social services departments. People
deemed dangerous to themselves or others are coerced under criminal
law or the 1983 Mental Health Act. More generally, people tend to arrive
at public services wanting an unhappy situation remedied: the experience
of illness, impairment, temporary dependency, having been a victim of
crime and so on. As Ian Greener observed in the context of the NHS,
what we see here is an unstable field of relationships and practices organised
around the problem of 'who, choosing what?' (Greener, 2003).

In this unsettled field of relationships between the public and public
services, the consumer orientation cannot contain the range of possible
challenges that may be made (Clarke, 2004b). To some extent,
consumerism in public services is already blurred by government
preoccupations with consultation and participation. These may be better
understood as processes of voice rather than choice. This wider
participation agenda links service/policy issues (about modernisation,
standards, improvement and so on) with political/governmental issues
(about activating citizens, communities and detached/disaffected or
excluded social groups in relation to concerns about political legitimacy).

In other directions, consumerism blurs into legal forms of claim-making: the individual and/or collective establishment of rights or entitlements that are enforceable through judicial processes.

While the provision of public services is not market-like in key ways, the promise of choice-making for members of the public using services will remain problematic. The consumer model of choice that dominates the contemporary debate assumes that wants are enforceable through the exchange of cash (or its equivalents) for commodities. The simple market image of the articulation of supply and demand requires the medium of money as a way of both signalling and enforcing wants. The political processes of decommodifying public services aimed to address (some of) the inequalities associated with market-mediated consumption. In the absence of other clear – and clearly effective – mechanisms for enforcing consumer choices, public services are made more unstable and contradictory by the promise of choice. It is unclear who gets to choose what – and how their choices are made effective. In the case of secondary education, for example, it appears that 'producers' exercise significant choice: expressed in the capacity of some schools to select their pupils (and their parents). Elsewhere, rationing and organisational priority-setting processes may narrow and delimit the field of user 'choice' (in social care, for example).

At the same time, service providers expend increasing effort on 'educative' work to ensure that consumer choices are informed, reasonable and responsible. Such efforts often involve trying to teach the public to think like the professionals – recognising the professional judgement of constraints, conditions and likely consequences. An 'informed public' is a public that is informed by the sharing of professional or organisational knowledge and, as a result, is able to make 'informed choices'. Of course, the circulation of other knowledge through social movements, networks and the Internet creates the conditions for both information and expertise to be contested. Choice – in such public service contexts – becomes rather blurred. It is blurred not because of 'producer hostility' towards the public but because the idea of choice lacks both clear specification and clear mechanisms that would enable its exercise and enforce the choices made. Service providers – and other critics – doubt whether this market-mimicking image of choice is either practical or appropriate to public provision that requires collective judgement about the relationship between resources and priorities. Such doubts persist even where there is support for the principle of making services more personal, more responsive and less demeaning, dehumanising and discriminatory. This unease about whether 'choice' is the best route to public service reform reflects the wider contradictions of consumerism.

The unstable politics of consumerism

It is possible to see consumerist approaches to public service reform as a progressive challenge to producer domination and bureau-professional paternalism; or as a regressive individualisation narrowing collective democratic engagement (and a front for marketisation/privatisation). These different views of consumerism are public service reflections of a wider debate about the value/significance of the consumer as a social/cultural identity. For example, Gabriel and Lang have argued that:

> The consumer has become a god-like figure, before whom markets and politicians alike bow. Everywhere it seems, the consumer is triumphant. Consumers are said to dictate production; to fuel innovation; to be creating new service sectors in advanced economies; to be driving modern politics; to have it in their power to save the environment and protect the future of the planet. Consumers embody a simple modern logic, the right to choose. Choice, the consumer's friend, the inefficient producer's foe, can be applied to things as diverse as soap-powder, holidays, healthcare or politicians. And yet the consumer is also seen as a weak and malleable creature, easily manipulated, dependent, passive and foolish. Immersed in illusions, addicted to joyless pursuits of ever-increasing living standards, the consumer, far from being god, is a pawn, in games played in invisible boardrooms. (1995, p 1)

In the context of public services, however, these different views imply *political* logics of consumerism. That is, both see the rise of consumerism as something more than a simple reflection of a wider 'consumer culture' in the changing world of public services. By contrast, both treat consumerism as the focus or expression of a political tendency. The first sees it as an expression of both social changes and popular challenges to the limitations of public provision:

> The society in which our public services now operate is vastly different to the post-war society for which much of the welfare state was designed. Traditional structures, such as the way families are organised, have changed. Contemporary society has broken away from previous centres of authority and is defined by much greater social pluralism and diversity of race and culture. Old myths that once united society no longer hold true. The

paternalistic delivery of public services, characterised by the 'doctor knows best' relationship between professionals and users, is increasingly challenged in an era of growing individualism. Vastly improved information flows fuel the emergence of informed and assertive users of public services.

In a world of increased pluralism, individualism and diversity of needs, it is increasingly difficult to know what users of services want. What is required above all is the active involvement of individuals in the determination of their own needs.... [B]oth choice and voice should be extended in order to rebalance services away from provider interests and towards the interests of users. When users are empowered, services become more responsive to rising expectations and demands. (NCC, 2004, p 7)

The alternative view sees it as a top-down, statist imposition on the public realm that de-politicises and de-collectivises it:

Consumerism is a model that prioritises the individual over the community, encourages passivity, downgrades public spaces, weakens accountability, and privatises citizenship. In T.H. Marshall's words: 'There is little that consumers can do except imitate Oliver Twist and 'ask for more'.... This is not only restrictive of citizens' domain of action. It may also be a problem for government. If the nature of consumer demand is that it is limitless, the result may be a citizenry that expects public services to match their private sector equivalents without recognising the constraints that limit public provision....

Rather than delivering a satisfied and pliable citizenry, consumerism may be fostering privatised and resentful citizen-consumers whose expectations of government can never be met. (Needham, 2003, p 33)

For us, thinking about the emergence of this hybridised citizen-consumer means exploring the ways in which these different forces intersect in the contemporary politics of public service reform (Clarke, 2004b; Clarke and Newman, 2005: forthcoming). On the one hand, the consumerist turn in public services is unimaginable without the range of popular challenges to public services (their concentrations of power, mono-culturalism, discriminatory policies *and* practices, and so on). Since the 1960s, social and user movements have been raising voices against the limitations, oppressions, discriminations and subordinations that were built into the processes and relationships of welfare/public services. It is, we think, impossible to see consumerism without hearing those critiques of, and challenges to, social democratic 'welfare statism' (Clarke, 2004b). The insistence on users as 'knowledgeable' owes much to the ways in which women's and disabled people's movements insisted on the power and value of self-knowledge in the face of the oppressive forms of knowledge embodied in professional or state power. Similarly, the question of 'diversity' of needs and wants emerges from the struggles against the normative presumptions of citizenship and its embodiment in the figure of the white, non-disabled, male, adult 'independent' citizen.

On the other hand, the consumerist turn is also unimaginable without neo-liberalism (and its distinctive insertion into the UK political cultural formation [see Clarke, 2004a]). So, consumerism relies on the neo-liberal (public choice) distinction between producer interest and consumer interest (and the implication that they are necessarily antithetical). It implies a particular sort of subject (a knowledgeable, choice-making *and rational* economic individual). Finally, consumerism collapses difference into diversity (Lewis, 2003) where diversity means an individualised field of equivalent but different needs/wants, rather than people being positioned in arrangements of structured, and unequal, differences. The rise of the citizen-consumer as the focus of public service reform is an attempt to appropriate multiple challenges to public services and to contain them within a neo-liberal framing of individuated choice. However, the contradictory and contested politics of public services are unlikely to be contained within this framing – and questions of inequalities, power and resources will continue to de-stabilise the politics, policies and practices of public provision.

Notes

[1] All three authors are part of a research project *Creating citizen consumers: Changing identifications and relationships*, based at the Open University, that is funded by the ESRC/AHRB Cultures of Consumption Programme (grant number: RES-143-25-008). It also involves Janet Newman and Louise Westmarland, to whom we are grateful for their contributions to the development of this chapter. The project has looked at three public services – health, policing and social care – in two different urban settings in England, in order to explore the shifting relationships between the public and public services.

[2] See, for example, the wide-ranging comments in the media following both Labour's and the Conservatives' evocation of choice (*The Daily Mail*, 'Comment', 24 June 2004, p 12; *The Daily Mirror*, 'Voice of *The Daily Mirror*', 24 June 2004, p 6; Jenni

Russell, 'I'm a patient, not a consumer', *The Guardian*, 26 June 2004, p 21; Barry Schwartz, 'Comment', *The Guardian, Society*, 23 June 2004, p 7; Dr Richard Taylor, MP, 'Competition is bad for our health', *The Guardian*, 29 June 2004, p 19).

[3] It is, of course, a problematic distinction, always tending to crowd out the complexities of private, household, domestic and personal relationships and practices (and the gendered division of labour through which they are organised). But the weight of this multiple distinction means that the citizen-consumer distinction often gets posed without reference to the (shifting) gendering of public and private spheres and practices (Wakefield, 2003). 'Welfare' is profoundly associated with women as producers and users (in all 'sectors'). In what ways, then, might a gender perspective illuminate the identity and behaviour of 'consumers' of public services? One critical element might be that women as consumers of public services typically mediate the service to others (in their roles as carers), as well as using services directly. Similarly, their involvement in producing welfare – as waged workers, as volunteers and as carers – suggests that the simple model of producers and users may need to be enriched.

References

Barnes, M., Newman, J., Knops, A. and Sullivan, H. (2003) 'Constituting the "public" in public participation', *Public Administration*, vol 81, no 2, pp 379-99.

Blair, T. (2003) 'Progress and justice in the 21st century', Fabian Society Annual Lecture, Fabian Society, 17 June.

Brown, G. (2003) *A modern agenda for prosperity and social reform*, London: Social Market Foundation, 3 February.

Bunting, M. (2003) 'Citizens or consumers?', *The Guardian*, 24 November.

Byers, S. (2003) 'The former Transport and Local Government Secretary's speech to the Social Market Foundation', *Guardian Unlimited*, 28 May.

Clarke, J. (2004a) 'Dissolving the public realm? The logics and limits of neo-liberalism', *Journal of Social Policy*, vol 33, no 1, pp 27-48.

Clarke, J. (2004b) 'A consuming public?', ESRC/AHRB Cultures of Consumption Lecture, The Royal Society, London, 22 April.

Clarke, J. and Newman, J. (2005: forthcoming) 'Constructing citizen-consumers: New Labour and public service reform', in J. Newman (ed) *Rethinking governance*, Bristol: The Policy Press.

Esping-Andersen, G. (1990) *Three worlds of welfare capitalism*, Cambridge: Polity Press.

Gabriel, Y. and Lang, T. (1995) *The unmanageable consumer*, London: Sage Publications.

Goodman, A. and Oldfield, Z. (2004) *Permanent differences? Income and expenditure inequality in the 1990s and 2000s*, London: Institute for Fiscal Studies.

Greener, I. (2002) 'Agency, theory and social policy', *Critical Social Policy*, vol 22, no 4, pp 688-705.

Greener, I. (2003) 'Who choosing what? The evolution of the use of "choice" in the NHS, and its importance for New Labour', in C. Bochel, N. Ellison and M. Powell (eds) *Social Policy Review 15*, Bristol: The Policy Press/Social Policy Association, pp 49-68.

Hetherington, P. (2004) 'Opinion', *The Guardian, Society*, 11 February, p 7.

Jackson, B. and Segal, P. (2004) *Why inequality matters*, London: The Catalyst Forum.

Langan, M. (ed) (1998) *Welfare: Needs, rights and risks*, London: Routledge/The Open University.

Leadbeater, C. (2004) *Personalising participation: A new script for public services*, London: Demos.

Le Grand, J. (1982) *The strategy of equality: Redistribution and the social services*, London: Allen and Unwin.

Lewis, G. (2003) '"Difference" and social policy', in N. Ellison and C. Pierson (eds) *Developments in British social policy 2,* Basingstoke: Palgrave Macmillan, pp 90-106.

Marquand, D. (2004) *The decline of the public*, Cambridge: Polity Press.

NCC (National Consumer Council) (2003) *Expectations of public services: Consumer concerns*, London: NCC.

NCC (2004) *Making public services personal: A new compact for public services* (The Report of the Policy Commission on Public Services), London: NCC.

Needham, C. (2003) *Citizen-consumers: New Labour's marketplace democracy*, London: The Catalyst Forum.

Schwartz, B. (2004a) 'Comment', *The Guardian, Society*, 23 June, p 7.

Schwartz, B. (2004b) *The paradox of choice: Why more is less*, New York, NY: Harper Collins.

SCIE (Social Care Institute for Excellence) (2004) *Has service user participation made a difference to social care services?*, Position Paper no 3, London: SCIE.

Sihota, S. and Lennard, L. (2004) *Health literacy: Being able to make the most of health*, London: NCC.

Smith, N. and Clarke, J. (2004) 'Creating citizen-consumers', Seminar for the Public Interest Network, Open University, March.

Wakefield, H. (2003) 'Women, modernisation and trade unions', *Soundings*, no 77, autumn, pp 44-56.

TEN

The challenges of measuring government output in the healthcare sector

Adriana Castelli, Diane Dawson, Hugh Gravelle and Andrew Street

Introduction

The government is a major actor in every economy. It sets policy, helps shape and maintain social structures, collects taxation and redistributes resources. Most governments also have an extensive role in either the provision or financing of a wide range of goods and services. Often political debate over the adequacy and quality of these public services draws on ideology rather than evidence. These debates include defining the boundaries between the public and private sector, and how the public sector might be reformed or re-organised. But such debates are usually restricted by the limited amount of information about what the public sector does and what it achieves.

There are a few areas of public policy where (relatively) independent data exist that can be used to inform debates about the impact of government policies. If policies are implemented to stimulate economic growth or redistribute income, the effect might be captured within a year or two in the National Accounts or in data compiled routinely by the Inland Revenue. But, in most areas of public policy, only limited data are collected on a routine basis. In recent years, there has been considerable international interest in finding ways of routinely collecting and reporting data on the goods and services being produced by the public sector. This is partly due to the importance of public production in overall economic activity, but another important driver has been the realisation that examination of the efficiency and effectiveness of public services requires data on what is actually being delivered.

Political concern with the output and efficiency of public services is not new. In the UK, Klein points to the early 1980s as the time when the debate started to shift from measuring inputs (the number of doctors and nurses employed in the health sector; the number of teachers in schools) to outputs (the number of operations performed; the number of children taught) (Klein, 2000). At a time when a political priority was to contain the growth of public expenditure, seeking ways to improve the efficiency with which resources were used became increasingly important. Performance indicators flourished, often a motley collection of whatever administrative data happened to be available (Pollitt, 1985; Hood, 1991; Smith, 1995). Concepts like 'value for money', other private sector principles and ways of thinking were introduced into the public sector (Griffiths, 1992; Pollitt, 1995; Webster, 1998).

While this concern with measuring output and efficiency in the public services has been part of the policy background for a quarter of a century, in recent years it has moved further up the political agenda. In the UK, this is because of the decision by the Prime Minister in 2000 to significantly increase public expenditure on the National Health Service (NHS) and on education. Politicians need to identify some benefit from all the extra expenditure in order to demonstrate that the money is well spent. They soon discovered they lacked the tools to measure whether the new investment was delivering more and better services. They lacked adequate information to measure 'value for money'. One consequence was that, in December 2002, the National Statistician commissioned Sir Tony Atkinson to conduct an independent review of the measurement of government output in the National Accounts (Atkinson, 2005). The terms of reference were: "To advance methodologies for the measurement of government output, productivity and associated price indices in the context of the National Accounts" (Atkinson, 2005, p 1). Particular requirements included consideration of:

- the differences in the nature and quality of outputs over time;
- the relationship between government outputs and social outcomes;
- the need for comparability with measures of private sector services' output and costs.

In this chapter, we explore some of the problems that must be overcome if the objectives of the Atkinson Review are to be reflected in future national statistics.

Interest in finding ways to measure output and value for money is not just a parochial UK phenomenon. In every country, statistics on the output of the economy are compiled into national accounts. Estimates of Gross

Domestic Product (GDP) are used by governments, business, academics and international organisations. A significant part of GDP is accounted for by public services, and the inadequacies of how we measure output for the public sector affects the value and reliability of the whole exercise.

Hence, interest in obtaining reliable data on the production of public services ranges from the technical (such as for the compilation of national accounts) to the highly political (to answer questions such as 'What has the Labour Party achieved by pouring money into public services?'). The challenge is that reliable data are not easy to come by.

First, we briefly discuss the main problems of measuring the output of public services and current official practice in compiling national statistics. Then, we examine the issues in depth using the example of one public service, the healthcare sector. Finally, we provide tentative conclusions on what is emerging as a major change in the way we monitor and measure the output of public services.

Government expenditure

Government expenditure on goods and services can be subdivided into collective services and individual goods and services. The former comprise services provided to society as a whole, whereas the latter include goods and services that are consumed, in the main, on an individual basis. Government expenditure on collective services is justified by their status as public goods, which people can neither be excluded from nor abstain from consuming. National defence is the classic example. For the countries shown in Table 10.1, government spending on collective services averages 32% of total government spending and 15% of GDP. The UK spends less than the average of these countries, spending proportionately less on general public services but more on defence.

A larger proportion of government spending is on individual goods and services such as healthcare, education, social protection, recreation services and cultural services, which together account for an average of 31% of GDP for these countries. A common justification for government provision of such services is that, left to the market, there would be general underprovision or socially unacceptable inequalities of access.

Of these individual services, government expenditure on social protection is the largest category, incorporating such things as sickness, disability, housing and unemployment benefits. The UK government spends proportionately more on health and education than the other European countries, where there may be a higher proportion of private expenditure on these services.

Table 10.1: Government expenditure in selected EU countries (2002)

Government expenditure	UK		Germany		Countries Spain		France		Italy	
	% of Govt exp	% of GDP	% of Govt exp	% of GDP	% of Govt exp	% of GDP	% of Govt exp	% of GDP	% of Govt exp	% of GDP
Collective services										
General public services	10.5	4.2	12.9	6.2	13.4	5.3	13.5	7.2	19.2	9.1
Defence	6.3	2.5	2.5	1.2	3.1	1.2	4.6	2.5	2.5	1.2
Public order and safety	5.2	2.1	3.3	1.6	5.3	2.1	1.9	1.0	4.1	1.9
Economic affairs	5.9	2.4	8.2	4.0	11.2	4.5	8.9	4.8	8.1	3.9
Environmental protection	1.4	0.6	1.2	0.6	2.4	1.0	2.2	1.2	1.8	0.8
Individual services										
Health	16.1	6.4	13.2	6.4	13.5	5.4	15.7	8.4	13.7	6.5
Education	12.6	5.0	8.6	4.2	11.1	4.4	11.2	6.0	10.2	4.9
Social protection	39.5	15.7	46.2	22.5	33.9	13.5	38.6	20.6	38.3	18.2
Housing and community amenities	1.3	0.5	2.3	1.1	2.8	1.1	1.9	1.0	0.3	0.1
Recreation, culture and religion	1.3	0.5	1.5	0.7	3.4	1.4	1.5	0.8	1.8	0.9
Total	100	39.7	100	48.6	100	39.9	100	53.5	100	47.6

Source: Eurostat online (2004) (www.epp.eurostat.cec.eu.int)

Four key challenges

Governments have faced four key challenges in developing measures of output and in demonstrating to taxpayers that resources are used to produce outputs that are good value for money.

First, the output of the public sector is often difficult to describe or measure. For instance, an argument for maintaining armed forces is that they deter aggression from other countries, but the extent to which defence spending reduces the threat of war can never be known.

Second, even if it is possible to count these outputs, it is difficult to measure their quality. For instance, it is fairly easy to measure the amount of airtime provided by public broadcasting corporations (such as the BBC), but much more difficult to assess the quality of television or radio programmes.

Third, it is difficult to measure change over time. Technological changes across many parts of the economy have led to improved standards of living. For example, rapid advances in the production of computer hardware have led to wider choice, greater functionality and lower prices. It is more difficult to assess whether the provision of education (say) is better now than it used to be. In the UK, it has simply been assumed that the quality of education has improved by 0.25% per annum (Atkinson, 2004, 2005). This is an extrapolation from GCSE exam results, but there is no direct evidence to support a constant rate of improvement over time.

Fourth, some means of weighting different goods and services is required in order to aggregate them into a single output index. For goods and services exchanged in the private sector, market prices provide an indication of their relative value to consumers and, in national accounting, prices are used to weight the different outputs for much of the economy. But such prices do not exist for government outputs. Even if we knew how many fires would remain burning and how many more crimes would be solved, what would be the change in total output of redistributing resources from fighting fires to fighting crime?

Official practice

Internationally, the need to compile national accounts has provided a motivation for greater standardisation in describing, measuring and valuing goods and services provided or purchased by government.

From the early 1960s to 1998, the output of the UK public sector, as in all national accounts, was valued simply by adding up expenditure on inputs, an approach termed the 'output=input' convention. The attraction of this approach is that it sidesteps the need both to measure and to place valuations on non-market outputs. But there are two main drawbacks to this convention:

1. It is circular and self-justifying. The value of output is however much the government chooses to spend on producing or purchasing it. By definition, the higher the level of spending, the better. Taxpayers may disagree.
2. Quality improvements that reduce expenditure appear to reduce output. For example, if a new pharmaceutical product means patients can now be treated more cost-effectively without having to be admitted to hospital, the output=input convention would show a fall in the 'output' of the health system because total expenditure has fallen.

The inadequacy of this convention led to recommendations from international bodies such as Eurostat for the development of measures of government output using methods that are independent of expenditure on inputs (Eurostat, 1995). In 1995, Eurostat published recommendations in the *European system of accounts* (ESA95), the aim being to produce a harmonised and reliable system of accounts across the European Union, thus improving cross-country comparisons of GDP growth (Eurostat, 1995). The main change was that government outputs were to be measured directly.

In 1998, the UK Office for National Statistics (ONS) began to update its methodology in constructing the National Accounts in line with ESA95 for health, education, and administration of social security (ONS, 1998). So, for instance, instead of reporting what was spent on education, the ONS started to measure how many pupils were taught. This move to counting activities is a first step toward measuring output but, as explained later, leaves much to be done. Similar changes were incorporated in the 2000 and 2001 *Blue books* for administration of justice, fire and personal social services, these being subsets of some of the expenditure categories listed in Table 10.1 (ONS, 2000, 2001).

In addition to a better understanding of outputs, the accurate compilation of national accounts also requires a procedure for summing divergent changes in the output of different goods and services. If, from one year to the next, agricultural production goes down and production of computers increases, determining whether overall output has changed is reasonably uncontroversial. The convention in national accounting is to weight the products by their respective market prices. The rationale is that these prices reflect the relative value that people place on these goods and services. The problem with applying this approach to the valuation of government output is that, by definition, market prices do not exist. Instead, the use of unit costs is recommended. This implies that relative costs reflect the relative value society places on these outputs – a dubious assumption.

A UK example: healthcare

To illustrate the problems in trying to assess whether health sector 'output' has increased over time, consider just two broad areas of activity undertaken by the health sector: hip replacements (H02) and the non-surgical treatment of fibrosis, menstrual disorders and endometriosis (M14). Annual data relating to these activities are available for England from the Hospital Episode Statistics for the period from 1996/97 to 2002/03. For both H02 and M14, the following three graphs plot the number of treatments provided (Figure 10.1), the median waiting time for admission to hospital for treatment (Figure 10.2), and the in-hospital mortality rate (Figure 10.3). The figures illustrate the challenges in determining overall output change.

What is the relative importance of each treatment? Over the period, more hip replacements (H02) have been undertaken, but there has been a decline in the amount of non-surgical treatment of fibrosis, menstrual disorders and endometriosis (M14) (Figure 10.1). In order to come to a view about the change in overall output, it is necessary to assess the

Figure 10.1: Activity for two NHS treatments (1997-2002)

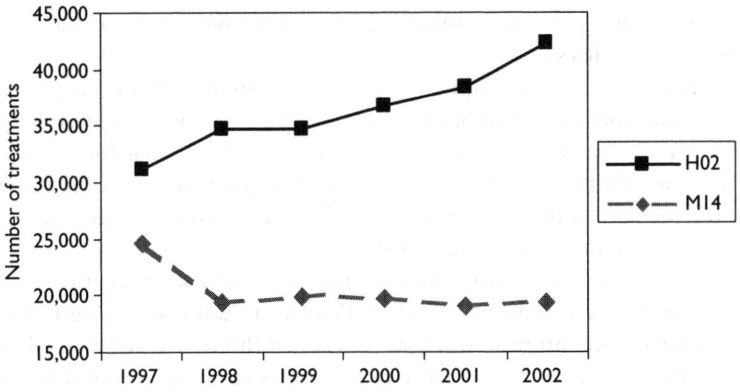

Source: Derived from Hospital Episode Statistics

**Figure 10.2: Median waiting times for two NHS treatments
(1997-2002)**

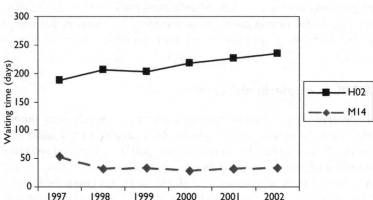

Source: Derived from Hospital Episode Statistics

relative value of each type of activity. Even though the total number of
treatments has increased over time, if M14 is highly valued and H02 is of
limited value, overall output might be judged to have decreased as a result
of the shift in activity.

It is not simply the receipt of treatment that patients value from the
health system. They also value the process of care delivery, and one
aspect of the care process is how long they have to wait for treatment.
Figure 10.2 shows that, over time, median waiting times have increased
for H02 and decreased for M14. Again, to assess whether waiting times
have improved overall, it is necessary to assess whether the inconvenience
or cost of a day spent waiting for a hip replacement differs from that of a
day spent waiting for non-surgical treatment of fibrosis, menstrual disorders
and endometriosis.

Furthermore, if the output of the health system is to be judged in
terms not only of the amount of activity produced but also how long
patients have to wait for treatment, some way of assessing the relative
values of activity and waiting times is required. How much of the value
of the increase in the number of hip replacements has been offset by the
increased waiting time for this treatment?

Healthcare is not valued in its own right but because of its impact on
health status. This impact is both difficult to measure and uncertain –
many healthcare interventions carry a risk that things will go wrong. For
some interventions, the mortality rate provides an indication of the risk
faced. The mortality rates for H02 and M14 are shown in Figure 10.3. A

Figure 10.3: In-hospital mortality rates for two NHS treatments (1997-2002)

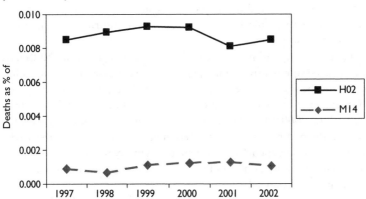

Source: Derived from Hospital Episode Statistics

falling mortality rate over time may be the result of improvements in medical practice or technological advances. As with changes in waiting times, in order to have accurate output measurement, it is necessary to place a value on changes in the risk of dying.

It is not a simple matter, then, to ascertain whether things have got better or worse over time, even when restricting attention to just two treatments. The complexities are compounded when trying to look at the health sector as a whole. We now consider how to address each of the key challenges identified earlier.

Describing healthcare outputs

It is not problematic to define the outputs of many sectors of the economy. For instance, the output of the motor industry can be assessed (albeit in crude terms) by counting the number of cars, trucks and other vehicles produced. But in other sectors, such as health, there is no readily available measure of output. A measure of health service output might be the 'treated patient'. But, because many patients receive care over long periods of time and in different settings (for example, first in general practice, later in hospital and finally in a hospice), and because data systems rarely track patients across settings, counting the number of treated patients is not currently possible.

The alternative is to count the number of activities undertaken, such as the number of visits to general practitioners (GPs), the number of diagnostic tests conducted, the number of operations performed and so on. This is rather like counting the number of tyres, engines and chassis that went into the production process of motor vehicles. Nevertheless, this has been the typical approach taken to measuring health service output (Atkinson, 2005).

Traditional ways of measuring and counting activity in the NHS have not been comprehensive. This partial approach provides a misleading picture of the level or rate of growth of NHS output. Figure 10.4 plots NHS expenditure against an index of NHS output for each year from 1990/91 to 2000/01. The main component of the output index is a count of the number of people treated in hospital. For most of the 1990s, increases in NHS expenditure were matched pretty much proportionately with increases in the output index – as spending increased, more hospital treatment was produced.

In 2000, the Labour government announced substantial and sustained increases in expenditure on the NHS. However, over recent years, the number of patients treated in hospital has risen less rapidly than expenditure, the result being a flattening of the input/output curve. Thus, if output is based primarily on the number of hospital patients, measured productivity (the ratio of output to input) has fallen, and it does not appear to indicate that the increased expenditure has secured good value for money.

Figure 10.4: Index of NHS outputs and inputs (1990/91-2000/01)

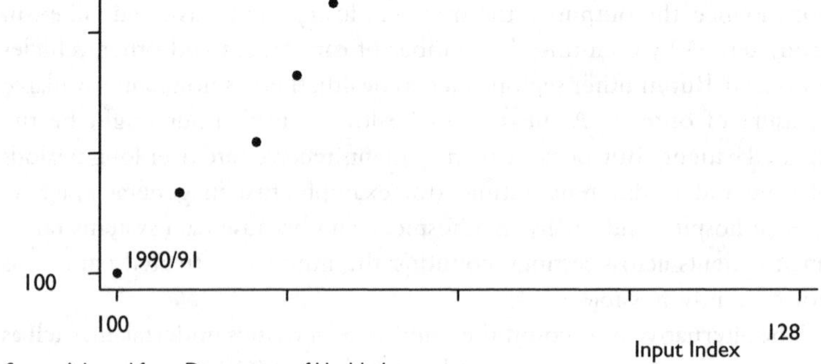

Source: Adapted from Department of Health data

But the evidence presented in Figure 10.4 does not show the full story, partly because many activities are ignored and partly because simply undertaking more activity is not the sole purpose of the NHS. Along with the funding increase, the Labour government has re-focused the objectives of the NHS, setting more demanding waiting-time targets, continuing the shift of care from the hospital to primary and community care sectors, giving patients greater choice, investing more in NHS facilities and so on. Progress against these objectives is not captured by an output index that concentrates almost exclusively on counting the number of hospital treatments but ignores other important outputs and objectives. Consequently Figure 10.4 cannot answer the question of whether or not the increased expenditure represents value for money. This has prompted the development of new measures of NHS productivity.

Measuring quality – the characteristics of output

In measuring the output of all goods and services, a key problem is measuring their 'quality'. Consider an output of the electrical goods industry: television (TV) sets. We know that purchasers consider a black and white TV to be qualitatively different from a colour TV and, judging from market behaviour, they place a relatively greater value on the latter type. One way to deal with this problem is to describe goods and services in terms of their 'characteristics': a TV can be black and white or colour, digital or analogue, flat screen or not and so forth. This bundle of characteristics is not always easy to describe and, moreover, is likely to change over time as a result of technical progress.

As for TV sets, we need to understand the characteristics of health services and how they change over time. Just counting patients treated is like just counting the number of TV sets produced. A key challenge is to identify those characteristics of healthcare that are of importance to patients and taxpayers, and how to measure them. There is unlikely to be universal agreement on what constitute the main characteristics of healthcare output, but important aspects include the following:

- the contribution made to improving health;
- having a choice about when and where care is delivered;
- the delay (waiting time) before receipt of care;
- the environment in which care is delivered.

Of these, perhaps the most important is the first, given that the main aim of any health system is to make a positive contribution to the health of the population. In essence, the measure of health outcome should indicate the improvement or 'value added' to health following contact with the health system. This has proved difficult to make operational in the health sector, mainly because of measurement difficulties. The fundamental difficulty is that the counterfactual – what health status would have been in the absence of intervention – is rarely observed. However, although health status measurement is becoming increasingly routine in many healthcare settings, this tends to involve comparisons of health states before and (sometimes) after intervention. The with/without and before/after measures of the value of contact with the health system are unlikely to be equivalent.

Figure 10.5 illustrates the problem. The figure plots an individual's health status, measured on the y axis using a scale where 1 indicates full health and 0 death, over time along the x axis. In this illustration, the individual suffers a decline in health status until time t_0 when the option of treatment is made available. Without treatment, the health profile would follow the dashed line, $h^o(t)$, with the patient dying at time t_2. If the patient accepts treatment, the time path $h^*(t)$ is followed. Treatment initially reduces health – the patient may be temporarily incapacitated even by successful surgery. After t_1, however, the patient begins a recovery and the treatment improves health status and lengthens life from t_2 to t_3. The net change in health status resulting from treatment can be calculated by subtracting the area where $h^*(t) < h^o(t)$ from the area where $h^*(t) > h^o(t)$. This difference is commonly referred to as the total number of quality-adjusted life years (QALYs) resulting from treatment. A QALY therefore captures the effect of treatment on both how long patients live and their quality of life over time. It is thus a more sophisticated measure

Figure 10.5: With and without treatment health profiles

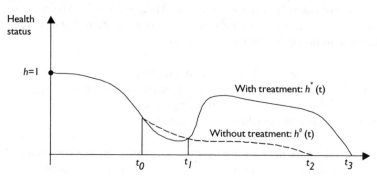

of the treatment effect than simply focusing on the mortality rates depicted in Figure 10.3.

A further complication in measuring QALYs is that to identify $h^*(t)$ it is necessary to measure health status continuously. Typically, however, only snapshot estimates at particular points in time are available. The timing of the snapshots is clearly crucial: the individual's health status appears quite different if measured at t_2 rather than at t_1. So a 'before and after' view can look very different depending on the point in time chosen to measure health status after treatment. The without treatment time path, $h^o(t)$, is typically not monitored, although the 'expert opinion' of clinicians has been used to estimate expected outcome in the absence of treatment.

These difficulties limit the usefulness of value-added measures in the health sector. Most critically, the difference between with/without and before/after measures of added value will depend on the patient's underlying health condition. For conditions where the without treatment time path $h^o(t)$ is likely to be constant, the with/without and before/after measures of added value may be in close agreement. But for other conditions the measures will diverge. Divergence is likely to be most noticeable where people, if left untreated, would be expected to suffer a deterioration in health over time, and where the purpose of the intervention is not to improve health but to stabilise the condition. In such cases, the before/after measure would suggest little or no change in health status, irrespective of the fact that the intervention might have been highly beneficial. Sole reliance on before/after measures will systematically favour interventions that lead to health improvements over those that stabilise or slow the deterioration of conditions. Consequently, such measures should not be used to make judgements about the relative value of different types of healthcare intervention unless some way can be found to measure expected health status in the absence of treatment.

In view of the difficulty of measuring the impact of interventions on health outcome, little progress has been made in incorporating such information into measures of the output of the health system. But, even when measures of other characteristics of output are available, these have not been routinely incorporated into NHS output measures either. For example, waiting times have long been a focus of political attention, and considerable effort has been addressed towards reducing both the number of people waiting for treatment and the length of time spent waiting. But, although the Department of Health has data on NHS waiting times for hospital admission (and, less comprehensively, for other health services), this information is not included systematically in the measure of output.

Yet, people attach value to how long they have to wait for treatment. If a patient does not have to endure the pain and incapacity of (say) an arthritic hip for two years but can have relief within three months, the quality of healthcare has improved. Failure to incorporate progress in reducing waiting lists underestimates the amount of NHS output.

People also value non-health-related characteristics of the health sector such as being offered a choice of provider, the quality of food, the pleasantness of staff, and whether they are treated with dignity and respect. There is unlikely to be consensus as to what constitutes the most important of these characteristics, and even less agreement about how they might be measured. Perhaps the best-known attempt to address this issue was the World Health Organization's (WHO) assessment of national health system performance (WHO, 2000). The WHO evaluation included how well each health system fosters personal respect (preserving dignity, maintaining confidentiality and allowing autonomy to participate in healthcare choices) and whether the system is client oriented (ensuring prompt attention, providing adequate amenities and access to social support networks, and allowing a choice of provider). The WHO study is instructive on the challenges faced in defining and measuring these characteristics. Primary data were missing for many countries, and substantial reliance was placed on expert opinion to impute information and to judge the relative importance of each of the characteristics (Williams, 2001; Nord, 2002). Similar problems are encountered when trying to measure and value such characteristics at national level.

Measuring change over time

Although we suggested earlier that it is fairly straightforward to count the output of the motor industry, simply counting the number of vehicles produced does not fully capture the output of the sector. An annual count of vehicles would imply there was no difference between a model *T* Ford and a Ford *Gti* that has better fuel consumption, a lower risk of breakdown and more safety features. For marketed goods and services, the improvement in quality tends to be measured in two ways. First, after controlling for inflation, if the real value of the good has increased, the assumption is that the increase in value is capturing an increase in quality – people are willing to pay more for the safety of cars with air bags relative to those without. A second approach is to use hedonic price techniques (Cockburn and Amis, 2001). These techniques are used to identify the proportion of the price related to the various characteristics of a good, and to look at how the mix of characteristics changes over time.

Improvements in quality over time have occurred for health services. The health system has moved from treating patients with mental illness by putting them in straitjackets and cold baths to counselling, psychotherapy and medications that can help many people lead normal lives. A patient who suffers a stroke, rather than facing early death or severe disability, is now presented with treatment options that promise survival with good quality of life. If we are interested only in measuring improvements in healthcare interventions over time (rather than trying to value each intervention relative to the others), reliance on before/after measures may not be subject to systematic bias across interventions. To measure improvements from one year to the next, we would need to compare $h^*(t)$ in a baseline year (year 0) with $h^*(t)$ in a later year (year 1). If technological changes have generated improvements in the quality but not length of life of people suffering from a particular condition, this would lead to an upward shift of the $h^*(t)$ time path, as illustrated in Figure 10.6. If both quality and length of life were improved, the year 1 time path would extend beyond t_3.

Quality changes in healthcare are not restricted to technological changes, such as new surgical techniques and new drugs. Other improvements are due to new methods of delivering services (for example, NHS Direct, Walk-in Centres), and new types of staff (for example, Primary Care Mental Health Specialists, GPs with special interests). If, for example, patients with minor problems find Walk-in Centres more convenient than making an appointment at a GP's surgery, the convenience value should be incorporated in a measure of NHS output.

Figure 10.6: Improved health profiles over time

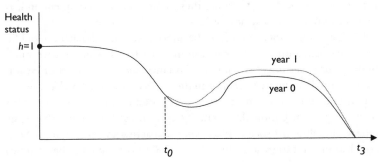

Valuing outputs and output characteristics

In most spheres of government activity, there are no final markets where patients buy outputs from producers. Since there are no prices to reveal patients' marginal valuations of government outputs, we have to find other means of estimating their value. There are three main competing approaches to imputing relative values for public sector outputs: extrapolating private sector prices; using contingent valuation methods; and costs.

The use of private sector prices requires a close match between private and public sector goods and services. Some NHS activities have close matches in the private sector (non-emergency ambulance transport is similar to a taxi service, for example). But the use of prices for private healthcare is problematic for at least two reasons.

1. Private healthcare outputs produce a different, and arguably more valuable, mix of outcomes (better quality 'hotel' services, shorter waiting times) so that the price of private health sector output may overstate willingness to pay for NHS output.
2. The private sector does not produce the full range of NHS outputs, and hence private sector prices are not available for the bulk of NHS output.

A way of measuring the social value attached to different outputs or characteristics of these outputs is to elicit the public's willingness to pay for them. Contingent valuation techniques have long been used to elicit population values for various aspects of environmental protection and are being used to gain some understanding of the relative values people place on different aspects of healthcare (Diener et al, 1998). The problem is that research studies generating these valuations are infrequent and, as such, can say little about how values change over time.

In view of the shortcomings of the alternatives, traditionally the public sector has relied on cost information in order to assess the relative value of different government outputs. For instance, the Department of Health has measured productivity change in the NHS using an index that weights activities by unit cost. This practice is consistent with recommendations of the European Union (Eurostat, 2001). However, it implies that costs reflect the value that society places on these activities at the margin. So, a cochlear implant to treat deafness (at £23,889) is assumed to be 15 times more valuable at the margin than a normal delivery in maternity care (at £1,598). The use of unit costs as weights reflecting the marginal social value of outputs rests on strong implicit assumptions unlikely to be valid for the NHS, including the equivalence of average and marginal costs.

Conclusion

Democratic societies need better measures of government output. Services typically provided by the public sector are essential to the fairness and quality of life of the population. Political debates on changes in the level of taxation degenerate into exchanges of prejudice in the absence of evidence on what is actually being provided. Given the importance of these services, our ignorance of what is being delivered can be a major impediment to informed political debate.

There is also a legitimate concern that public services are produced efficiently. Too often in the past pressure on governments to 'improve' efficiency has resulted in programmes to cut costs irrespective of whether the cuts in expenditure reduce output of much greater value than the cost savings. An example is the series of 'cost efficiency targets' set each year for many UK public services that required departments to cut unit costs by some 1-3% per annum. Better measures of the value and quality of output can be used to marshal evidence in support of cases for spending more where the marginal benefit is high and identifying areas where the marginal benefit is low. Efficiency is important in a resource-constrained world, but we only achieve efficiency if the cost of an activity is related to its benefit. The issue of efficiency will not disappear from the policy agenda of the UK or any other country. Improved measures of public sector output ought to lead to a more informed debate.

Further, individuals and organisations producing public services need better information on output so that they can monitor and improve performance. In healthcare, for example, routine collection of data on health outcomes would make it possible for doctors, hospitals and the NHS to identify situations where things may be substandard, and to take preventative action. We should not have to wait for things to go badly wrong, when only corrective measures can be taken. In much of manufacturing industry, quality control is central to the monitoring of production. These types of process should be introduced more widely in the public sector.

The present era is sometimes described as the 'information age', yet there is still limited information on many public services. There are clear improvements that can be made. In the area of healthcare, a few basic changes in the type of and way in which information is collected would shed greater understanding on changes in the quality and level of healthcare provided by the NHS. Of fundamental importance is the routine collection of data on the health outcomes of NHS patients. We pointed out earlier some of the problems in interpreting data on health outcomes. There is no counter factual so we rarely know what would have happened in the absence of treatment. However, routine monitoring may give us an insight into whether outcomes are improving or falling over time and, for particular interventions, whether some individuals or organisations are better at undertaking them than others. These are important issues requiring further research as to when and for how long outcomes from a medical intervention should be measured. Without data on health outcomes, it is not possible to assess the effectiveness of policy initiatives such as, for example, whether substituting inpatient treatment for GP-led care improves the health of patients. It is perfectly feasible to introduce systems for collection of outcomes data, and it is likely the NHS will start this process in the near future.

Another major step forward would be to link information on individual patients who receive care in different settings. This would help us measure changes in the treatment of patients with chronic conditions in particular. Rather than counting the activities of the health service, the patient should be the centre of attention – what treatments is the patient receiving, who from and are they doing any good? This would be considerably more informative than simply adding up the number of GP consultations, operations and drugs prescribed.

These conclusions were endorsed by the final report of the Atkinson Review (Atkinson, 2005, ch 8). Its key recommendations included:

- Obtain better estimates of the treatment provided by GPs. The vast majority of NHS patients are treated in primary care, yet most of our data on activity and output relate to hospitals.
- Measure output in terms of whole courses of treatment for a patient (rather than simply counting activities). At present this is not feasible, but Atkinson believes that current developments in IT systems should make it possible in future.
- Routinely collect data on health outcomes. This would contribute to dealing with at least two problems. First, where the introduction of cost-reducing treatments results in the same or better health outcomes, we would observe an increase in the productivity of healthcare rather than a fall in NHS output, as is currently the case. Second, data on health outcomes could be useful in measuring quality change over time, a central focus for the National Accounts.

The main challenges of quantifying the output of health services apply to all other public services. These services are not easily defined; their quality is difficult to measure; it is a challenge to assess how services change over time; and it is not straightforward to calculate their social value. However, the importance of making progress in this area has been recognised. Following publication of the Atkinson Review, it was announced that a new UK Centre for the Measurement of Government Activity was to be established within the ONS. Given that government plays a substantial role in the economy and the services it provides or funds have such a major impact on the quality of life of the population, improved measurement and monitoring of government outputs is an essential ingredient of policy debate and democratic accountability.

Acknowledgement

The authors are grateful to the referees and the editors of this volume for comments on earlier drafts and to the Department of Health for financial support. The views expressed are those of the authors only.

References

Atkinson, T. (2004) *Atkinson review: Interim report. Measurement of government output and productivity for the National Accounts*, London: The Stationery Office.

Atkinson, T. (2005) *Atkinson review: Final report. Measurement of government output and productivity for the National Accounts*, Basingstoke: Palgrave Macmillan.

Cockburn, I.M. and Amis, A.H. (2001) 'Hedonic analysis of arthritis drugs', in D.M. Cutler and E.R. Berndt (eds) *Medical care output and productivity*, Chicago, IL: University of Chicago Press, pp 305-62.

Diener, A., O'Brien, B. and Gafni, A. (1998) 'Health care contingent valuation studies: a review and classification of the literature', *Health Economics*, vol 7, pp 313-26.

Eurostat (1995) *European systems of accounts ESA95*, Luxembourg: Office for Official Publications of the European Communities.

Eurostat (2001) *Handbook on price and volume measures in national accounts*, Luxembourg: Office for Official Publications of the European Communities.

Griffiths, R. (1992) 'Seven years of progress: general management in the NHS', *Health Economics*, vol 1, no 1, pp 61-70.

Hood, C. (1991) 'A public management for all seasons', *Public Administration*, vol 69, no 1, pp 3-19.

Hospital Episode Statistics (http://www.dh.gov.uk/PublicationsAndStatistics/Statistics/HospitalEpisodeStatistics/fs/en).

Klein, R. (2000) *The new politics of the NHS*, Harlow, Essex: Prentice Hall.

Nord, E. (2002) 'Measures of goal attainment and performance in the *World health report 2000*: a brief, critical consumer guide', *Health Policy*, vol 59, no 3, pp 183-191.

ONS (Office for National Statistics) (1998) *United Kingdom National Accounts: The blue book 1998*, London: ONS.

ONS (2000) *United Kingdom National Accounts: The blue book 2000*, London: ONS.

ONS (2001) *United Kingdom National Accounts: The blue book 2001*, London: ONS.

Pollitt, C. (1985) 'Measuring performance: a new system for the National Health Service, *Policy & Politics*, vol 13, no 1, pp 1-15.

Politt, C. (1995) 'Justification by works or by faith? Evaluating the new public management', *Evaluation*, vol 1, no 2, pp 133-54.

Smith, P.C. (1995) 'Performance indicators and control in the public sector', in A.J. Berry, J. Broadbent and D. Otley (eds) *Management control: Theories, issues and practices*, Basingstoke: Macmillan, pp 163-78.

Webster, C. (1998) *The National Health Service: A political history*, Oxford: Oxford University Press.

WHO (World Health Organization) (2000) *World health report 2000*, Geneva: WHO.

Williams, A. (2001) 'Science or marketing at WHO? A commentary on world health 2000', *Health Economics*, vol 10, no 2, pp 93-100.

ELEVEN

Social investment perspectives and practices: a decade in British politics[1]

Alexandra Dobrowolsky and Jane Jenson

Introduction

The social investment perspective has been influential for a least a decade. It frames social policy expenditures as investments rather than expenditures, forecasting future dividends from spending now, and describes social policy as supporting larger objectives – namely, propelling economies into the 21st century, and positioning states as innovative and competitive players in the global marketplace. The claim is that good economic outcomes depend on good social policy. A core concern is creating incentives for most adults to enter the labour market. Income supplements, particularly those that 'make work pay', are both popular and described as 'investments' because not only are they less costly than social assistance payments, they also foster a culture of inclusion and break the cycle of poverty. At the same time, however, the social investment perspective makes individuals responsible for 'investing in themselves' and their children. There are significant incentives to families to accumulate assets.

Here we trace the embrace and adaptation of the social investment perspective in Britain, from the early 1990s through to the likely election of a third government led by Tony Blair. We ask about the 'domestication' of the perspective and the particular policies and programmes that have been adopted, focusing on four particularly important policy goals: reducing child poverty; reforming learning; increasing quality childcare services; and promoting the accumulation of assets. In these four policy domains, our analysis seeks to uncover the reasons for the choices made, by attributing weight not only to institutional factors but also to the interests, ideas and identities of the actors involved.

The social investment perspective in general

In the mid-1990s, straightforward neo-liberalism, represented by Thatcherism and Reaganism had hit both an ideational and a political wall; the promised cutbacks in state activity and massive savings in state expenditures failed to materialise and social problems deepened. Poverty rates steadily mounted, and fears about social cohesion haunted policy makers, including the most economistic, who had rarely given it much previous attention. In international organisations as well as on the centre-left, old analyses were giving way to new ideas. In his influential formulation, Anthony Giddens wrote (1998, p 117): "In place of the welfare state we should put the social investment state, operating in the context of a positive welfare society". As early as 1994, the Organisation for Economic Co-operation and Development (OECD) was preparing the social investment perspective, arguing for a continuing need to spend rather than simply cut back in the social realm (Deacon, 2001, p 74). The OECD high-level conference, *Beyond 2000: The new social policy agenda*, in Paris in 1996, concluded with a call for a 'social investment approach for a future welfare state' which:

> requires that social expenditures be focussed on areas where returns are maximised in the form of social cohesion and active participation in society and in the labour market. As with all investment, this implies taking a long-term view of the costs and benefits.... Such an approach implies greater investment in children and young adults, as well as the maintenance of human capital over the life course[2].

Three ideas discussed at this high-level meeting continued to shape the social investment perspective. These were the need to (1) redesign systems of social protection so as to provide clearer incentives to work, save and invest; (2) reform learning systems in general and, in particular, have what the OECD termed 'state-dominated' education include lifelong learning and incentives for investing (sometimes by borrowing) in one's own human capital; and (3) foster adaptations in corporate and local community governance (OECD, 1997, pp 23-4).

We recall the position of the OECD in detail *not* because we want to imply that it simply spread the idea of social investment. Rather, in its documents we find, in summary form, the principal elements that have shaped the social investment perspective and practices over the last decade. These are the beliefs that good social policy requires a future time orientation; good economic outcomes depend on good social policy, because social inequities may undermine economic innovation; good social policy depends less on how much is spent than on where investments are made; fiscal prudence is a value in itself; investments are necessary in social inclusion as well as human capital, in order to ensure that flexibility and innovation are maximised; governance matters, expressed in public–private partnerships and revamped public administrations[3].

All this has brought an important shift in policy instruments, following from the idea of fiscal prudence. There is a clear preference for tax-based instruments for determining eligibility for benefits, with eligibility determined by income-testing rather than by means-testing and payment via tax credits (Myles and Quadagno, 2000, p 159).

Despite various policy communities reworking the components, the basic framework is widespread, especially in the Anglo-American world[4]. The social investment perspective serves centre-left politicians and parties whose programmes depend on the promise to improve on post-1945 systems of social protection, without totally abandoning basic principles of social justice. It aids, then, in transforming the identity of centre-left political formations and meeting their fundamental political interest in attaining office.

The elaboration of the ideas of social investment has had an unanticipated outcome: 'children' now provide a more important frame for social and economic policy analysis than in the post-war welfare state (Jenson, 2001; Dobrowolsky, 2002; Lister, 2003). Improving the life chances of children is sometimes the key metaphor, used by reformers inside and outside the state (Dobrowolsky and Saint-Martin, 2005).

In political terms, a child-focused version of the social investment perspective has facilitated adjustments to the identity of centre-left political formations. They can claim to reject any return to the 'bad old days' of taxing and spending and to be learning from the best of neo-liberalism, while maintaining their traditional values and commitments to social justice. In doing so, they promise to make investments that will pay off, and children appear as good investments. In partisan competition for the middle classes, moreover, a focus on education and preparation of young people for the new economy resonates quite well (Bonoli, 2001). Thus, a social investment perspective that borrows from the left and the right serves political parties that seek to broker a broad spectrum of interests and appeal to a wide variety of voters.

In ideational terms, children matter because human capital formation matters (Saint-Martin, 2000). Social investment is primarily about human capital formation and increasing the capacity of everyone to participate in paid work. Such ideas cast government spending in a very different light than in the post-1945 years. Income transfers and credits to 'end child poverty' and 'make work pay' frame spending very differently from 'the dole'. Benefits for the unemployed can be reduced, while increased 'investments' in education and health as well as child benefits can be justified (Powell, 1999, p 21).

The language as well as the instruments of the social investment perspective appeared in Britain in the mid-1990s. Social investment provided an idea set for thinking about income security, early learning and education as well as assets. The language of investment was used most explicitly to justify spending on health and education. An emphasis on investment also informed the government's enthusiasm for fostering private savings and individuals' own investment habits, as well as childcare and anti-poverty measures. In all cases, there were important changes in governance practices included in the policy redesign.

Social investment: its multiple purposes

Notably, the main value underpinning the social investment perspective is that well-being comes from employment. Markets are assumed capable of providing sufficiently for most people[5]. The social investment perspective is an ideational frame for politicians and policy makers to conceptualise ways of ensuring that everyone now – and in the future – will contribute to their own well-being through their own earnings and savings[6]. This underlying principle has tangible effects: it organises understanding of and actions on child poverty; it accounts for the emphasis on schools and learning; it makes sense of the sea-change that the commitment to publicly funded childcare represents; and it underpins the enthusiasm for distributing assets and encouraging savings.

The social investment perspective did not arrive with Tony Blair and his guru, Anthony Giddens. The Labour Party had been striving to recast its identity since its disastrous defeats at the hands of the Conservatives. While the notion of modernising the party was most obviously expressed by the label 'New Labour' that Tony Blair promoted (Fairclough, 2000), work on altering the party's identity had begun before he became leader in 1994. It began under Neil Kinnock (1983-92), and party modernisers gained ground during John Smith's brief leadership (1992-94).

John Smith established the Commission on Social Justice (CSJ) in 1992, symbolically choosing the 50th anniversary of the Beveridge Report. Housed within the Institute for Public Policy Research (IPPR), this independent review was charged with producing policy ideas. Many supporters and certainly several leaders judged that the Beveridgian paradigm was out of date, while others continued to believe that the work had hardly begun. The Commission had to navigate among a range of groups struggling to shape the identity of the party (Alcock, 2002, pp 242-3)[7].

The Blair government's overall framework, focusing on opportunity more than substantive equality and on investment rather than spending, can also be found in the report of the CSJ, as the Commission called for an 'Investor's Britain' (Powell, 1999, p 14):

> Investors argue for collective action and above all collective investment – whether it is public, private, voluntary or a partnership of all three – to promote individual opportunity. The first and most important task for government is to set in place the opportunities for children and adults to learn their personal best. By investing in skills, we raise people's capacity to add value to the economy, to take charge of their own lives, and to contribute to their families and communities. (CSJ, 1994, pp 119-20)

The CSJ advanced now familiar policy positions that shaped the identity of New Labour: the advantages of spending on employability programmes rather than welfare; lifelong learning; and work for all. It made the point too that social justice – that is, a modernised welfare state – is "an economic not merely a social necessity" (Borrie, 1996). The report also promoted a child focus for social investment: "the investment we make in babies and young children is wholly inadequate"; "children are not a private pleasure or a personal burden; they are 100% of the nation's future … the best indicator of the capacity of our economy tomorrow is the quality of our children today" (CSJ, 1994, pp 122, 311). Finally, it concluded that "the best way to help the one in three children growing up in poverty is to help their parents get jobs" (CSJ, 1994, p 313). While Tony Blair rarely directly acknowledges any debt to the CSJ, the Commission's skill in finding the middle ground within the divided party identified a path for New Labour when it took office.

From social inclusion to social investment: the child poverty strand

> Tackling child poverty will both improve individuals' life chances and contribute to the development of an educated and highly-skilled workforce. The Government has an ambitious, long-term goal to eradicate child poverty by 2020. The Government's strategy is to provide financial support for families, with work for those who can and support for those

who cannot; and to deliver high quality public services, which are key to
improving poor children's life chances and breaking cycles of deprivation.
(HM Treasury, 2004a, p 90)

This document, prepared in advance of the 2005 budget, summarises the
multiplicity of purposes for fighting child poverty. Indeed, reducing child
poverty has been one of the big policy ideas of the Labour government
since 1999 when Tony Blair pledged to end it in a generation. Then he
identified the principles of social investment underpinning the anti-poverty
strategy in terms of good and bad: "good spending on areas we want
money spent like Child Benefit and pensions is going up. Bad spending
on the bills of economic failure is coming down" (Blair, 1999, p 17). One
result of such understandings has been increases in child and family benefits
as well as earnings supplements since 1997[8].

Improving opportunities is the underlying goal. As the Chancellor of
the Exchequer Gordon Brown described it in the Foreword to *Tackling
child poverty*: "Our children are our future and the most important
investment we can make as a nation is in developing the potential of all
our country's children. Together we can ensure that no child is left
behind"[9]. Providing new opportunities implied rebalancing rights and
responsibilities. Income transfers and credits to 'lift' children and families
out of poverty were no gift, as Gordon Brown bluntly said: "Being a
parent brings with it rights and responsibilities. The Government will do
all it can to support parents, but in turn it is right that parents fulfil their
responsibilities too" (HM Treasury, 2001a, pp iii–iv).

The strategy is wide-ranging: it is meant to help both individuals and
the economy; it expects employment for – almost – all; its success depends
on both income and services. This strategy has emerged from a number
of institutional locales, including the Prime Minister's Office, the Social
Exclusion Unit (SEU) and the Treasury, over the life of the two Labour
governments.

Before efforts to address child poverty could be made, however, there
had to be policy ideas about the *reasons for* their poverty. The focus on
child poverty led directly and immediately to parental employment or,
more correctly, to non-employment. First, poverty was the result of
'worklessness'. The UK experienced an increase in workless households
prior to 1996, resulting in a child poverty rate after taxes and transfers of
20%, a 'score' higher than all OECD countries except Italy and the US
(UNICEF, 2000, pp 13–14, 15). While a correlation between worklessness
and poverty might seem obvious, the underlying notion was that, without
employment, social transfers of the residual sort Britain had always provided

could not move people out of poverty. Thus, the main idea about how to end child poverty was to combat 'worklessness' (HM Treasury, 2001a, chapter 2; 2003, p 5) by moving parents into employment.

In addition, however, income supplements and support for employed parents would have to be increased. Most were provided in the social investment way – that is, as tax credits – and were 'child-tested'. Arguments for the necessity of supplementing earned income followed from several observations. First, many parents of young children earn low wages. Second, the wage structure makes it increasingly difficult to support a family with one earner. Third, the birth of a child pushes a significant number of families below the poverty line, and this occurs more in the UK than elsewhere (for example, HM Treasury, 1999, p 21).

Thus, child poverty was related to access to work and parental income, but it was also necessary to justify focusing on *child* poverty, rather than poverty pure and simple. A key notion is that child poverty is time-sensitive; children are young for only a few years. Moreover, the effects of child poverty go well beyond the present. Reports of think-tanks and foundations as well as academic studies all found long-term consequences to a childhood spent in low income; even a few years of poverty could be reflected in lower levels of educational achievement and earnings as well as greater involvement with the police (for example, Hobcraft, 1998; Gregg et al, 1999). These observations were quickly incorporated into the idea set of policy makers, and government documents began presenting the science[10]. Such findings are foundational in the social investment perspective. That Britain had one of the highest rates of child poverty in Europe was not only unjust; it would also be very costly for the future.

Also important was another key idea: that poverty involves more than low income – it leads to social exclusion. This, in turn, calls for a multi-pronged strategy. Incomes had to rise, to be sure, but so too did services in neighbourhoods and support for parents. Indeed, science was invoked to impress upon parents the importance of their role:

> Children need a supportive, loving environment in which they can grow, and young people need guidance, role models and clear boundaries to enable them to develop into adults. Evidence shows time and time again that where these factors are not present in the home, the child is at risk of failure. (Blair, 2003)

Thus, the government would support not only *parents* but also *parenting* and relationships[11]: "The quality of the parents' relationship is crucial to their parenting capabilities and a critical factor affecting children's well-being.... Within Government, the Lord Chancellor's Department provides core funding for several national relationship support organisations..." (HM Treasury, 2001a, p viii, chapter 4).

A third key idea related to governance. Fighting childhood poverty meant relying on the voluntary sector. Along with the Comprehensive Spending Reviews' proposals for investment in health and education, investments in communities were front and centre for the Treasury (for example, HM Treasury, 1999, p 6; 2001a, chapter 3; Brown, 2000). Programmes such as Sure Start and the New Deal for Communities were intended to provide community-based interventions that would combine new instruments for fighting poverty and public–private partnerships.

Human capital – the most obvious social investment

The New Labour government moved quickly on another core theme in the social investment perspective: that of individuals' responsibility for investing in their own human capital by learning. These initiatives intersected with direct investments intended to restructure the economy by increasing competitiveness and reducing the productivity gap with other countries as well as with the objectives of higher social mobility and lower poverty. Equally important was the emphasis on restructuring government so that investments in public services, especially education, would pay off. Introducing the White Paper on Public Service Agreements, Chief Secretary, Stephen Byers (1998) said: "For too long people have focused on how much money is spent on public services. It is now time to move on and consider the more important issue – how the money is spent and what people get in return for their money".

We will deal with skills and education separately, because they partially addressed separate population categories and were initially rooted in quite different idea sets. They also had different potential consequences for the Labour Party's fortunes – that is, its political interests.

Upgrading skills

Learning has been a constant theme in international discussions of employability, and is at the core of the social investment perspective. In the 1998 Green Paper, *The learning age: A renaissance for a new Britain*, individuals were encouraged to invest in their own training and learning throughout the life course, with some financial support from the state (Kendall and Holloway, 2001, p 166). More recently, the Learning and

Skills Council (LSC) (LSC, 2003) has instituted a certification scheme, labelling local LSCs that meet the criteria as 'Investors in People'. Spending on learning exemplified the opportunity-in-exchange-for-responsibility theme and the 'enabling state' (Brown, 2000). It would be the arm in the fight against childhood poverty, helping parents to upgrade skills and to ensure children did not follow their parents along the low-skill road. Improving skills was closely linked to welfare reform. For example, lone parents were targeted in the Department for Education and Employment (DfEE) strategy *Skills for life* (DfEE, 2001a, p 17), and basic skills counselling became part of their 'New Deal'. Other groups 'at risk of exclusion' were targeted too. It also became part of the battle against crime, as David Blunkett, then Secretary of State for Education and Employment, explained: in addition to earning £50,000 less on average over their working lives, "people with low basic skills ... are more likely to have health problems or turn to crime" (DfEE, 2001a, Foreword).

Again, the ideas about *why* there was a skills gap were central drivers of the solutions selected. Three main ideas about the structure of employment, under-employment and non-employment can be found. First was the belief, widely shared across the OECD world, that the labour force constantly needs new skills and upgrading. This idea clearly shaped the education agenda, as we see later, but it also underlay ideas about ensuring that individuals could engage in a lifelong upgrading of skills. It brought Individual Learning Accounts (HM Treasury, 1999, p 36) – launched in 2000 and closed down in 2001 due to allegations of fraud and mismanagement.

A second idea was that some people were under-employed because they had lost their human capital, having stayed too long out of the labour force. New Deals were the prescription in this diagnosis, targeting both the long-term unemployed and women risking their human capital by staying home to care for children[12]. The third idea, and probably the one that has been the most influential in shaping policy, was that people had lost – or never had – the basic skills needed for labour force participation. While the New Deals might offer some basic skills training, the major focus in this strand of the analysis was children: "The seed of inequality in adulthood is denial of opportunity in childhood. Education is the most important transmission mechanism – people with few skills and qualifications are much less likely to succeed in the labour market" (HM Treasury, 1999, p 7). Thus, the 'skills agenda' would include a heavy dose of investment in schooling.

Not surprisingly, then, investing in learning was at the top of New

Labour's agenda. Initiatives for skills upgrading came from the Treasury and the Department for Education and Skills (DfES – previously DfEE), along with the Prime Minister, an active participant in framing the analysis. Tony Blair (2002) summed up his ideas in a major speech about welfare reform when he said the investment strategy of his government was directed towards aiding those lacking sufficient training and skills (such as lone parents, the long-term unemployed and those with disabilities). However, in the Prime Minister's view, if people made claims for support for their learning, it became their responsibility to accept basic skills training if they needed it, and then to look for work.

New governance arrangements, of two types, were part of the package. Investments would be in communities as well as individuals, and therefore partnerships were important. As part of an emphasis on neighbourhood effects and the need to invest disproportionately in places of disadvantage, means-tested Education Maintenance Allowances were piloted for the over-16s at risk of leaving school (although they were later extended). Initiatives for the very young, such as Sure Start, were also part of the learning agenda. Education Action Zones (EAZs) were instituted as public–private partnerships to provide alternative approaches to learning, and Excellence in Cities targeted funds for teaching and welfare workers – that is, 'joined-up governing' in inner cities (for a summary of EAZs, see HM Treasury, 1999, p 36; for an evaluation as well as description of Excellence in Cities, see Ofsted, 2004). Ambitions for the new governance were high. The EAZ's 'education action forums' were to act "as an investment in social capital ... they could prefigure a revived civil society within which parents and other community members are 'empowered' to take more control of local services" (Gewirtz, 2000, p 360).

The second adjustment to governance involved civil service reform, where the goal was to mimic as well as partner with the private sector and to develop services similar to those provided by private agencies. For example, three of the four dimensions of a new welfare strategy sketched by Tony Blair in his 2002 speech involved changed work activities of public sector employees. The Prime Minister (Blair, 2002) described the redesign of the Department for Work and Pensions' employment services and the new Jobcentres Plus[13] in the classic terms of the social investment perspective: "Job Centre Plus [sic] exemplifies both an active welfare state and our vision for public services". Public servants would no longer simply hand out benefits, an approach that was "demoralising and unsatisfying for staff as well as claimants". The state itself would "invest in its own employees" to ensure that they too would become the kind of workers needed in the knowledge-based economy, capable of innovation and decision making. Termed personal advisors, government workers would then be empowered to put together a package to match the needs of each individual – childcare, new suit, bus pass, tools or whatever.

In new governance terms, the Prime Minister also stressed the payoffs from experiments with public-private partnerships as well as the lessons to be learned from the private sector: "The best Employment Zones – run by Working Links, a PPP, or by the private sector – are achieving impressive job outcomes and are popular with claimants. And we're picking up some valuable lessons" (Blair, 2002).

Despite this promotion of one of the key themes of the social investment perspective, the commitment to training and lifelong learning has been quite limited. Britain remains a low spender on active labour market policies. These measures still clearly emphasise 'employment first', and making work pay. There has been some change over time, however (Grover and Stewart, 2000), especially in Labour's second term in office, as the government began to pay more attention to building skills, sustaining people in work and recognising that people are not going to be enticed into work by low-paid jobs (Finn, 2003, p 710).

Education and the competitiveness agenda

In comparison to the Conservatives, New Labour was "thoroughly dirigiste in its approach to school reform" (Driver and Martell, 2002, p 50). Educational reform was a goal dear to the Prime Minister, and many proposals for far-reaching educational changes were publicly and enthusiastically promoted by Tony Blair. Indeed, throughout his time in office, education for the 'new economy' is one of the big investment ideas to which the Prime Minister has remained devoted. Consequently, significant funds have been allocated to the education system, increasing 39% between 1993 and 2004 (AUT, 2004), and the government has set a target of 50% of young people aged 18-30 going into higher education by the year 2010.

From the very start of his leadership, Blair called for ways to update traditional Labour Party principles such as justice and progress by applying "them in a different way for the modern world – stressing education, skills, technology, design and invention and the role of small business" (MacGregor, 1998, p 265; Bullen et al, 2000, pp 441-2). And so, in the 1997 election, "'Education, education, education' headed the manifesto and education was declared to be the Party's first priority" (Muschamp et al, 1999, p 101).

By 1999, in his Romanes Lecture at Oxford University[14], Tony Blair used a social investment perspective to talk of education:

> Our number one priority for investment is education. The reason for this is simple. In the 21st century, as we forge a new progressive politics on the centre-left, the battle of this century between the 'economic' and the 'social' will end.... The liberation of human potential – for all the people, not just a privileged few – is in today's world the key both to economic and social progress. In economic terms, human capital is a nation's biggest resource. Brainpower, skills and flexibility – not cheap manual labour – are the key to competitiveness and productivity.

In calling for greater flexibility in education, Blair was both echoing the OECD's concerns about existing 'state-dominated' education quoted earlier and foreshadowing what would be his commitment to experimentation in public-private partnerships in education, as well as an emphasis on standards and testing. When it comes to education, then, three refrains recur: target setting, competition and choice.

For example, when the 2004 budget announced more spending for education, the Secretary of State for Education, Charles Clarke, promised that what he constantly called 'the investment' would "make a reality of our commitment that every school that meets the standard will have the opportunity to gain specialist status; and will allow a continued expansion in the number of academies" (Clarke, 2004). This educational assessment process also gives priority to 'competitiveness'. Within the educational system, institutions compete to receive the highest marks from Ofsted inspections[15] and other assessment exercises. Universities, subjected to Research Assessment Exercises (RAE), the results of which shape funding support, face tighter competition between those programmes and departments judged to be in the highest class and those in the middle.

Social investment, as noted in our introduction, is meant to improve economic competitiveness. Investments in education were framed as key to the competitiveness agenda for the British economy when the Chancellor of the Exchequer focused on productivity, competitiveness and investment, and in the Treasury task forces and other initiatives. By 1998, these ideas had been applied to the 'productivity gap', in a White Paper on Competitiveness and in 'Productivity Roadshows'.

The investment for competitiveness and productivity also informed the debate around the White Paper on higher education and the subsequent consultation documents (DfES, 2003b, 2003c). So too did the idea of choice, however. In effect, if spending on education has increased significantly, it has not been to the advantage of higher education; total public spending on higher education and student support fell by 7%, and public spending on higher education as a proportion of GDP was actually "slightly higher in 1994-95 than it was 10 years later" (AUT, 2004). This trend, which reflects a commitment to individuals and families investing in their own futures, underpins the discussions of higher education reform – both the White Paper, *The future of higher education* (DfEs, 2003b) and the accompanying *Widening participation in higher education* (DfES, 2003c). Analysis in these documents found that individual investments were significantly class biased; those from less privileged backgrounds were a smaller proportion of those at university than in 1960 (DfES, 2003c, p 7). Non-participation by students of manual or working-class backgrounds was analysed as due to lack of 'aspiration' more than discrimination in admissions. Therefore, universities able, as of 2006, to charge differential fees, would have to do more to attract good students (explaining their offerings and the funding options available) as fees rose significantly. Choice would, in other words, extend across the board, from universities through private academies to childcare centres; education is presented holistically in this social investment perspective.

To illustrate, Charles Clarke, Secretary of State for Education, displayed proficiency in the language of the social investment while presenting the 2004 budget numbers for his department:

> [They] would provide the necessary investment to achieve excellence in standards of education and skills and take forward the radical agenda for children and families ... in every area, investment would be matched by reform ... the investment would make huge progress in ensuring every child matters, giving every child the best start in life. (Clarke, 2004)

With such use of familiar terms, as well as the responsibilities of the DfES, Ofsted and other agencies, we see the extent to which early childhood education has risen to the top of Labour's social investment agenda.

Investing in children: childcare for children as well as parents

> When we came to power, we inherited one of the worst set of childcare and family friendly provisions in Europe and one of the worst records on child poverty in the industrialised world. We have a lot more to do but we are turning that round – making a real and sustained difference

to the lives of millions of children and parents.... Together we need to build a childcare system that meets the needs of today's family life, that is secure enough to fulfil children's opportunities.... We must, above all, ensure the best possible start in life for all our children who are our strength and our future. (Blair, 2004)

Thus far in this chapter, we have seen that a focus on child poverty was the major way the Labour governments deployed the social investment perspective for welfare reform. Attention to early learning and childcare has been an important part of this focus with the result that there has been a sea-change in the childcare policy domain, involving both levels of provision and forms of governance (Harker, 1998). In education and learning, the social investment perspective was predominant because skills and schooling are easily described as 'human capital', one of the key organising principles of the perspective, and childcare has been positioned as part of 'lifelong education'.

Childcare, as a third big idea in the British social investment perspective, merits its own attention. Over the two Labour governments, it has always been treated as a support for working parents. But any childcare discussion goes well beyond its costs to working parents. There is always a consideration of whether and when non-parental care is appropriate and the advantages of formal over informal care. On these issues, the British government still continues to be much less convinced than many other countries that high-quality educational care – and more than part-time nursery school – is good for all children.

New Labour has always had clear ideas about the needs of children who are at risk of suffering from childhood poverty – they need high-quality publicly supported services to compensate for disadvantage at home. For the rest, the government continues to promise parental choice, while providing its own glowing picture of the advantages to *all* children of high-quality early education[16]. Even getting to this somewhat schizophrenic position has taken a number of years.

Prior to 1997, "the official government view [was that] childcare should be 'primarily a matter of private arrangement between parents and private and voluntary resources except where there were special needs'" (Randall, 2002, p 224). As the high costs of care were recognised as a barrier to taking a job, however, the practice of linking a childcare benefit to supplements for low earnings became the norm (Randall, 2002, pp 231-2). The Major government began annexing childcare to the agenda of welfare reform and employability, and then the Labour government followed suit.

In the first Labour government, the 1998 Green Paper, *Meeting the childcare challenge*, maintained an employability lens for childcare, promising investments that would help parents to enter and stay in the labour force. Particular attention was paid to lone parents, who were described as both facing costs and forming a potential pool of paid childcare workers (DfEE, 1998, section 3.1, para 2.22).

This introduced a slippery notion of quality that continues to shape ideas about childcare in British policy circles. It promised a National Childcare Strategy whose aim was "to ensure good quality, affordable childcare for children aged 0 to 14 in every neighbourhood". But it immediately went on to say that there were many ways to provide 'quality' care including "formal childcare, such as playgroups, out of school clubs and childminders. And it includes support for informal childcare, for example relatives or friends looking after children". Public support for formal care was described as 'filling gaps' (DfEE, 1998, para ES4). Therefore, as substantial investments in the form of both increased tax credits and support for infrastructure were made over the next years, the emphasis on the mix of informal care and part-time care remained.

After 1997, the Labour government also immediately reaffirmed "the Conservative pledge, and indeed funding commitment, to provide nursery education for all four-year-olds" (Randall, 2002, p 234), a year later extending it to cover all children aged three and over. Local education authorities were tasked in spring 1997 with developing Early Years Partnerships with the voluntary and private sector, and then producing Early Years Development Plans to show how a half-day nursery school place would be created for all children aged four and over. In other words, the governance structure for the nursery portion of the childcare package was instituted as a partnership from the start. Then, as Vicky Randall perceives (2002, p 235): "When the new childcare policy was launched in March 1998 it was in a sense grafted onto this Early Years policy. The existing local partnerships were expanded so as to constitute Early Years Development and Childcare Partnerships". This was the route taken whereby childcare was incorporated into the DfEE (later DfES).

This history of partnerships for creating nursery spaces had two consequences. First, because nursery schools only provide half-day services, parents were still left searching for care the rest of the day, for younger as well as for school-age children. This need would supposedly be met by providing tax credits for purchasing care from home-based childminders or by informal care. In this way, the legitimacy of informal care has remained high and of family daycare providers (childminders) even higher. The 10-year strategy for childcare presented in 2004 reinforces this legitimacy, both by including informal care on the tray of choices and by seeking ways to increase the qualification levels of home-based carers (childminders) (HM Treasury, 2004b).

A second result of this history was that community-based institutions and partnerships became the governance model, this time for the childcare component of social investment to tackle child poverty. Sure Start is, of course, the classic example of the way the social investment perspective shaped childcare and other early childhood thinking, sharing the logo 'Investing in our future', with the DfEE[17]. While always asserting that 'all children' and their parents deserve the highest quality services and supports, the initiative was targeted to poor children in disadvantaged neighbourhoods.

The debt to the social investment perspective's ways of understanding the dangers of childhood poverty was deep. Sure Start was built on an understanding of the health as well as social and educational challenges arising from disadvantaged childhood, and it focused on training for parenting as well as employability measures and services for children. The childcare component, in the 2001 Service Delivery Agreement, came via a commitment to providing all children in a Sure Start area "access to good quality play and learning opportunities, helping progress towards early learning goals when they get to school". This went along with a target "to reduce by at least 12% the number of 0- to 3-year-old children in Sure Start areas living in households where no one is working" by 2004 (DfEE, 2001b, p 5).

A similar debt to the social investment perspective is apparent in the ways that regulation of childcare developed. Following the National Childcare Strategy, there were both a new set of regulations and the decision to assign oversight of childcare providers to Ofsted (www.ofsted.gov.uk/howwework). But in addition to regulations, beginning in 2002, Sure Start moved to add a certification programme, Investors in Children. This is described as a quality assurance scheme that will accredit organisations providing childcare and early education (such as nurseries, out of school clubs, crèches, pre-schools, play groups) as well as childminders[18]. In a childcare regime like Britain's that is demand-driven, parents need some sort of signal from providers in order to identify 'quality'. This is the announced goal of the Investors in Children programme.

By the second Labour government, in other words, childcare as a service even within Sure Start had expanded beyond poor children. This shift to a more general frame was further confirmed when in 2003 changes to improve families' balance of work and family life were incorporated into the 'Work–Life Balance Campaign'. Childcare was one of the many measures on the list of things (including maternity leave, flexible working and so on) to support parents. Providing better childcare would allow the government to achieve its goals for employment, child poverty and productivity (HM Treasury, 2003, p 21).

As the preparations for the 2005 election went forward, childcare rose to the top as one of the big ideas for the next term. In the process, other ideas about childcare gained in importance. In *Balancing work and family life: Enhancing choice and support for parents* (HM Treasury, 2003) and *Choice for parents, the best start for children: A ten year strategy for childcare* (HM Treasury, 2004b, especially Appendix A), early childhood education was an investment target, benefiting everyone. A thoroughly modern welfare state would recognise that in the 21st century, fostering a better balance between work and family life was a win–win situation from the social investment perspective.

> Enabling parents to balance work and family responsibilities can make the difference between their participation in the labour market or their exclusion. For the employer, it can make the difference between being able to retain a valued member of staff or incurring the costs of recruitment and further training. And for children it gives them the best possible start in life. (HM Treasury, 2003, Foreword)

The 10-year strategy was still to be a prudent one, of course: "we know that we cannot build universal childcare or better work–life provision over night.... That's why we are developing a long-term strategy with crucial milestones..." (Blair, 2004). When pre-electoral promises about future investments were laid on the table, prudence continued to be the trump card.

Investing in investing: assets and savings

Not long after his second electoral success, Tony Blair (2002) described his vision of welfare reform. In the speech, he saved his greatest enthusiasm and his most upbeat description of the future for one idea that built directly on the social investment perspective:

> But if we are serious about transforming the welfare state, our strategy has to be about more than helping people into work and relieving poverty. To enable people to be independent and make their own choices, they need the back-up of having some savings in the bank or a nest-egg.

> Money put aside changes your horizons. It makes you plan, brings
> responsibility, offers protection and opportunity. And I want to ensure
> that those on lower incomes – and the next generation – can share those
> advantages.

Such ideas about the wide range of benefits from fostering savings and
acquisition of 'assets' are the purest expression of the social investment
perspective. Not surprisingly, the Labour government has been enthusiastic,
with the Institute for Public Policy Research (IPPR) playing a major
role in promoting this aspect of social investment. It claims paternity of
the so-called baby bonds that eventually became the Child Trust Fund, as
well as shadowing the thinking in the Treasury about instituting the
measures (Regan, 2001).

In his speech, Blair projected his understanding of British identity: it
was to be "a nation of savers and asset-holders". Assets and savings have
been portrayed as a fourth dimension of the extension of opportunity for
all, and they have been among the big ideas since the earliest days of New
Labour. In 1997, for example, Individual Savings Accounts were described
this way: "We want to build the savings culture. That is good for individuals.
It is good for businesses and is therefore good for the country as a whole"
(Darling, 1997). Both the 1997 and 2001 election manifestos promised
measures to promote savings, and in 2001 the ideas went out for
consultation (Emmerson and Wakefield, 2001). When the White Paper,
Savings and assets for all (HM Treasury, 2001b), was launched, the rhetoric
was ratcheted up further: Brown suggested the initiatives had the potential
of "creating a democracy where wealth ownership is genuinely open to
all" (Brown, 2001).

The final form of the Child Trust Fund was announced in the 2003
Budget where it was characterised as a long-term savings and investment
account. Coming into effect in April 2005 for eligible children born on
or after September 2002, the government will provide a lump sum, in
amounts that vary by family income. Families can themselves make
contributions to the accounts. The goal is to help build up a useful stock
of assets for when children reach the age of 18. Financial education is
included in the package so as to create the 'saving culture'. All children
will receive financial education to help them manage their money with
future needs in mind. Parents are responsible for its management until
children reach the age of 16, at which point they may take over. They
may not withdraw from the fund until age 18.

Savings Gateway programmes are also being piloted. For every £1 put
into an account, up to a limit, the government will deposit a matching

amount. These savings package are really like learning the savings habit 'with training wheels', given the upper limit is the relatively modest £375. Indeed, the pilots are run through the DfES Community Finance and Learning Initiative at five sites.

Both the Child Trust Fund and the Savings Gateway pilots involve partnerships with the private sector, in particular the banking institutions that will handle the new accounts.

Conclusion

This chapter has traced the ways that four big ideas in the social investment perspective have been deployed by the British Labour Party since the early 1990s. To map the 'domestication' of this perspective in Britain, we examined welfare reform, especially as it has focused on child poverty, learning, childcare and savings. These idea sets, we contend, have contributed to re-shaping the identity of the Labour Party, tying it to its targeted constituency on the centre-left and promoting new state–society relations particularly via innovations in governance forms.

In each case, ideas drawn from the social investment perspective were used to justify the spending choices of the Labour government. These included emphasising a future orientation, increasing incentives to seek paid employment and being attentive to human capital. Thus, welfare reform focused on children, because they appeared to be the best place to wager for the future. Just as one would predict from the social investment perspective, investments in human capital, from early childhood through later working life, received an injection of funds. This spending was increased, even as traditional patterns of spending (for example, on higher education) declined in relative terms. The British government has also gone quite far along the 'investing in investing' road, committing substantial funds to its various schemes, including the Child Trust Fund.

Childcare provides somewhat of a counter example. Services have been improved and Britain did take significant steps towards continental Europe's (and now the OECD-endorsed) reliance on early childhood education and care, compared to its own past. Yet, Britain has not moved beyond a traditional liberal emphasis on parental 'choice' about childcare arrangements and support for informal, family-based care. Parents, armed with ever more generous childcare credits, have been left to make their purchases in the market, including the market for informal care, or even to provide care themselves. British policy remains wedded to some traditional visions of motherhood, and therefore continues to excuse female heads of lone-parent families from taking paid work. With its 10-year

Strategy for Childcare also building in mechanisms for financing informal and home-based care, Britain continues to be an outlier in the policy directions of the OECD world[19].

Obviously, ideas are important. The implementation of the social investment perspective has essentially completed the re-making of the Labour Party's identity as a party that spends wisely and is not afraid of working in partnership with business. While conflicts between the current Prime Minister and future leadership contenders are newsworthy and intense, the departments they head are moving in parallel directions. For instance, Gordon Brown may have a penchant for starting important policy statements with a reference to William Beveridge, but the Treasury has nonetheless taken the lead in transforming attention to poverty into a concern with child poverty, leaving other categories of poor citizens to fend for themselves. It was also the Treasury that launched the *Savings and assets for all* consultation and has worked carefully to link the discussions of investments in human capital to the competitiveness agenda. Therefore, rather than a party identity that is profoundly ambivalent, as it was in the 1980s, there is now evidence of significant consensus around the social investment perspective. Put differently, while interests within the Labour Party remain deeply antagonistic, nevertheless, as the 2005 election looms, the overriding interest in retaining power – the long-standing goal of any political party – remains predominant.

It is also helpful to assess the effects of the British version of the social investment perspective on the identity of citizens themselves. Such an analysis would, to be effective, require a whole article of its own. However, we can find some elements of, at least, the state's notions of that identity. Each of the four policy domains projected an identity on to individuals and the country as a whole, providing descriptions of what it means to be British.

Parents were identified in the anti-poverty discourse as responsible when they responded to the incentives to take up work and to care well for their children. Yet, this also came with the thinly veiled message that there were also 'some parents' who were irresponsible or, at least, in need of training. Their children were in need of special attention, services and support.

While the skills and learning agenda projected an image of responsible individuals busy making investments in their human capital, the almost photographic negative was that of an adult lacking basic skills and, in the case of parents, likely to pass this lack to the next generation. Therefore, while programmes might target skills training for adults, the greatest attention had to go to children and to educational experiments that would better foster social mobility, so they could escape from the negative influence of their families rather than from (as one might have said in the past) the negative influence of their social circumstances.

In strong contrast, the other two policy domains projected a more consistently positive identity on citizens. Parents were encouraged to make their own childcare choices, even if they selected forms that experts considered to be less developmentally advantageous. Certainly the notion of the 'savings culture' granted a fair amount of discretion to parents and adolescent children to make choices about the disposal of accumulated assets. Here they were encouraged to think about themselves as market players and certainly not in terms of class or any other form of solidarity. In other words, there were mixed messages being sent out that were certainly not neutral in class terms.

This recognised, we can conclude by noting that after more than eight years of Labour government, much of the social investment perspective has been institutionalised. It now pervades key departments, which have been re-designed – and often renamed – better to participate in its dissemination. As a result, the next steps for analysis become ones that take the social investment perspective as a given.

Notes

[1] This chapter is part of the project 'Fostering social cohesion: a comparison of new policy strategies', supported by the Social Sciences and Humanities Research Council of Canada (SSHRC).

[2] See www.oecd.org/. The conference report is OECD (1997).

[3] These ideas are summarised in OECD (1997). Jenson and Saint-Martin (2003a) provide a synthetic presentation of the perspective.

[4] The social investment perspective *has* influenced European policy analysis (Esping-Andersen, 2002; Jenson and Saint-Martin, 2003b). That is why it is not a synonym for the 'third way', the latter having little resonance in continental European politics (Bonoli, 2001).

[5] This assumption about the capacities of markets also underpinned social policy thinking after 1945. However, notions about 'full employment' have clearly changed. Then it meant half the population – that is men. Now it means almost everyone.

[6] The British government is very careful to distinguish between 'work for those who can and support for those who cannot'. The result is an ongoing tussle about who is grouped among the 'cannot'. British lone parents can still substitute childcare for paid work, a practice that has been eliminated in most other jurisdictions. The New Deal for lone parents is meant to foster, without compelling, their labour force participation (Sumaza, 2001). The goal is 70% of lone parents in employment by 2010. In addition, New Deal work obligations have been extended to partners of unemployed men under 25 and women under 45 without dependent children (Bryson, 2003, pp 83-4).

[7] The CSJ was not alone: "The Adam Smith Institute's Omega project on the reform of the welfare state and public services; the IPPR's Social Justice Commission which laid the foundations for Labour's new ideas on welfare and redistribution; the Fabian Society's Commission on Tax and Citizenship, and the IPPR's Commission on Private–Public Partnerships" (Gamble, 2002, p 307) were all important locales for identity work.

[8] "Total spending on child-contingent support has risen markedly since 1975. Total spending has risen from £10 billion to £22 billion per year in 2003 prices. This is an increase from … 3.4% to 4.7% of total government spending…. The increase in child contingent support since 1999 is much more significant than the total increase between 1975 and 1999" (JRF, 2004, pp 2-3).

[9] This Foreword and the document contain many echoes of US discourse. During the Clinton presidency, welfare reform included marriage incentives, and this document promises spending on 'good relationships'. President George W. Bush claims his educational reforms will ensure "that no child is left behind"; indeed that is the title of the programme. The Chancellor of the Exchequer also echoed a much earlier President when he described his government's anti-poverty strategy as "the war against child poverty" (Brown, 2000).

[10] Cross-sectional and panel studies were cited, documenting both long-term effects of childhood poverty for outcomes such as truancy *and* greater intergenerational inequality (HM Treasury, 2001a, p 2). See also *Every child matters* (DfES, 2003a, chapter 1).

[11] Many reported findings about good parenting and youth outcomes came from the SEU's Policy Action Team 12 on young people. Parenting support was viewed primarily as a service for parents of children in trouble with the law (HM Treasury, 2001a, pp 5, 47-8). Additional data are reported in *Every child matters* (DfES, 2003a, pp 20-1, for example).

[12] For example, *Tackling poverty and extending opportunity* (HM Treasury, 1999, p 47) used a pseudo-gender frame: "Partners of the unemployed, mainly women, are themselves disproportionately likely to be unemployed. In the past, the benefit system has assumed that partners of the unemployed cannot or do not want to work, denying them help and opportunities. The New Deal for the long-term unemployed now provides new opportunities for partners aged over 25 to receive the help they need to get back to work. For the under 25's partners of the 18-24's without children will in future be brought into the New Deal for young people".

[13] Creating 'Jobcentre Plus' involved merging the Employment Service and the parts of the Benefits Agency that had offered services to those of working age into a 'single window', a favourite term in the new governance discourse.

[14] See the Prime Minister's website (www.pmo.gov.uk/output/page5.asp).

[15] 'Standards' have been at the heart of the school reforms and a significant preoccupation of Labour governments (David, 2003, pp 358-9). Since 1992, the Office for Standards in Education (Ofsted) has inspected all schools in England as well as teacher training institutions and youth work. In 2001, Ofsted took over responsibility for inspecting all education for those aged 16-19 and childcare facilities, including childminders. Its inspection reports on individual schools are available (www.ofsted.gov.uk).

[16] The title of *Choice for parents, the best start for children: A ten year strategy for childcare* (HM Treasury, 2004b) combines the option to 'choose' informal care, whether parental, familial or other, with the code phrase common to early childhood educators that the 'best start' is one that includes formal early childhood education.

[17] Other significant innovations in addition to the National Childcare Strategy and Sure Start are the Neighbourhood Childcare Initiative, the Out of School Childcare Initiative, and Early Years Development and Childcare Partnerships (Grover and Stewart 2000, p 240).

[18] See www.surestart.gov.uk/ensuringquality/investorsinchildren

[19] The OECD has come out strongly, for both child development and human capital reasons, in support of relatively short (12 months) parental leaves coupled with significant spending on early childhood education and care (OECD, 2001).

References

Alcock, P. (2002) 'Welfare policy', in P. Dunleavy, A. Gamble, R. Heffernan, I. Holliday and G. Peele (eds) *Developments in British politics* (revised edn), Houndmills: Palgrave, pp 238-56.

AUT (Association of University Teachers) (2004) *UK higher education, public spending and GDP*, AUT research report, April (www.aut.org.uk/media/html/spendingandgdp1.html).

Blair, T. (1999) 'Beveridge revisited: a welfare state for the 21st century', Beveridge Lecture, Toynbee Hall, in R. Walker (ed) *Ending child poverty: Popular welfare for the 21st century*, Bristol: The Policy Press, pp 7-18.

Blair, T. (2002) 'PM speech on welfare reform', 10 June (www.pmo.gov.uk/output/Page1716.asp).

Blair, T. (2003) 'Prime Minister's speech on the launch of the children's Green Paper, *Every child matters*', 8 September (www.pmo.gov.uk/output/Page4426.asp).

Blair, T. (2004) 'Prime Minister's speech to the Daycare Trust', 11 November (www.pmo.gov.uk/output/Page6564.asp).

Bonoli, G. (2001) 'The third way and political economy traditions in Western Europe', Paper prepared for presentation at the workshop 'Third ways in Europe', European Consortium for Political Research – Joint Sessions, Grenoble, 6-11 April.

Borrie, Lord (1996) 'Is social justice affordable?', Speech to the Centre for the Understanding of Society and Politics, Kingston University, 20 March (www.kingston.ac.ik/cusp/Lectures/Borrie.htm).

Brown. G. (2000) 'The James Meade Memorial Lecture', London School of Economics, 8 May (speech 60-00 on www.hm-treasury.gov.uk).

Brown, G. (2001) Statement by Chancellor Gordon Brown at the press launch of the *Savings and assets for all* consultation, 26 April (speech 54-01 on www.hm-treasury.gov.uk).

Bryson, A. (2003) 'From welfare to workfare', in J. Millar (ed) *Understanding social security: Issues for policy and practice*, Bristol: The Policy Press, pp 77-101.

Bullen, E., Kenway, J. and Hay, V. (2000) 'New Labour, social exclusion and educational risk management: the case of "gymslip mums"', *British Educational Research Journal*, vol 6, no 4, pp 441-56.

Byers, S. (1998) 'Public services for the future – modernisation, reform and accountability', 17 December (speech 212-98 on www.hm-treasury.gov.uk).

Clarke, C. (2004) 'Stability and steady investment in children and every stage of education', 18 March, press archive no 2004-41 (www.dfes.gov.uk).

CSJ (Commission on Social Justice) (1994) *Social justice: Strategies for national renewal. Report of the Commission on Social Justice*, London:Vintage.

Darling, A. (1997) 'Speech by The Rt Hon Alistair Darling MP, Chief Secretary to the Treasury, at the Proshare Annual Awards Dinner', 3 December (speech 155-97 on www.hm-treasury.gov.uk).

David, M. (2003) 'Education', in P. Alcock, A. Erskine and M. May (eds) *The student's companion to social policy* (2nd edn), Oxford: Blackwell, pp 355-61.

Deacon, B. (2001) 'Les organisations internationales, l'union européenne et la politique sociale globalisée', *Lien Social et Politiques*, vol 45, pp 73-87.

DfEE (Department for Education and Employment) (1998) *Meeting the childcare challenge*, Cm 3959, Norwich: The Stationery Office.

DfEE (2001a) *Skills for life: The national strategy for improving adult literacy and numeracy skills*, Nottingham: DfEE (www.dfee.gov.uk/readwriteplus).

DfEE (2001b) *Sure Start: Making a difference for families and children*, London: DfEE.

DfES (Department for Education and Skills) (2003a) *Every child matters*, Cm 5860, Norwich: The Stationery Office.

DfES (2003b) *The future of higher education*, Cm 5735, Norwich: The Stationery Office.

DfES (2003c) *Widening participation in higher education*, London: DfES (www.dfes.gov.uk).

Dobrowolsky, A. (2002) 'The future of the child and New Labour's strategic "social investment state"', *Studies in Political Economy*, vol 69, pp 43-73.

Dobrowolsky, A. and Saint-Martin, D. (2005) 'Agency, actors and change in a child-focused future: problematising path dependency', *Journal of Commonwealth and Comparative Politics*, vol 43, no 1, pp 1-33.

Driver, S. and Martell, L. (2002) *Blair's Britain*, Cambridge: Polity.

Emmerson, C. and Wakefield, M. (2001) *The saving gateway and the Child Trust Fund: Is asset-based welfare 'well fair'?*, London: Institute for Fiscal Studies.

Esping-Andersen, G. (2002) *Why we need a new welfare state*, Oxford: Oxford University Press.

Fairclough, N. (2000) *New Labour, new language?*, London and New York, NY: Routledge.

Finn, D. (2003) 'The "employment-first" welfare state: lessons from the New Deal for young people', *Social Policy and Administration*, vol 37, no 7, pp 709-24.

Gamble, A. (2002) 'Policy agendas in a multi-level polity', in P. Dunleavy, A. Gamble, R. Heffernan, I. Holliday and G. Peele (eds) *Developments in British politics* (revised edn), Houndmills: Palgrave, pp 290-307.

Gewirtz, S. (2000) 'Bringing the politics back in: a critical analysis of quality discourses in education', *British Journal of Education Studies*, vol 48, no 4, pp 352-70.

Giddens, A. (1998) *The third way: The renewal of social democracy*, Cambridge: Polity Press.

Gregg, P., Harkness, S. and Machin, S. (1999) *Child development and family income*, York: Joseph Rowntree Foundation.

Grover, C. and Stewart, J. (2000) 'Modernising social security? Labour and its welfare-to-work strategy', *Social Policy and Administration*, vol 34, no 3, pp 235-53.

Harker, L. (1998) 'A national child care strategy: does it meet the child care challenge?', *Political Quarterly*, vol 69, pp 458-63.

HM Treasury (1999) 'Tackling poverty and extending opportunity', in the *The modernisation of Britain's tax and benefit system*, no 4, London: HM Treasury (www.hm-treasury.gov.uk).

HM Treasury (2001a) *Tackling child poverty: Giving every child the best possible start in life*, a pre-budget document, London: HM Treasury, December (www.hm-treasury.gov.uk).

HM Treasury (2001b) 'Saving and assets for all', in *The modernisation of Britain's tax and benefit system*, no 8, April, London: HM Treasury (www.hm-treasury.gov.uk).

HM Treasury (with Department of Trade and Industry) (2003) *Balancing work and family life: Enhancing choice and support for parents*, Norwich: HM Treasury, January (www.hm-treasury.gov.uk).

HM Treasury (2004a) *Opportunity for all: The strength to take the long-term decisions for Britain*, a pre-budget document, Norwich: HM Treasury, December (www.hm-treasury.gov.uk).

HM Treasury (2004b) *Choice for parents, the best start for children: A ten year strategy for childcare*, Norwich: HM Treasury, December (www.hm-treasury.gov.uk).

Hobcraft, J.N. (1998) *Intergenerational and life-course transmission of social exclusion: Influences of childhood poverty, family disruption and contact with the police*, CASEpaper 15, London: London School of Economics and Political Science.

Jenson, J. (2001) 'Rethinking equality and equity: Canadian children and the social union', in E. Broadbent (ed) *Democratic equality: What went wrong?*, Toronto: University of Toronto Press.

Jenson, J. and Saint-Martin, D. (2003a) 'New routes to social cohesion? Citizenship and the social investment state', *Canadian Journal of Sociology*, vol 28, no 1, pp 77-99.

Jenson, J. and Saint-Martin, D. (2003b) 'Building blocks for a new welfare architecture: is LEGO™ the model for an active society?', Paper presented at the meeting of the RC19 of the International Sociological Association, University of Toronto, August (www.individual.utoronto.ca/RC19_2003/papers.html).

JRF (Joseph Rowntree Foundation) (2004) *Findings*, January (www.jrf.org.uk/knowledge/findings/socialpolicy/pdf/124.pdf).

Kendall, I. and Holloway, D. (2001) 'Education policy', in S.P. Savage and R. Atkinson (eds) *Public policy under Blair*, Houndmills: Palgrave, pp 154-73.

LSC (Learning and Skills Council) (2003) *Corporate plan to 2005: Championing the power of learning*, London: LSC (www.lsc.gov.uk).

Lister, R. (2003) 'Investing in the citizen-workers of the future: transformations in citizenship and the state under New Labour', *Social Policy and Administration*, vol 37, no 5, pp 427-43.

MacGregor, S. (1998) 'A new deal for Britain?', in H. Jones and S. MacGregor (eds) *Social issues and party politics*, London: Routledge, pp 248-72.

Muschamp, Y., Jamieson, I. and Lauder, H. (1999) 'Education, education, education', in M. Powell (ed) *New Labour, new welfare state?: The 'third way' in British social policy*, Bristol: The Policy Press, pp 101-21.

Myles, J. and Quadagno, J. (2000) 'Envisioning a third way: the welfare state in the twenty-first century', *Contemporary Sociology*, vol 29, no 1, pp 157-67.

OECD (Organisation for Economic Co-operation and Development) (1997) *Societal cohesion and the globalising economy: What does the future hold?*, Paris: OECD.

OECD (2001) *Starting strong: Early childhood education and care*, Paris: OECD.

Ofsted (Office for Standards in Education) (2004) *Excellence in cities: The primary extension*, document HMI 2394, London: Ofsted (www.ofsted.gov.uk).

Powell, M. (1999) 'Introduction', in M. Powell (ed) *New Labour, new welfare state?: The 'third way' in British social policy*, Bristol: The Policy Press, pp 1-27.

Randall, V. (2002) 'Child care in Britain, or, how do you restructure nothing?', in S. Michel and R. Mahon (eds) *Child care policy at the crossroads: Gender and welfare state restructuring*, London: Routledge.

Regan, S. (ed) (2001) *Assets and progressive welfare*, London: IPPR.

Saint-Martin, D. (2000) 'De l'état-providence à l'état d'investissement social?', in L. Pal (ed) *How Ottawa spends 2000-2001: Past imperfect, future tense,* Toronto: Oxford University Press, pp 33-58.

Sumaza, C.R. (2001) 'Lone parent families within New Labour welfare reform', *Contemporary Politics,* vol 7, no 3, pp 231-46.

UNICEF (United Nations Children's Fund) (2000) *A league table of child poverty in rich nations,* Innocenti report card no 1, Florence, Italy: Innocenti Research Centre (www.unicef-icdc.org).

Part Three:
New Labour

A rootless third way: a continental European perspective on New Labour's welfare state, revisited

Daniel Clegg

Introduction: the continental perspective, revisited

A considerable amount of intellectual effort has been devoted to assessing the varying and multi-faceted implications of New Labour's so-called 'third way' for the reorganisation of the British welfare state in recent years. In an abundant and still growing literature, the Blair government's policies and initiatives in the social domain have been picked apart and examined in detail (for example, Powell, 2002). But, in the many fine and fine-grained analyses of different policy areas, the broader question first posed by White (2001) – has New Labour found the key to the 'progressive future' for state welfare? – has tended to be somewhat sidelined. Focusing in policy terms principally on initiatives at the interface between the welfare state and the labour market, this chapter seeks to refocus attention on this question by adopting a macro-political and historical, as well as comparative (cf also Bonoli and Powell, 2003; Lewis and Surender, 2004), perspective on New Labour's search for a new balance between social justice and economic competitiveness 'for the 21st century'. Specifically, it seeks to evaluate the strengths and weaknesses of the Blairite third way against the form of welfare capitalism conventionally practised in the 'conservative-corporatist' or 'Bismarckian' welfare states of continental Europe's heartlands. The chapter's main argument is that this comparison throws light on an insufficiently recognised, and as yet largely unresolved, dilemma facing progressives engaged in social reform – namely, the apparent conflict between the goals of promoting the short-term effectiveness of social policy reform and of ensuring its longer-term political legitimacy or 'solidity'.

Comparisons between British welfare policy 'New Labour style' and continental European social protection have been drawn before, and have tended to emphasise either similarities or differences. In an early attempt to get a comparative and historical 'handle' on the Blairite third way, Marquand (1998) suggested that certain *parallels* could be drawn with the tradition of Christian Democracy that has done so much to shape post-war public policy in much of continental Europe. Navarro (1999) reached a similar conclusion. Likewise, Seeleib-Kaiser (2002) found in New Labour's discourse evidence that they are caught up in what he sees as a broader 'Christian Democratisation' of social democracy in Europe. Importantly, each of these assessments was based as much on the third way's apparent embrace of certain procedural *leitmotifs* related to recasting the role of the state – the promotion of 'community', of 'civil society' and of 'partnership' – as it was on the actual detail of the Blair government's substantive policy orientations. For, with respect to the latter, and particularly through the emphasis on restructuring the work–welfare interface, New Labour hardly seems to have been treading a continental European path.Van Kersbergen and Hemerijck (2004) have recently argued that, as the social policy profiles of continental European states are above all characterised by crippling 'welfare *without* work' passivity, any parallels between them and the British third way are counter-intuitive at best. For these authors, the comparative story is more one of *contrasts*. Rather than being interpreted as a form of alignment of the British welfare state with its continental neighbours, New Labour's agenda should instead be seen as offering some possible solutions to the more glaring programmatic impasses in which many of the latter still find themselves.

When comparing third ways cross-nationally, it is of course important to distinguish clearly between discourses, values and actual policy practices (cf Bonoli and Powell, 2002; Powell, 2003), and in this case British discourses – for example, around themes such as 'partnership' and 'civil society' – have arguably often been compared with continental European practices. Nonetheless, it remains that the continental European social policy tradition has been held up both as the model and prototype for a third way in welfare in certain respects, and as its antithesis in others. This chapter submits that in this apparent paradox there is in fact an important lesson for reflections on the progressive future of social policy in Europe. The key here is to distinguish not between discourses, values and policy mechanisms or goals, but to differentiate between different *types* of goals, and more closely examine their compatibility.

The third way credentials of traditional continental European social policy rest above all on its highly successful institutionalisation of a genuine 'one-nation' consensus around the need to balance economic competitiveness and social solidarity. Such a consensus is crucial to the third way, and almost implicit in the term itself. In continental Europe, it has what could be called its 'roots' in the existence of cooperative and participatory – or 'co-determinative' – social governance institutions, which have traditionally 'taken the edge off' distributive conflict over social policy questions. But these very social governance institutions have become, under fast changing socioeconomic conditions, important obstacles to the pursuit of a certain number of substantive policy reforms, particularly at the interface between the social protection and the labour market (cf Clasen and Clegg, 2004). The British welfare state legacy contained no equivalent machinery for institutionalised power sharing and consensus building and, sporadic participatory rhetoric notwithstanding, New Labour has done little in office to foster its development. The absence of societal embedding, or the 'rootlessness', of British social policy has made the pursuit of a 'new supply-side agenda' (cf Blair and Schröder, 1999) rather less complicated for New Labour than for governments in continental Europe, and explains the comparative effectiveness of recent British reforms in areas like welfare-to-work. But it also raises troubling questions as to the genuine entrenchment of these policies, and the possibilities for building on them on the future. In sum, although promoting short-term effectiveness *in* social policy and building longer-term legitimacy or societal consensus *over* social policy can both be seen as necessary steps on the road to a progressive future in welfare, the comparison between the New Labour experience in Britain and continental European social policy dynamics suggests that these goals are perhaps less easily reconcilable than is often assumed.

This argument is developed more fully across the three main sections that follow. The first of these briefly provides the historical context, contrasting the statism of post-war British social protection with the very explicit attempts in almost all continental European countries to embed social policy in broader social relations via the development of devolved social governance institutions in which private actors were represented and participated actively in social policy development. Section two demonstrates how these institutions today play a somewhat ambiguous role in continental European social policy. While arguably continuing to play a vital part in sustaining the legitimacy of a generic 'middle way' in social policy, it is shown how they have in recent years come into conflict increasingly often with specific programmatic attempts to adapt it to a radically changed labour market context from that existing at the time of their creation. 'Social partnership' has, in short, often worked against pragmatic reform. The New Labour experience with welfare-to-work policies can then be read, it is suggested in the third section, as a sort of mirror image of this continental European dilemma. In the absence of any major governance obstacles, the Blair governments have been able to 'fine tune' the work–welfare interface with relative ease, but for the same reason have been able to fashion only a seedling 'social investment state' that risks, furthermore, proving highly vulnerable to winds of future political change. A final section briefly summarises the argument and draws out some of its implications.

The procedural dimension of 'welfare state' construction: continental Europe and Britain compared

Comparisons of what are commonly referred to as 'welfare states' have, in many respects understandably, tended to concentrate principally on the substance of the social policies that they are made up of, whether this dependent variable is operationalised through social expenditure or through more fine-grained analyses of the eligibility and entitlement criteria in social programmes. However, some of the most conspicuous differences between social protection systems – and particularly between the mid-century welfare state model in Britain, on the one hand, and the comprehensive social security systems established in the same period in continental European states, on the other – are less about substance and content than they are about procedure and process. Nor is this merely a story of different 'means' being used in the pursuit of similar 'ends'. In many of the states of continental Europe, utilising specific procedures and processes for making and administering welfare policy has been an end – or goal – in itself.

This is perhaps most obvious in those countries where the task of welfare system construction and consolidation was, in the immediate post-war years, assumed mainly by Christian Democrats. Christian Democracy is distinguished from competing political ideologies, such as social democracy and liberalism, by having a guiding principle – subsidiarity – that is procedural rather than substantive. In keeping with the principle of subsidiarity, the goal of Christian Democratic social policy was thus more to reinforce the capacity of social actors to regulate society than it was to protect individuals against social risks per se (Van Kersbergen, 1995, 1999). The 'organisational expression' of this aspiration in the welfare sphere was the insistence that normally antagonistic private actors – with respect to the most important areas of social policy at mid-century, essentially trades unions and employers' associations – should assume (or retain) the responsibility for the governance of public social policies (van Kersbergen and Hemerijck, 2004, p 172). In countries with a strong Christian Democratic tradition, such as the Netherlands and Germany, social protection institutions thus developed at least partly autonomously from government, and came to serve a double function: protecting individuals against social risks, and acting as "intermediary organs between state and society" (van Kersbergen, 1999, p 357).

It was not only in those states where Christian Democracy was electorally dominant that the concern with the procedural dimension of social policy manifested itself, however. Christian Democratic parties were never more than a marginal actor in the French political landscape (Kalyvas, 1996). Nonetheless, the construction of the French social protection system was also explicitly premised on using social policy to build the capacity of social actors, ensuring that the direct role of the supposedly omnipotent French state remained limited (Palier, 2001a). In the absence of any explicit reference to subsidiarity, this was justified by the need to establish a form of democracy specific – and 'appropriate' – to the social sphere, something that the French refer to as *démocratie sociale* (social democracy). Like subsidiarity, *démocratie sociale* associated the sphere of social policy with a form of 'input legitimacy' that differed significantly from that on which state action is commonly based, namely representative or parliamentary democracy. Characterising social protection systems based on such assumptions as 'welfare states' is indeed somewhat misleading. Rather than being reduced to a simple activity, among others, of elected govern*ment*, continental European social policy was historically grounded in participatory gover*nance*, in which the role of private actors was less important than the role of public office-holders.

Against this continental European backdrop, the procedural exceptionalism of the Britain's welfare state – and here, the consecrated expression *is* appropriate – model is striking. As Crouch (1999, p 438) has described, the social reforms of the post-war Labour government reflected an "almost Jacobin" belief in the state's "lack of a need to consult with or embed itself in the wider population". In this respect at least, the Labour government largely followed the recommendations of William Beveridge, whose famous report proposed a welfare state based on "a unity of responsibility, management and control within a public service context" (Perrin, 1992, p 44). The result was the creation of what Harris (1992, p 116) has rightly characterised as "one of the most uniform, centralised and bureaucratic and 'public' welfare systems in Europe, and indeed the modern world".

Back in continental Europe, the precise details of social governance arrangements have varied considerably within continental European social policy, both between states and across different policy domains – for example, pensions and unemployment insurance – within the same state (Ebbinghaus, 2002). However, in all continental European social protection systems, public social policy-making space has conventionally been shared to some degree with private actors, and this is a categorical difference with the 'elite-led' British welfare state model (cf Crouch, 1999, p 448). Despite the recent wave of reforms in European social policy, this historical distinction between the British welfare state and the social protection systems of its continental neighbours retains much of its pertinence today. A more explicit evaluation of the strengths and weaknesses of each model seems a crucial dimension of any meaningful reflection on the optimal progressive future for social welfare provision.

The social protection systems of continental Europe: political success and policy failures

The social governance frameworks that underpin the social protection systems of continental Europe have both important virtues and some very real drawbacks. On the one hand, they have played a rather discreet but nonetheless crucial role in moderating the political demands made on, or against, collective social provision. The result has been a widespread societal acceptance of the need to find a balance between social solidarity and economic competitiveness, and a natural coalescence around a model of social citizenship based upon both rights and duties. The social governance of welfare provision has thus long acted as a 'conduit' for the principles that are today expressed by proponents of the third way in Britain. The problem is that the operation of these same institutions has more recently become a constraint on certain attempts to bring the public policies that conventionally concretised these principles into line with a radically changed economic and labour market context.

The most striking political benefit of the social governance structures in continental social protection systems has been in helping to temper employers' hostility to social provision. Granting employers a role in the governance of public social policies was initially crucial – as Mares (2003) has shown in historical research on the French and German cases – in helping to facilitate agreements between organised labour and those sections of capital whose substantive opposition to social security was least resolute. The particular 'variety of capitalism' (cf Hall and Soskice, 2001) that these historical compromises favoured – based on real and durable investments in a skilled and secure workforce – in turn generated an independent dynamic in which social security was aligned with the interests of the great number of employers during the 'thirty glorious years' of welfare expansion after the war. As industrial sectors have declined and pressures for increased flexibility have grown, however, the mediating effect of social governance structures has once again become inherently and directly important. As well as representing the procedural status quo, participation in the governance of social security is a source of key political resources (access to decision makers) and material resources (access to sources of finance) for the organisations representing employers' interests. The result of this is that even the most self-consciously radical proposals for the restructuring of public welfare made by employers in continental European countries will usually articulate policy preferences that are compatible with social governance, and thus intrinsically – if often tortuously – reconcilable with the very different interests of other social actors. The existence of social governance institutions in this way helps to explain why the countries of continental Europe were almost entirely spared any neo-liberal attack on social provision of the kind that characterised the UK and the US, but also some Scandinavian countries, in the 1970s and 1980s.

Inversely, but logically and just as importantly, social governance has also encouraged the moderation of left-wing demands on social welfare. In part because the close relationship between welfare and work justified their participation in social governance institutions, labour movements in continental Europe never fully embraced an ideal of universal social citizenship totally disconnected from labour market status and performance. Even in the years of rapid welfare expansion, access to social protection remained strongly conditioned by labour market status, through the medium of contributory social insurance. A 'lid' was thus kept on demands for the extension of social rights. In the more recent period, social governance has at times also smoothed the path to retrenchment. Once again, it is the French case that perhaps offers the most compelling evidence for this, given that in France, unlike the Netherlands or Germany, the broader industrial relations context does not appear a priori to be well suited to the search for consensus and compromise. But a (shifting) majority of the main five French trade union confederations have, on a number of occasions throughout the 1980s and 1990s, helped to negotiate some very significant cuts in social benefits, notably in the area of unemployment insurance (Daniel, 2000; Clasen and Clegg, 2003). These actors have effectively accepted reductions in benefit and (particularly) coverage rates as the price of maintaining their governance role within unemployment insurance. Organised labour's willingness to swallow otherwise bitter policy pills in return for the maintenance of the social governance status quo can also be seen in other policy areas, such as pensions (cf Bonoli, 2000, pp 50-1), and across a number of continental social protection systems (Natali and Rhodes, 2004).

In short, after facilitating but stabilising the growth of social provision in continental Europe, social governance institutions have on occasions helped to facilitate, but stabilise, its selective retreat. Under governments of both right and left, social policy development has tended to remain relatively 'balanced'. If the 'welfare state' is always a compromise institution, then this compromise has in other words been particularly stable in continental Europe, in no small measure because of the pre-eminent role played by the 'social partners' in welfare regulation. It is in this sense that the continental European model of social protection can be considered a political 'success'.

The now well-known problem faced in continental Europe is that, in a context of profound social and economic change, the costs and benefits of this compromise have been increasingly inequitably distributed. With the progressive tertiarisation of developed economies and the growing social heterogeneity resulting from this, those whose interests are represented by conventional social governance actors are a dwindling minority of the population, but it is they who have nonetheless benefited disproportionately from the adjustment pattern of continental welfare states. As has been well described by Hemerijck et al (2000), under increased competitive pressures the social partners have had incentives to use their managerial control of social protection schemes to create relatively generous 'cushions' for older workers, who are both the main category of unionised workers and whose high wages and dwindling productivity makes them employers' favourite targets in downsizing exercises. Meanwhile, most negotiated cuts to social protection have focused, inversely, on those with the less solid and continuous labour market attachments (for example, younger workers and women). Furthermore, these latter categories find it increasingly difficult to enter stable jobs, and often any job at all, as the rising cost of social protection – caused by population ageing, but also the outlays needed to keep the more privileged sections of the jobless in subsidised long-term inactivity – tends to price them out of jobs, especially as social security in continental Europe is largely financed out of payroll taxes (cf Scharpf, 1997). The result is that continental European countries have followed a 'high productivity-low employment' adjustment path that, irrespective of its economic viability in the medium term, poses increasingly urgent problems of social cohesion in the short term (Esping-Andersen, 1996).

In the crucial short term, policy makers can arguably do little to reverse adjustment patterns that have been internalised by social and economic agents. But they can, in principle, make some seemingly technical adjustments that help to attenuate their most inequitable distributive consequences, and which might eventually set in motion an adjustment trajectory more compatible with the 'general interest'. Here, however, social governance institutions have represented a significant obstacle to reform. Even though widely accepted in principle, for example, suggestions to harmonise various social security schemes more closely with the work of the public employment services, to prevent the former becoming 'inactivity traps', have thus often come up against the unwillingness of the social partners to see the autonomy of social governance institutions undermined. And, as contributory financing provides the rationale for devolved social governance, proposals to shift the financing of social security away from payroll taxes and on to more 'employment friendly' forms of revenue can provoke similar objections (cf Palier, 1999). While the social partners' shared interest in preserving the autonomy of social governance institutions helps them arrive at seemingly difficult agreements over the re-setting of conventional social policy instruments, it also makes them hostile even to apparently distributively anodyne policy proposals which, because they introduce new policy instruments or bring together previously distinct policy domains, challenge the existing division of procedural labour in social and economic policy. The capacity for policy innovation in continental European social protection systems thus seems to be limited by their institutional set-up.

The seemingly obvious solution to these problems of policy coordination is to reduce the influence of autonomous social governance institutions and increase the role of the state. This indeed resumes fairly well the procedural thrust of much social policy reform in continental European countries in recent years (Wierink, 2000; Palier, 2001b; Vail, 2003; Häusermann et al, 2004). But the move towards greater statism in social protection has been tentative – or 'fumbling' (cf Jobert, 1996) – and is still far from total; and this is not only because elected politicians have lacked the courage to take on entrenched cross-class interests. The stability of the continental European-style social contract is perhaps too often dismissed as evidence of 'conservatism'. Regardless of the obstacles that it might put in the way of technically optimal social policy design implemented through 'clean', top-down reform, encouraging the 'ownership' of social compromise by collective interests, and through them by the majority of citizens they (ideally) represent, is an ambition to which many progressives on the European continent in fact remain strongly attached. Although the difficult search for a new model of social governance may complicate the path to straightforward programmatic reform, this often appears to be seen as the price that must be paid for the elaboration of a modernised social compromise that will have 'staying power'. If this is indeed the case, then progressives in Britain may very possibly come to regret the fact that New Labour's third way has rarely paid more than lip-service to the goal of institutionalising consensus and power-sharing.

New Labour's 'third welfare state way': from policy successes to political failure?

Except in its most restrictive sense, social compromise was never really a feature of post-war British social politics and social policy, except perhaps in the few very immediate post-war years. Even during the largely stillborn efforts to develop a British-style corporatism in the 1960s – the era of 'beer and sandwiches at number 10' – social policy was rarely on the menu. The somewhat nostalgic notion of a longer-lasting 'post-war consensus' has come to be increasingly challenged by historians, particularly with reference to the welfare state (Lowe, 1993). In fact, it could indeed be said that the lack of any institutional articulation between industrial relations and social policy led inevitably to the relationship between 'the economic' and 'the social' being seen in zero-sum, oppositional terms (cf Rhodes, 2000). The British Labour movement's lack of institutionalised commitment to what elsewhere came to be perceived as the 'social wage' meant that, as the post-war decades passed, social policy issues were increasingly articulated essentially in terms of social rights by the political left in Britain, which thus turned its back on the more reciprocal vision of solidarity that had inspired William Beveridge. This rights-based discourse in turn paradoxically legitimised and inspired the notion that social provision was a 'burden' on the economy, the sort of argument that helped to stymie the expansion of the British welfare state in the post-war decades and, under the Conservative governments of the 1980s and early 1990s, played a crucial role in its retrenchment.

New Labour's third way for welfare seemed set to challenge this legacy on at least two levels. First and more obviously, the 'welfare-to-work' agenda that was central to the third way broke openly with attachment to unconditional social rights that had become so important to the British left by the 1970s. This was captured in the expression "no rights without responsibilities", the first 'rule of thumb' for third way politics identified by New Labour's intellectual *eminence grise*, Anthony Giddens (1998, p

64). The practical translation of this principle fed into some clear, 'no-nonsense' policy proposals; "unemployment benefits, for example," wrote Giddens (1998, p 5), "should carry the obligation to look for work, and it is up to governments to ensure that welfare systems do not discourage active search". But on a second, and today less often remembered level, the British third way also initially presented itself as a vehicle for "political emancipation and a more meaningful form of democracy in terms of involving citizens in the political process" (Schmidtke, 2002, p 13). This was the sense of Giddens' second 'rule of thumb', "no authority without democracy" (Giddens, 1998, p 72), with its implicit critique of classic, representative forms of democratic legitimisation. In the social domain, such ideas resulted in essentially procedural recommendations along the lines that "the reconstruction of welfare provision has to be integrated with programmes for the active development of civil society" (1998, pp 117-18), and the revitalisation of calls for the transition from a 'welfare state' to a 'welfare society' (1998, p 117).

At least on the surface, then, the ambition of the third way thus seemed to be to not *merely* to offer welfare *policies* that broke with those promoted under the 'dutiless individualism' of either neo-liberalism or British 1970s-style social democracy (cf Plant, 1998), but *also* to create the framework for a radically different form of welfare *politics* from that which had nourished these dutiless individualisms in the first place. In this respect, the third way at first looked like a new label for the idea of the 'stakeholder society'. This concept – which New Labour used liberally in a brief period just prior to their first General Election victory (see especially, Labour Party, 1996, pp 8-9) – was first popularised in Will Hutton's (1995) critical analysis of the organisation of the British political economy, which argued for changes in the procedures of both corporate and political governance that were inspired largely by the perceived superiority of the 'Rhineish' or continental European experience.

It is the first of the two levels of the British third way's initial agenda for the reform of social provision that has received the bulk of attention in academic analyses, and understandably so; it has also received by far the most attention in the social policy initiatives of the Blair governments to date. From the 'New Deals' through the massive expansion of in-work tax credits to the street-level integration of labour market and social security services, 'no rights (to social support) without responsibilities (to work)' has offered New Labour a coherent macro-narrative for concrete reforms that have sought to re-work – and in certain cases dissolve – the frontier between social provision and labour market policy. The 2002 government policy paper, *Full and fulfilling employment*, even explicitly cites the notion of 'rights and responsibilities', calling it a "fusion ... central to delivering work for those who can and security for those who cannot" (DTI, 2002, p 59).

During the same period, erstwhile hopes for a fundamental shake-up in the procedural framework for British social policy making have been consistently disappointed. Although Frank Field was in 1997 named Minister for Welfare Reform and asked to 'think the unthinkable', it was soon clear that his stakeholding-inspired ideas for an overhaul of the British welfare state, organised around the development of devolved and cooperatively managed social insurance (cf Field, 1996), were a little too unthinkable for New Labour realists (cf Driver and Martell, 2002, p 68). If anything, social policy has actually become *more* centralised and state-led under New Labour, reinforcing British exceptionalism not only with respect to their continental European neighbours, but also relative to states such as Ireland that have more recently embraced participatory forms of social governance (Jobert, 2002, pp 419-20; Daly and Yeates, 2003, p 95). The British third way is still a 'welfare state way'. Although Tony Blair repeatedly extols the virtues of 'enabling government' (for example, Blair, 2003), in British social policy practice under New Labour this has, at least at the national level, essentially been interpreted in the very narrow, individualistic sense of the government enabling – if not forcing – individuals to work (or train, save for retirement and so on) through the 'intelligent' deployment of incentives and sanctions in public policy. 'Partnership' in social policy has meanwhile been largely reduced to the use of private firms and voluntary organisations at the delivery level, a continuation of a pre-existing trend towards 'contracting out' that, as Crouch (2004, pp 100-1) has recently argued, is premised upon and reinforces "a Jacobin model of centralised democracy and a citizenship without intermediate levels of political action". At least in the most directly 'economic' and historically centralised domains of the British welfare state (social security and labour market policy), 'partnership', 'civil society' and 'democratising democracy' seem to have been little more than empty slogans designed to legitimise an essentially technocratic form of political steering for social policy (Rummery, 2002, p 243).

The Blair governments' unwillingness to relinquish the levers of policy control is in many ways quite understandable. The centralised, 'elitist' framework of British social policy has always rendered systemic reform relatively uncomplicated (Crouch, 1999, p 440), and thus represents a valuable institutional resource for governments seeking to enact specific policies. With respect to social security and labour market policy, this policy-making framework has facilitated the adoption of reforms that –

however insistently the third way rhetoric of the Blair government endeavours to play up their originality – lie squarely within the pragmatic agenda of 'compensated commodification' or 'flexibility plus' that has been gradually taking form in the recommendations of social policy specialists and international organisations since the early 1990s at least (cf Clasen and Clegg, 2004, pp 92-4). As Bonoli and Powell (2002, p 64) note, the capacity of the Labour government to adopt these reforms has been enhanced by the fact that there have been "few alliances, social pacts and social partners to stand in the way", as they so often have done in continental European countries. Inversely, Lewis (2004) has pointed out that in sectors of the British welfare state where (albeit rather different) forms of 'partnership' *do* actually exist (personal social services, childcare), they have tended to represent a real constraint on the pursuit of substantive policy objectives.

Unsurprisingly, technocratic political steering has improved the 'output efficiency' of British public policies at the work–welfare interface. After nearly two full terms of New Labour government, UK unemployment is at its lowest level for 25 years, while employment levels have reached an all-time high. The combination of a consistently dynamic and flexible labour market and the New Deal for young people has furthermore facilitated the all-but-total eradication, since 1997, of long-term unemployment among the under-25s. Intensive investment in a variety of tax credits has helped to 'make work pay' (better) even within a deregulated labour market, and contributed to a sharp diminution in poverty rates among certain groups, particularly working parents (Brewer et al, 2004). The flexible, 'evidence-based' targeting of labour market measures such as the various 'options' within the New Deal programme have allowed the substitution effects that so often bedevil such programmes to be largely avoided (White and Riley, 2002). The Jobcentre Plus initiative, through which the delivery of benefits to all working-age people has now been linked to the provision of individualised labour market counselling, has been repeatedly presented as a model in recent debates over unemployment protection reforms in both France and Germany. In short, through programmatic and administrative reform, New Labour has been able to enhance equity on a number of fronts while adhering to a stable macroeconomic and relatively restrictive fiscal policy.

For two overlapping reasons, however, some scepticism is admissible regarding claims that New Labour has laid the foundations for an optimal new compromise between competitiveness and solidarity. The first of these relates to the social limits of their initiatives to date. Notwithstanding a context of steady economic growth and the government's capacity to 'fine tune' policy instruments at will, the New Deals, for example, have done little to reverse the sharp increase in inactivity among unskilled, working-age men, which had been seen under the Conservatives (Faggio and Nickell, 2003; Gregg and Wadsworth, 2003). Among the young, they have had difficulty in helping those with the highest barriers to employment (Finn, 2003). In both examples, the central problem is funding. Even under New Labour, active labour market policy has commanded far lower resources in Britain than in most of its European neighbours (cf Powell and Barrientos, 2004) – including almost all the purportedly 'passive' continental countries, as well as some states, such as Denmark, where unemployment is very low – and has thus placed little emphasis on more resource-intensive objectives such as skill formation (Clasen, 2005). To date, the New Deal has been a "modest success at modest cost" (Blundell et al, 2003, p 18). It is widely recognised that further progress in improving equality of opportunity in the labour market – 'converting the try' of the first two terms of social security and labour market reform – will require greatly increased investment.

While it might be argued that the 'plus' side of the 'flexibility plus' equation can be built up over time and into the future, it is here that a second, more political, misgiving regarding New Labour's reform model becomes pertinent: it is not clear that there is much structural glue holding the compromise together. New Labour's very explicit break with the ideals of the British left in the 1970s and 1980s – making use of the 'counter-scheduling' tactic also employed by Clinton's Democrats in the US (King and Wickham-Jones, 1999) – may have temporarily restored its electoral credibility among voters of the centre and right. For the moment, furthermore, these voters seem to appreciate the pragmatic 'what works' approach taken by New Labour, allowing the party to have a degree of electoral success that is the envy of centre-left parties elsewhere in Europe (cf Bonoli, 2003). But, skilfully playing the political game is not the same as changing the terms of the game itself. Should New Labour endeavour to mobilise the significant resources needed for a more ambitious social investment strategy, they would clearly open a larger window of political opportunity for the Conservative opposition. Indeed, in the absence of any real 'attachment' of business or other societal interests to programmes like the New Deal, the British right may well see its interest to be in the search for a compelling narrative with which to sell their dismantlement. The announcement at the 2004 Conservative Party conference that the 'lamentable' New Deal would be scrapped by a future Tory government suggests this search is already underway. Should it prove successful, then even the current modest levels of investment in the unemployed – 'productive' or otherwise – will quickly be vulnerable. In short, although New Labour may have tried to promote a "depoliticised politics" (Newman, 2004, p 84), they have done little structurally – at least in the domain of social security and labour market policy – to avert the eventual re-emergence of partisan conflict over social policy.

Conclusion: the virtues and limits of a rootless third way

The comparison with continental European social policy arguably brings both the most important virtues *and* the most serious limits of the British third way, as a progressive agenda for the reform of the welfare state, into particularly sharp focus. On the positive side of the equation, the policies that have been pursued by the Blair governments seem, at least in the domains of work and welfare, to have been more responsive to the 'general interest' within a post-industrialising economy and society than the policy trajectory followed in most continental European countries. On the negative side, however, a basic commitment to the reconciliation of social and economic goals still appears to be far more widely and deeply shared on the European continent, even if under new conditions the fruits of this consensus are often no longer either economically or socially virtuous. The conclusion that results from this comparison of recent social policy developments in Britain and continental Europe can be rephrased as a 'progressive dilemma'; while statism seems to be the most reactive and flexible framework for effective social policy development, policies developed within this framework will, lacking any roots in broader society, be inherently vulnerable to conflict and contestation.

Having arguably long used the language of partnership as a camouflage for essentially technocratic political steering, there are signs that within New Labour itself there is a growing openness about the virtues of Britain's welfare centralisation from a social policy-making perspective, as well as growing concern about its political limits. On the one hand, a recent Department of Trade and Industry publication pointed out that in Britain, "unlike many other countries, most social benefits are paid centrally by governments rather than by the social partners of local government. This makes a 'rights and responsibilities' or 'activation' agenda possible as the central delivery of help and support can be linked to the administration of paying benefits" (DTI, 2002, p 60). On the other hand, however, the dispersion of power and responsibility over public policy is increasingly presented within Blairite 'progressive politics' circles as a means of building trust and legitimacy, and ensuring that New Labour's policies will be 'legacy policies' (for example, Browne and Thompson, 2003). The growing interest in a 'new localism' can be seen in this context. What is still lacking, however, is any compelling model of how centrally defined core policy goals might be 'steered' or 'levered' within a devolved policy-making framework drawing in multiple stakeholders with conflicting interests (cf also Lewis, 2004, p 224).

Although the British experience undoubtedly carries some important lessons for social policy makers on the European continent, in this last respect New Labour may in turn benefit from observing ongoing adjustment of the social governance arrangements prevalent in continental Europe. This could seem a paradoxical suggestion, given that social governance is currently 'under pressure'. Not only has it, as shown earlier, acted as a clear brake on the pursuit of some 'general interest' policies in recent years but, in sustaining an increasingly inequitable and exclusive mainstream consensus, it may also have contributed to enhancing the electoral appeal of those whose political ideas are situated defiantly and definitively outwith the political mainstream. But, precisely because of the growing urgency of the challenges, attempts to rework the continental European social compromise have been gathering pace in recent years. One important question that has arisen is, short of reclaiming unique control of social policy, how can the state deploy its authority to ensure that collective actors sharing public space act in the interest of the whole public, and not their narrower constituencies? A related question is, beyond the conventional 'social partners', how can the representation of a broader variety of interests be assured within a reformed social and labour market governance framework? Neither of these questions has an obvious answer, but close examination of the inevitably laborious and drawn out attempts to update social compromises in continental Europe is likely to provide the best clues. If these institutionalised social compromises can be updated without being uprooted, it may be there that the contours of the true success stories – that is, both policy and political successes – of the next phase of welfare state development will begin to emerge.

References

Blair, T. (2003) *Where the third way goes from here*, launch text for the 2003 'Progressive Governance' Conference, London, April (www.progressive-governance.net/php/article.php?sid=9&aid=35).

Blair, T. and Schröder, G. (1999) *Europe: The third way/Die neue mitte*, London: The Labour Party.

Blundell, R., Reed, H., Van Reenan, J. and Shephard, A. (2003) 'The impact of the New Deal for young people on the labour market: a four-year assessment', in R. Dickens, P. Gregg and J. Wadsworth (eds) *The labour market under New Labour*, Basingstoke: Macmillan, pp 17-31.

Bonoli, G. (2000) *The politics of pension reform: Institutions and policy change in Western Europe*, Cambridge: Cambridge University Press.

Bonoli, G. (2003) 'Social democratic party policies in Europe: towards a third way?', in G. Bonoli and M. Powell (eds) *Social democratic party policies in contemporary Europe*, London: Routledge, pp 197-213.

Bonoli, G. and Powell, M. (2002) 'Third ways in Europe?', *Social Policy and Society*, vol 1, no 1, pp 59-66.

Bonoli, G. and Powell, M. (2003) *Social democratic party policies in contemporary Europe*, London: Routledge.

Brewer, M., Goodman, A., Myck, M., Shaw, J. and Shephard, A. (2004) *Poverty and inequality in Britain: 2004*, Institute for Fiscal Studies (IFS) Commentaries C96, February, London: IFS.

Browne, M. and Thompson, P. (2003) 'Trust and legitimacy: why the left needs to learn to share power!', *Progressive Politics*, vol 2, no 2.

Clasen, J. (2005) 'From unemployment to worklessness: the transformation of British unemployment policy', in J. Clasen, M. Ferrera and M. Rhodes (eds) *Welfare states and the challenge of unemployment: Reform policies and institutions in the European Union*, London: Routledge.

Clasen, J. and Clegg, D. (2003) 'Unemployment protection and labour market reform in France and Great Britain: solidarity versus activation?', *Journal of Social Policy*, vol 32, no 3, pp 361-81.

Clasen, J. and Clegg, D. (2004) 'Does the third way work? The left and labour market policy reform in Britain, France and Germany', in J. Lewis and R. Surender (eds) *Welfare state change: Towards a third way?*, Oxford: Oxford University Press, pp 89-110.

Crouch, C. (1999) 'Employment, industrial relations and social policy: new life in an old connection', *Social Policy and Administration*, vol 33, no 4, pp 437-57.

Crouch, C. (2001) 'Welfare state regimes and industrial relations systems: the questionable role of path dependency theory', in B. Ebbinghaus and P. Manow (eds) *Comparing welfare capitalism: Social policy and political economy in Europe, Japan and the USA*, London: Routledge, pp 105-24.

Crouch, C. (2004) *Post-democracy*, Cambridge: Polity.

Daly, M. and Yeates, N. (2003) 'Common origins, different paths: adaptation and change in social security in Britain and Ireland', *Policy & Politics*, vol 31, no 1, pp 85-97.

Daniel, C. (2000) 'L'indemnisation du chômage depuis 1974: d'une logique d'intégration à une logique de segmentation', *Revue Française des Affaires Sociales*, vol 54, nos 3-4, pp 29-46.

Driver, S. and Martell, L. (2002) *Blair's Britain*, Cambridge: Polity.

DTI (Department of Trade and Industry) (2002) *Full and fulfilling employment: Creating the labour market of the future*, London: DTI.

Ebbinghaus, B. (2002) *Varieties of social governance: Comparing the social partners' involvement in pension and employment policies*, Max Planck Institute for the Study of Societies Working Paper, Cologne: MPIfG.

Esping-Andersen, G. (1996) 'Welfare states without work: the impasse of labour shedding and familialism in continental European social policy', in G. Esping-Andersen (ed) *Welfare states in transition*, London: Sage Publications, pp 66-87.

Faggio, G. and Nickell, S. (2003) 'The rise in inactivity among adult men', in R. Dickens, P. Gregg and J. Wadsworth (eds) *The labour market under New Labour*, Basingstoke: Macmillan, pp 40-52.

Field, F. (1996) *Stakeholder welfare*, London: Institute for Economic Affairs.

Finn, D. (2003) 'The employment-first welfare state: lessons from the New Deal for young people', *Social Policy and Administration*, vol 37, no 7, pp 709-24.

Giddens, A. (1998) *The third way: The renewal of social democracy*, Cambridge: Polity.

Gregg, P. and Wadsworth, J. (2003) 'Workless households and the recovery', in R. Dickens, P. Gregg and J. Wadsworth (eds) *The labour market under New Labour*, Basingstoke: Macmillan, pp 32-9.

Hall, P. and Soskice, D. (eds) (2001) *Varieties of capitalism: The institutional foundations of comparative advantage*, Oxford: Oxford University Press.

Harris, J. (1992) 'Political thought and the welfare state 1870-1940: an intellectual framework for British social policy', *Past and Present*, no 135, pp 116-41.

Häusermann, S., Mach, A. and Papadopoulos, Y. (2004) 'From corporatism to partisan politics: social policy making under strain in Switzerland', *Swiss Political Science Review*, vol 10, no 2, pp 33-59.

Hemerijck, A., Manow, P. and Van Kersbergen, K. (2000) 'Welfare without work: divergent experiences of reform in Germany and the Netherlands', in S. Kuhnle (ed) *The survival of the European welfare state*, London: Routledge, pp 106-27.

Hutton, W. (1995) *The state we're in*, London: Jonathan Cape.

Jobert, B. (1996) 'Le retour tâtonnant de l'etat', in F. d'Arcy and L. Rouban (eds) *De la cinquième république à l'Europe: Hommage à Jean-Louis Quermonne*, Paris: Presses de Sciences Po, pp 315-28.

Jobert, B. (2002) 'Une troisième voie trés britannique: Giddens et l'etat providence', *Revue Française de Sociologie*, vol 43, no 2, pp 407-22.

Kalyvas, S. (1996) *The rise of Christian Democracy in Europe*, Ithica, NY: Cornell.

King, D. and Wickham-Jones, M. (1999) 'Bridging the Atlantic: the Democratic (Party) origins of welfare-to-work', in M. Powell (ed) *New Labour, new welfare state? The 'third way' in British social policy*, Bristol: The Policy Press, pp 257-80.

Labour Party (1996) *New Labour: New life for Britain*, London: Labour Party.

Lewis, J. (2004) 'What is New Labour? Can it deliver on social policy?', in J. Lewis and R. Surender (eds) *Welfare state change: Towards a third way?*, Oxford: Oxford University Press, pp 207-27.

Lewis, J. and Surender, R. (eds) (2004) *Welfare state change: Towards a third way?*, Oxford: Oxford University Press.

Lowe, R. (1993) *The welfare state in Britain since 1945*, Basingstoke: Macmillan.

Mares, I. (2003) *The politics of social risk: Business and welfare state development*, Cambridge: Cambridge University Press.

Marquand, D. (1998) 'The Blair paradox', *Prospect*, no 30, May, pp 19-24.

Natali, D. and Rhodes, M. (2004) *The new politics of the Bismarckian welfare state: Pension reforms in continental Europe*, EUI working paper 04/10, Florence: European University Institute.

Navarro, V. (1999) 'Is there a third way?', *International Journal of Health Services*, vol 29, no 4, pp 667-77.

Newman, J. (2004) 'Modernising the state: a new style of governance?', in J. Lewis and R. Surender (eds) *Welfare state change: Towards a third way?*, Oxford: Oxford University Press, pp 69-88.

Palier, B. (1999) *Du salaire différé aux charges sociales: Les avatars du mode de financement du système français de sécurité sociale*, EUI Working Paper, EUF 99/11, Florence: European University Institute.

Palier, B. (2001a) 'De la démocratie à la refondation sociale', *Informations Sociales*, no 95, pp 80-95.

Palier, B. (2001b) 'Reshaping the policy-making framework in France', in P. Taylor-Gooby (ed) *Welfare states under pressure*, London: Sage Publications, pp 52-74.

Perrin, G. (1992) 'The Beveridge Plan: the main principles', *International Social Security Review*, vol 45, nos 1-2, pp 39-52.

Plant, R. (1998) *New Labour: A third way?*, London: European Policy Forum.

Powell, M. (ed) (2002) *Evaluating New Labour's welfare reforms*, Bristol: The Policy Press.

Powell, M. (2003) 'Social democracy in Europe: renewal or retreat?', in G. Bonoli and M. Powell (eds) *Social democratic party policies in contemporary Europe*, London: Routledge, pp 1-20.

Powell, M. and Barrientos, A. (2004) 'Welfare regimes and the welfare mix', *European Journal of Political Research*, vol 43, no 1, pp 85-105.

Rhodes, M. (2000) 'Desperately seeking a solution: social democracy, Thatcherism and the "third way" in British welfare', *West European Politics*, vol 23, no 2, pp 161-86.

Rummery, K. (2002) 'Towards a theory of welfare partnerships', in C. Glendinning, M. Powell and K. Rummery (eds) *Partnerships, New Labour and the governance of welfare*, Bristol: The Policy Press, pp 229-45.

Scharpf, F. (1997) *Employment and the welfare state: A continental dilemma?*, Max Planck Institute for the Study of Societies Working Paper, Cologne: MPIfG.

Schmidtke, O. (2002) 'Transforming the social democratic left: the challenges to third way politics in an age of globalisation', in O. Schmidtke (ed) *The third way transformation of social democracy*, Aldershot: Ashgate, pp 3-27.

Seeleib-Kaiser, M. (2002) 'Neubeginn oder ender der sozialdemocratie? Eine untersuchung zer programmatischen reform sozialdemokratischer parteien und ihrer auswirking auf die parteiendifferenzthese', *Politische Vierteljahresschrift*, vol 43, no 3, pp 478-96.

Vail, M. (2003) 'Rethinking corporatism and consensus: the dilemmas of German social protection reform', *West European Politics*, vol 26, no 3, pp 41-66.

Van Kersbergen, K. (1995) *Social capitalism: A study of Christian Democracy and the welfare state*, London: Routledge.

Van Kersbergen, K. (1999) 'Contemporary Christian Democracy and the demise of the politics of mediation', in H. Kitschelt, P. Lange, G. Marks and J. Stephens (eds) *Continuity and change in contemporary capitalism*, Cambridge: Cambridge University Press, pp 346-70.

Van Kersbergen, K. and Hemerijck, A. (2004) 'Christian Democracy, social democracy and the continental "welfare without work" syndrome', in N. Ellison, L. Bauld and M. Powell (eds) *Social Policy Review 16*, Bristol, The Policy Press/Social Policy Association, pp 167-86.

White, M. and Riley, R. (2002) *Findings from the macro-evaluation of the New Deal for young people*, London: DWP.

White, S. (ed) (2001) *New Labour: The progressive future?*, Basingstoke: Macmillan.

Wierink, M. (2000) 'Réforme des structures de la protection sociale et révision de la place des partenaires sociaux', *Chronique Internationale de l'IRES*, no 64, pp 26-38.

THIRTEEN

Welfare after Thatcherism: New Labour and social democratic politics

Stephen Driver

Introduction

New Labour promised to be a radical government – a government that would chart a 'third way' between 'old left' and 'New Right'; a government that would 'think the unthinkable' on welfare reform. New Labour has never been short of political ambition. But where have these ambitions taken the Labour government over two terms in power? Is this a government of neo-liberals or neo-social democrats? This chapter will argue that the Labour government has taken welfare beyond Thatcherism. It has put egalitarian policy making back on the political agenda, and the debate around choice and diversity in the public services marks an attempt to re-think collective public services within the social democratic tradition.

Welfare and the making of New Labour

Social policy has been at the heart of much of what might be thought of as new about New Labour. During the party's policy review after 1987, it was clear that Labour modernisers had little ambition to defend the welfare state status quo. This was partly about politics. While voters wanted good schools and hospitals, they did not appear to like voting for a party with a reputation for taxing and spending. In the run-up to the 1992 General Election, Labour's leaders endlessly repeated the mantra that a Labour government would only spend what it earned – a foretaste of Labour's strategy during the 1997 campaign. Unfortunately in 1992, the party's fiscal message was blown apart by 'Labour's tax bombshell':

raising taxes to pay for higher pensions and child benefit. This was not a mistake that New Labour would make.

Tony Blair, when Shadow Home Secretary, had done his bit to shift public perceptions. Labour: soft on crime? Not a chance. But behind the hard sell was some hard thinking on what a government of the left should do about the welfare state. Blair, as party leader, enthusiastically endorsed the final report from the Commission on Social Justice, set up by his predecessor, John Smith, which called for a radical change in centre-left social policy.

The central theme of this new direction was that a Labour government should use the welfare state to promote work not welfare. This demanded reforms to social administration, as well as to the rights and responsibilities of citizens to welfare entitlements. More education and training to boost human capital, as well as more family and childcare support to promote opportunities for the poorer sections of the community, were central to this new agenda for social justice. A better-educated and better-trained workforce, supported by a social security system that helped the unemployed back into work, would deliver social justice *and* economic success (Commission on Social Justice, 1994).

Many of these themes were not exactly new to 'old' European social democracy. Swedish social democracy had been constructed on a welfare settlement that demanded responsibilities from those receiving welfare in return for the state's active labour market policies. But they were controversial in the British social democratic context that had supported welfare rights and a strong sense that those on welfare should be provided with generous benefits without strings attached (see Deacon and Mann, 1999).

Many on the left condemned the Commission on Social Justice as a sell out to the New Right (see Cohen, 1994). Labour, the left accused, had not only abandoned the means to deliver social justice but any real socialist value of social justice. Equality? What equality? Those leading the reforms were unrepentant. Blair, in a 1995 lecture to the Fabian Society celebrating 50 years of what he called "the greatest peacetime government this century", told his audience that Labour had to move on, whatever its past achievements. "We need a new settlement on welfare for a new age," Blair said, "where opportunity and responsibility go together." The party's new social policies, he continued, "should and will cross the old boundaries between left and right, progressive and conservative" (Blair, 1995, pp 2, 14). This was not exactly a message for Labour's core voters – or socialist academics.

In the run-up to the General Election, Labour made a virtue out of *not* arguing for extra funding for health, education and social security. Reform of the welfare state could be achieved without significant increases in public expenditure – and thus higher taxes. Services and standards could be improved in other ways. This was all part of 'thinking the unthinkable' on welfare reform. During the election campaign, Blair and Brown went out of their way to bury Labour's image as a tax-and-spend party. As Labour's manifesto put it: "The level of public spending is no longer the best measure of the effectiveness of government action in the public interest. It is what money is actually spent on that counts more than how much money is spent ... New Labour will be wise spenders, not big spenders".

The Conservative legacy

Labour's return to government in 1997 and its two terms in office have to be set in the context of 18 years of Conservative government after 1979, as well as a broader picture of massive economic, social and cultural change. The governments of Margaret Thatcher and John Major set about reforming the welfare state. In many ways, they had to. Or at least they had to do something to address the accumulation of problems facing the welfare state and British society in the late 1970s. These were challenges that Labour ministers and social democratic writers wrestled with in the dog days of the Callaghan government. These problems were not unique to Britain. Promoting growth without sparking inflation; lengthening dole queues; facing up to the new international division of labour; financing social provision; improving the quality of public services; addressing changing patterns of family, community and cultural life: these were problems that parties on the left and right the world over were having to come to terms with and find politically convincing answers for.

In Britain, the Tories got there first. Their approach was hardly consensus conservatism. This was radical Tory politics that fused classical liberalism with traditional conservative themes. This radicalism was much in evidence as Conservative ministers set about the welfare state, even if their reforms fell short of what many of their supporters urged – and what critics feared.

Central to these reforms was to make the supply of welfare subject to market (or market-like) forces. This was done in three ways. First, the Conservatives introduced internal or quasi markets into public sector organisations – health and education being the main test beds for these reforms. The objectives of these reforms were to raise standards and efficiency by attaching resource allocation to consumer choice (parents and patients) and encouraging providers (schools and hospitals) to compete for these resources.

Second, the Conservatives sought to bring private investment and private provision into the public sector through public–private partnerships and by encouraging private welfare in areas such as pensions and housing. Public–private partnerships were developed across the public sector, including health, education and the prison service. Public–private partnerships were part of a third area of Conservative reforms to public sector provision: the introduction of private sector management, either directly or indirectly, to the provision of public services.

These reforms to the supply of welfare were accompanied by attempts to restrict entitlements to, and control public spending on, welfare. Both were high on the New Right agenda to limit welfare dependency and promote an enterprise economy. But neither was altogether successful in terms of government objectives. While entitlements to some social security such as unemployment benefit were tightened, other forms of welfare were introduced that increased dramatically, such as disability benefits. The growth of means testing did little to lift the net of welfare dependency. Attempts to control public spending on welfare, despite changes such as the switch from earnings-related to prices-related benefits, were little more successful. The best that can be said is that Conservatives slowed the growth in public spending. The government's share of national income still averaged 44% during these Conservative years.

Where did these years of Tory reforms leave Labour? If we strip away all the specific pledges made in 1997 to cut primary school class sizes and hospital waiting lists, when Labour returned to power it promised two basic things. First, Labour would not govern like Labour governments had done in the past by just taxing and spending. Labour could tackle poverty and social exclusion, and improve public services in other ways. Second, Labour would move Britain on from the market-based reforms of the Thatcher/Major years. Labour would 'modernise' the welfare state, not privatise it, finding new ways to deliver collective services.

Both promises, of course, were highly political. Past Labour governments had not just taxed and spent; and the Conservatives had not abandoned – and were not about to in 1997 – the welfare state for the market. But both commitments said something important about the political identity of New Labour – and how a New Labour government might reform the welfare state. If Labour were going to deliver, it would have to find some way of tackling the issues that Labour and the left had always addressed, while at the same time dealing with the legacy of 18 years of Conservative government.

Taxing and spending

Labour's initial response to dealing with the Conservative legacy was strictly short term: stick to Kenneth Clarke's fiscal plans. Combined with the long-term move to cede control of monetary policy to the Bank of England, this helped reassure sceptics that this was a Labour government that knew what to do with the economic levers of power. The 'windfall tax' on the privatised utilities did, as promised, fund the New Deal; and Gordon Brown found extra money (£2.2 billion) for health and education from the contingency fund in 1999. Otherwise, this was Gordon Brown at his most prudent. During the first term, the annual increase in public spending fell to 1.3%. By 1999, the share of government spending as a proportion of gross domestic product (GDP) had fallen to 37.4% – a 30-year low.

The 2000 comprehensive spending review changed all this. Along with the government's monetary policy and constitutional reforms, the review stands as one of the defining features of Labour in power over two terms. Public spending was back on the political agenda and it would stay there until the 2005 election.

In 1997, Labour inherited a growing economy. By 2000, Treasury coffers were filling as strong growth, higher taxes and tax takes increased government revenues. The current account was in surplus. The three-year review set out the government's spending plans for the rest of the Parliament and beyond. The package committed Labour to increase public expenditure by £68 billion over three years – the equivalent of more than £1,000 for every person in the country (Dilnot and Emmerson, 2000). After three years of a shrinking state, the size of government was set to grow again. Following the 2000 spending review, the rate of increase in public spending rose during the second term of the Blair government to 4.5% per year. The share of national income being spent by the government increased to 41.5% by 2004 (Chote et al, 2004). However, this remains substantially below the average for European Union member states prior to enlargement in 2004.

Where did all the extra money go? The big winners after 2000 were those areas of public policy closest to voters' hearts. Since the 2000 review, there have been big increases in spending on health and education – both averaging a little above or below 7% a year. With Labour's commitments to expand further nursery places for two-year-olds and to build children's centres in every community, education, like health, did well again in the 2004 review, with annual real spending set to grow by 5.2%. These increases in spending on health and education, as well as housing subsidies, were twice as valuable to those on the lowest incomes as top earners in 2000-01 (Hills, 2004).

While the 2004 spending review planned increases on health and education beyond Labour's second term, the review did mark a tightening of Labour's spending plans. If Labour do win a third term, overall public spending growth is planned to fall from 6.6% in 2003 to an annual rate of 4% until 2006 and 2.7% thereafter. In terms of social policy, the big loser will be social services: the growth in spending will fall from 6% per year in 2003 to under 2% in 2007-08 – a growth rate below the rate of growth of the economy.

Since 2000, economic growth rates have ensured that Labour's spending plans have not broken the Treasury's golden rules on public borrowing over the economic cycle. Despite recent widespread concerns (for example, Ernst & Young, 2005) that the government was on course to break its fiscal rules, and for taxes and borrowing to increase further (or public spending to be cut more than planned), Gordon Brown's reputation as a prudent chancellor with a purpose is (just about) intact. But how effective has all this spending been in tackling those issues central to Labour and social democratic politics? The next section will examine Labour's record on poverty, social exclusion and equality, before looking at the reform of public services.

Poverty, social exclusion – and the question of equality

Central to Conservative reforms to the welfare state was making work more attractive than welfare. This was done by tightening entitlements, cutting benefit rates and piloting welfare to work. But has Labour set a political agenda for welfare beyond Thatcherism: one that combines a commitment to poverty reduction and social inclusion as well as to equality and social justice? Or has New Labour, as Andrew Glyn and Stewart Wood have argued, "disentangled the traditional social democratic aims of promoting equality and eliminating poverty in ways that many on the left find both unacceptable (in respect of greater inequality in the top half of the distribution) and unconvincing (in respect of the near-exclusive emphasis on the labour market)" (Glyn and Wood, 2001, p 65)?

Central to Labour's anti-poverty drive was to get the unemployed and the economically inactive back into work (HM Treasury, 1998). Essentially, poverty would be addressed through the labour market, not the benefit system. This required Labour re-thinking social security entitlements, part of its wider rights and responsibilities agenda. Labour modernisers argued that post-war social democracy had neglected the responsibilities of those in receipt of state help. Instead, the government should promote a clearer balance between the duties of the state to provide welfare and the duties of the welfare recipient in return for the right to public support. This meant tightening employment tests for those claiming social security – and in return, providing help in looking for and getting work. For young people, the tests are tough and kick in after six months. The New Deals for lone parents and disabled people – New Deals that cover key groups that are economically inactive – are effectively voluntary, although in both cases the government has attempted to push through policies to tighten the rules covering these groups.

The carrots to go with the stick of the work test have included policies to 'make work pay' and to provide extra childcare for working parents. The minimum wage and working tax credits are designed first and foremost to remove disincentives to take jobs. But these labour market reforms also help with the government's anti-poverty drive. Labour's wider family policies are aimed in part at supporting parents with dependent children, especially in deprived communities, find and sustain employment by providing family support (Sure Start and new children's centres), and by increasing the supply and quality of early years childcare and education places. While these elements of Labour's welfare reforms were written off prematurely as 'symbolic differences' with Conservative social policy (Grover and Stewart, 1999), they mark a continued commitment to social justice and cast doubt on an easy neo-liberal convergence thesis (Rhodes, 2000).

How successful have these policies been in tacking poverty, promoting social inclusion and bringing about social justice? In terms of employment, the Labour government's record is impressive. Since 1997, helped by a buoyant and well-managed economy, Britain has enjoyed high levels of employment, rising incomes and better standards of living. There is an important debate, as there is in the US, about how effective the government's welfare-to-work programme has been in reducing unemployment compared to the boost to employment from economic growth (see Anderton et al, 1999; Riley and Young, 2001; Blundell et al, 2003). While the balance between active labour market policies and economic growth is always difficult to call, since 1997, the numbers working have increased by just over 2 million to 28.5 million. The overall rate of economic activity stands now at 74.8%.

However, the rates of economic inactivity have not fallen to anywhere near the same degree. Since the mid-1990s, those who are economically inactive but want to work have fallen by a seventh. This compares to a halving of official unemployment figures over the same period. As the report *Monitoring poverty and social exclusion 2004* from the New Policy Institute shows (Palmer et al, 2004), while the number of unemployed for two years or more and claiming out-of-work benefits has fallen sharply – in 2004, only 70,000 were long-term unemployed claimants compared with 440,000 in 1995 – the number of long-term sick or disabled claimants increased by a third over the same period. Four fifths of long-term claimants are sick or disabled, one fifth lone parents (Palmer et al, 2004). By 2004, 2.7 million people, 7.5% of the working-age population (and over 150,000 under 25), claimed an Incapacity Benefit. In his 2004 pre-budget statement, Gordon Brown announced a £40 'return to work' credit. The following February, Alan Johnson, the Work and Pensions Minister announced that Incapacity Benefit paid to 2.7 million people in 2004 would be scrapped to new claimants and replaced by new separate allowances for those whose impairments prevented them from taking work.

What about income distribution? During the 1980s, the income gap between rich and poor widened as a result of fiscal policy, deregulation, globalisation, new technology, changing patterns of work and a booming economy that stretched income differentials. During the early 1990s, the income gap stabilised as the British economy sank into recession, but it grew again as the economy took off in the second half of the 1990s. Since Labour came to power, the gap has widened between rich and poor although, as the very rich get richer, the poorest are catching up with the middle. This, as Hills (2004) argues, has been one of major drivers for the fall in poverty rates, especially for children, under Labour. Since the mid-1990s, there has been a steady decline in households living below the official poverty line (Palmer et al, 2004). In 2003/04, 22% of the population (12.4 million people) were in poor households, a fall from 2002/03. The real losers in the battle against poverty are working-age adults without dependent children. The levels of poverty among this population have grown since the mid-1990s.

The impact of government policy on the distribution of income has been equalising, certainly by comparison with Tory fiscal policy, especially in the High Thatcherite years of the 1980s (Clark et al, 2001). Between 1997 and 2001, according to the Institute for Fiscal Studies, the post-tax income of an average household in the bottom decile of income rose by 8.8%. Higher income groups benefited proportionally less; and the highest 30% of earners saw their post-tax income fall. Comparing the tax and benefit regimes in 1997 and 2004, whether adjusted for prices or earnings, the poorest are considerably better off and the richest worse off (Hills, 2004).

The pattern of winners and losers under Labour is complicated by consumption and direct taxes. The real winners of Labour's redistributions have been the working poor, especially those with dependent children. The impact of substantial increases to Child Benefit, as well as the introduction of the Working Families' Tax Credit, has been to redistribute income to those in work and with children. The biggest losers are those households not in work and without dependent children – households which, in the main, have seen benefits rise only with inflation.

How can we make sense of this record on employment, poverty and inequality, especially in terms of Labour and social democratic politics? Critics accuse Labour of putting work first to the neglect of social justice – thus marking continuity with Conservative social policy making (see Levitas, 1998; Lister, 2000; Peck and Theodore, 2000; Glyn and Wood, 2001). Even those in sympathy with the party's reformers have raised concerns that New Labour's third way ideas could all too easily lead the government away from social democracy and the values of the left (White, 1998).

Labour has explicitly made it a policy objective, even for groups such as lone parents, to boost employment levels as a way of tackling poverty and social exclusion. This can appear like work at any cost, even for those such as parents with young children and other caring responsibilities. Programmes like Sure Start that have been set up to support families with pre-school children do have employment-related objectives. But much of the energy of these local programmes is directed at supporting parents bringing up their young children – and many programmes have difficulty reaching those parents already at work.

If Labour does win a third term, there remain important challenges for the government: to reduce levels of economic inactivity; and to support those escaping poverty to stay out. But the problem for Labour's critics is that the government's record since 1997 on both employment and poverty is impressive. It certainly stands the social democratic test of putting the interests of the poor first through delivering near full employment and higher incomes for those at the bottom of the income distribution.

Labour's record on equality, however, is harder to judge. Its 'supply-side egalitarianism' is not a strategy to narrow the income gap between rich and poor. Policies to create more equal or just minimum starting points (or incomes) in life are aimed at poverty levels, as well as the opportunities that different groups in society have of making a go of it. The absence of an explicit equality commitment by Labour, reinforced by the widening income gap between rich and poor since 1997, infuriates the left. The problem, as John Hills (2004) shows, is that living standards have risen under Labour. Government policies, despite their significant redistributional effects, have not been enough to stop inequalities in disposable income rising. But, still the gap between the bottom and the middle has narrowed under Labour. While this has done more for poverty than overall inequality, it marks a social democratic shift in public policy after 1997 (see Oppenheim, 2001). Dealing with the Conservative legacy has in part been about changing government priorities to target resources on the poor. The Labour government has put egalitarian policy making back on the policy agenda – even if, for political reasons, *New* Labour does not always trumpet its achievements.

That the government could have done more to reduce inequality may have less to do with Labour's social democratic intent and more with the limits of the state in an open market society such as Britain. Indeed, balancing the competing demands of social justice and economic efficiency has been one of the central policy dilemmas for social democratic politics and philosophy for 50 years or more. How to achieve greater equality of opportunity and outcome through public policy, without undermining the capacity of the economy to generate wealth and higher living standards for all, is a problem shared by different generations of Labour ministers such as Tony Crosland and Gordon Brown. The Labour government has not abandoned the central ambitions of social democratic political economy – to intervene to change the distribution of rewards and opportunities in the economy and society.

If the Labour government has put egalitarian policy making back on the political agenda, how does Labour's record on the public services stand the test of social democracy? Is the debate around choice and diversity in the public sector challenging the underlying principles of the social democratic welfare state, or setting a new direction for collective action after Thatcherism?

'Modernising' the public services

The collective provision of public services was central to social democratic politics in Britain in the post-war period. For social democracy, the governance of public services is important. Left to private enterprise and the market, access to education, healthcare, housing and social security is rationed by ability to pay. Certain goods should be removed from the market, funded collectively through taxation and provided 'free' by the state on the basis of need.

Labour entered government in 1997 not simply to defend key public services such as health and education but to reform them. Indeed, it promised forms of governance that would offer a 'third way' between traditional forms of public and social administration *and* the reliance on markets as mechanisms to reform the delivery of public services. A Labour government would re-think collective public services – not abandon them to the market.

In practice, improving standards in public services for the incoming Labour government meant walking a tightrope between the Conservatives' market-based structural reform and Labour's traditional support for increased public funding for collectivist institutions. Labour promised that standards could be improved without more structural reform. But, in education, grant-maintained schools were abolished and replaced with a new category of 'foundation schools', back in the local education fold, but with more autonomy than local government-maintained schools. In health, the internal market was 'abolished' but the central element of that market, the split between the purchasing GPs and the providing trust hospitals, was retained. This was public sector reform at its most confusing or, at least, politically expedient: a new government making good on policy promises accumulated over a long period in opposition.

The funding settlements announced in 2000 made clearer what Labour's intentions were for the public services. The review, as we have seen, committed Labour to substantial increases in spending on collective public services, notably health and education. But these funding increases have come with strings attached: 'modernisation' – New Labour shorthand for public sector reform. 'Modernisation' encompasses changes to working practices, working culture and ethos, terms and conditions of employment and, fundamentally, what Labour and social democracy understand by public services and the role of the state in the provision of those services. This is a political minefield for any government, especially a Labour government and its New Labour leadership.

Key to these plans for public sector reform is the idea of delivery. Behind the rather innocuous message that services should be delivered well – who could object? – was New Labour's signal to voters and to public sector trades unions that this government would be different. The interests of consumers would come before the producers of services; and governments should be pragmatic about how a service is delivered to the consumer. Both messages challenged Labour's traditional attachment to public sector institutions, those who work in those institutions and the trades unions that represent those workers.

Labour's reform agenda was outlined in *Modernising government* (Cabinet

Office, 1999) and *Reforming our public services* (Office of Public Services Reform, 2002). The public services, the government argued, should become more 'customer-focused' – and that within a national framework the delivery of services should be devolved and delegated "to the front line, giving local leaders responsibility and accountability for delivery, and the opportunity to design and develop services around the needs of local people" (Office of Public Services Reform, 2002, p 10). The devolution of public policy making, it was argued, would lead to innovations in public policy, as individuals are encouraged to behave more entrepreneurially and to take risk. Furthermore, devolution would underpin strategies that sought to develop 'joined-up' policies and multi-agency partnership working.

In practice, there has been a tension between the setting of objectives and targets by central government and the devolutionary tendencies of the other aspects of the government's public sector reform programme. The centripetal forces in British government and politics are well established: the Whitehall-centred culture of public administration; the dominance of the Treasury in that centralist culture; the desire for governments (Labour no less) to 'get things done'; and the 'control freak' tendency of New Labour brought from opposition into government.

But, there is also an important difference of view between those Labour modernisers who see public sector reform as a process whereby the extra resources must be made more accountable against targets set by central government (the Brown/Treasury view) and those who see the need for far greater diversity – and autonomy – in the supply of public goods (the Blair/Downing Street view). In practice, the Labour government in policies on health and education has veered between centralist national plans and local devolved governance – and the coherence of the reform programme has suffered.

Overlaying this centre–local debate is the role of the private sector and market forms of governance in the delivery of public services. New Labour has embraced the managerial reforms introduced by the Conservatives across the civil service, local government and the wider public sector. The government expects the new public management to deliver better results by the more effective and efficient use of resources by public sector managers. The new public management has no hostility to the private sector in the provision of public goods. As long as public providers can show 'best value' (or just plain 'value for money'), government and auditors are happy.

Involving the private sector in the provision of public goods – and social welfare in particular – understandably rings alarm bells for social democrats. Labour's modernisation plans have embraced the Conservative's Private Finance Initiative (PFI). There continues to be a robust debate about the value to taxpayers of these private finance deals to build new hospitals, schools, prisons and roads. Studies of early hospital PFI deals by the National Audit Office show savings compared to publicly funded projects – although concerns were raised about the longer-term inflexibility that such deals could bring to responding to changing health needs (*Economist*, 2004). While this debate on the value for money of PFI procurement is important, it does not go to the heart of the *political* controversy over private sector involvement in the delivery of public services. Privately financed public services not only bring in private sector management and private sector ways of doing things, the PFI also breaches the great political divide for social democrats between public collective services and private markets.

The logical extension of the PFI is to bring in more private sector businesses to deliver public services, and to allow the public sector to behave more like the private sector. Labour has taken this step and signed concordats with the private health sector to supply the capacity the government desperately needs to cut hospital waiting lists – and, in so doing, has drawn the private sector into the public sector. Moreover, the government is set to extend this policy by guaranteeing that all NHS patients should be offered a choice of secondary healthcare facilities, one of which will be from the private sector – as long, that is, as the computer booking system works.

This is a red rag to the left – one they see challenging the founding principles of the welfare state: that health, education and other social services should be available to all on the basis of need and free at the point of use. The revival of quasi-markets also raises tensions within the government. While the Brown/Treasury view has been open to private finance (and to the markets that supply that finance), giving greater autonomy to public agencies, whether foundation hospitals or 'independent state schools', is viewed with suspicion. This is partly Treasury worry about the ability of these agencies to bear risk – and who will pick up the tab if things go wrong. But, it also reflects the unresolved tensions within New Labour about how best to reform the public services – and how these reforms are underpinned by social democratic values.

The problem Gordon Brown has with greater diversity and autonomy in public service provision – what he sees as 'marketisation' – is that they will undermine the unity, ethos and political economy of that provision – and they will not work (Brown, 2003). Brown's fear that markets undermine the public service ethos of organisations such as the NHS follows longstanding concerns about the impact of new public management from Margaret Thatcher's Efficiency Unit onwards on the culture of the civil service and public service more broadly (see Bogdanor, 1999). In Brown's Britain, choice in the public sector must be limited: to the booking of hospital appointments, not to which hospital a patient attends. Diversity and choice in health and education lead to a 'two-tier' system that undermines the unity and equity of the system. The Chancellor's views appeared to be supported by Lord Browne of Madingley at the Davos World Economic Forum in 2005: the head of British Petroleum criticised the spread of what he called 'pseudo markets' in the public sector.

Blairites such as Alan Milburn (whose views on the NHS shifted markedly between the Treasury and the Department of Health), Stephen Byers and the current Health Minister, John Reid, do not see it this way (see Milburn, 2004; Reid, 2005). Their perspective gives far greater weight to increasing the diversity of public sector provision – a diversity that embraces the private and voluntary sector – and to a more radical notion of 'personalised' public services: certainly one that encompasses notions of consumer choice and implies competition between service providers.

How can the Labour government manage to combine commitments to greater choice and diversity in public service provision – and the inevitable role of markets in making that choice and diversity possible – with traditional social democratic commitments to collective and universal state provision available to all on the basis of need?

Seen from the funding end, the government is supporting collective public service provision through public funds – supplemented by some private finance. These funds come with strings attached in terms of central government objectives and targets, and the accounting frameworks that are part of the new public management. From this end of the welfare state, the worry is not choice but whether taxpayers are getting value for money from the extra funds being spent on schooling and healthcare.

The political problems for the government, both internally and with its supporters on the backbenches and beyond, is at the delivery end. The government's modernisation programme challenges established systems and cultures of working – managerial, professional and employee. The challenge to public sector trades unionism, professional or non-professional, will no doubt intensify as private sector management spreads even further across the public sector. But the opposition of the unions to public sector reform is a red herring for social democratic politics – it is to confuse the interests of those working in the public sector with those the public sector serves. The important question is whether modernisation – certainly in its more radical Blairite guise – undermines social democratic political economy.

The core of the social democratic welfare state is the distribution of resources on the basis of needs, not property rights. The New Right challenge to this welfare state was that individuals should become more privately responsible for their own and their family's welfare. This meant that the market and private enterprise should have a much greater role in serving welfare needs. In the end, Thatcherism made only minor incursions into the social democratic state – largely in housing and pensions. In health and education, quasi-markets, not private enterprise, were as far as the Tories got.

Conservative reforms to the NHS did open up the possibility of different treatment with GP fundholders who, potentially, could cut a better deal with secondary providers in the internal market than non-fundholders. Labour's reforms to health, first with the introduction of Primary Care Trusts, then with practice-based commissioning, have closed that route by, in effect, making all GPs fundholders.

Introducing choice and diversity challenges social democratic political economy where those choices are attached to property rights. But, where choices remain attached to public money and those choices reflect needs, not private resources, they do not. There are important questions about how far greater choice and diversity exacerbate the local and regional variations in the quantity and quality of public services that have always existed. But these questions are little different to the debate around how far devolution, or even local accountability, of government gives rise to unacceptable regional variations in public policy across the UK.

The Brownites (and the Liberal Democrats), by insisting that only a unified welfare state can improve standards for all, remain stuck in a post-war British time warp when only nationalised monopoly provision is seen as capable of serving welfare needs and advancing social democracy. For all Brown's fuzzy talk of giving greater accountability of public services to local patients, parents and communities, the Chancellor cannot escape the very visible hand of central government (however much he pleads his innocence). This is a peculiarly insular view of social democratic governance – certainly one not shared by social democrats in other European countries.

The Blairites, rather than being the gravediggers of social democracy, are simply acknowledging the limits of the British welfare state first exposed in the 1970s. The quasi-markets, which, in effect, the government is being drawn back to, challenge public service providers to improve standards whether or not choice leads to exit: the potential for such an exit – 'contestability' – might be just as significant as whether welfare consumers actually switch suppliers (Le Grand, 2003). By arguing for greater choice and diversity in social provision, the Blairites are re-thinking collective action, not undermining it. And they are doing it in ways that are meaningful to voters. The central principle of the social democratic state remains intact: services such as health and schooling are free at the point of use. The Blairites want to reform the provision of welfare, not its financing. They are not that radical.

Conclusion

Thatcherism exposed the limits of British social democracy. The challenge from the New Right forced the Labour Party to re-think collective action and the provision of welfare. New Labour was never about to return Britain to a state of welfare before Thatcherism. To use Andrew Gamble and Tony Wright's words: "Too much has changed. And too much was wrong" (Gamble and Wright, 1999, p 6).

After two terms in power, far from abandoning social democracy for neo-liberalism, the Labour government has put egalitarian policy making back on the political agenda. Dealing with the Conservative legacy has in part been about changing government priorities to target resources on the poor. Moreover, by diverting extra funding to health and education, and challenging rights-based welfare entitlements, the government has given life to the welfare state and collective public service provision. It has done so in ways that are consistent with social democratic political economy – that put individual needs above private resources, and that offer relief from free market forces. The fact that the government is trying to reform these services shows that Labour has learnt the hard lessons of Thatcherism. The status quo is not an option if welfare provision is to keep pace with the demand for welfare. While the politics of choice will no doubt dominate the battles any third-term Labour government has with itself and with public sector trades unions, the future of British social democracy depends on Labour continuing to re-think collective action in radical ways.

References

Anderton, B., Riley, R. and Young, G. (1999) *The New Deal for young people: Early findings from the Pathfinder areas*, London: Employment Service/National Institute of Economic and Social Research (ESR34).

Blair, T. (1995) *Let us face the future: The 1945 anniversary lecture*, London: Fabian Society.

Blundell, R., Reed, H. and Van Reenen, J. (2003) 'The impact of the New Deal for young people on the labour market: a four year assessment', in R. Dickens, P. Gregg and J. Wadsworth (eds) *The labour market under New Labour*, London: Centre for Economic Performance, pp 17-31.

Bogdanor, V. (1999) 'Whitehall falls prey to the time and motion men', *The Times*, 12 September.

Brown, G. (2003) 'A modern agenda for prosperity and social reform', Speech to the Social Market Foundation, London: Cass Business School, 3 February.

Cabinet Office (1999) *Modernising government*, Cm 4310, London: The Stationery Office.

Chote, R., Emmerson, C. and Oldfield, Z. (2004) *The IFS green budget*, London: Institute for Fiscal Studies.

Clark, T., Myck, M. and Smith, Z. (2001) *Fiscal reforms affecting households, 1997-2001*, London: Institute for Fiscal Studies (IFS Election Briefing Note 5).

Cohen, G.A. (1994) 'Back to socialist basics', *New Left Review*, no 207, pp 3-16.

Commission on Social Justice (1994) *Social justice: Strategies for national renewal*, London: Vintage.

Deacon, A. and Mann, K. (1999) 'Agency, modernity and social policy', *Journal of Social Policy*, vol 28, no 3, pp 413-36.

Dilnot, A. and Emmerson, C. (2000) 'Ministers' challenge lies in delivery', *Financial Times*, 19 July.

Economist (2004) 'PFInancing new hospitals', *The Economist*, 10 January.

Ernst & Young (2005) *Economic outlook for business*, no 30, winter (www.ey.com/global/download.nsf/UK/ Economic_Outlook_for_Business_-_winter_05_01/$file/ EY_ITEM_Economic_Outlook_Winter_Jan_05.pdf).

Gamble, A. and Wright, T. (1999) 'Introduction', in A. Gamble and T. Wright (eds) *The new social democracy*, Oxford: Blackwell.

Glyn, A. and Wood, S. (2001) 'Economic policy under New Labour: how social democratic is the Blair government?', *Political Quarterly*, vol 72, no 1, pp 50-66.

Grover, C. and Stewart, J. (1999) 'Market workfare: social security, social regulation and competitiveness in the 1990s', *Journal of Social Policy*, vol 28, no 1, pp 73-96.

Hills, J. (2004) *Inequality and the state*, Oxford: Oxford University Press.

HM Treasury (1998) *Persistent poverty and lifetime inequality: The evidence*, London: HM Treasury/Centre for Analysis of Social Exclusion.

Le Grand, J. (2003) *Motivation, agency and public policy: Of knights and knaves, pawns and queens*, Oxford: Oxford University Press.

Levitas, R. (1998) *The inclusive society? Social exclusion and New Labour*, Basingstoke: Macmillan.

Lister, R. (2000) 'To Rio via the third way: New Labour's welfare reform agenda', *Renewal*, vol 8, no 4, pp 9-20.

Milburn, A. (2004) 'Power to the People', Speech to the Social Market Foundation, London, 8 December.

Office of Public Services Reform (2002) *Reforming our public services*, London: Cabinet Office.

Oppenheim, C. (2001) 'Enabling participation? New Labour's welfare-to-work policies', in S. White (ed) *New Labour: The progressive future?*, Basingstoke: Palgrave.

Palmer, G., Carr, J. and Kenway, P. (2004) *Monitoring poverty and social exclusion 2004*,York:Joseph Rowntree Foundation (www.poverty.org.uk/reports/mpse2004.pdf).

Peck,J. andTheodore, N. (2000) '"Work first": workfare and the regulation of contingent labour markets', *Cambridge Journal of Economics*, vol 24, pp 119-38.

Reid, J. (2005) 'Social democratic politics in an age of consumerism', Speech at Paisley University, 27 January (www.labour.org.uk/ac2004news?ux_news_id=socdemoc).

Rhodes, M. (2000) 'Desperately seeking a solution: social democracy, Thatcherism and the "third way" in British welfare', in M. Ferrera and M. Rhodes (eds) *Recasting European welfare states*, London: Frank Cass.

Riley, R. and Young, G. (2001) 'Does welfare-to-work policy increase employment? Evidence from the UK New Deal for young people', London: National Institute of Economic and Social Research (www.niesr.ac.uk/pubs/dps/dp183.PDF).

White, S. (1998) 'Interpreting the third way: not one road, but many', *Renewal*, vol 6, no 2, pp 17-30.

FOURTEEN

A progressive consensus in the making?

Peter Robinson and Kate Stanley

Introduction

The experience of Britain's Labour government since 1997 illustrates that social democracy can mean different things at different times even when it is the same government that is in office. The reform project of the Labour government, as one might perceive it in 2005, is not the project that one might have expected to see given the language and policies that Labour emphasised at the time of its 1997 election victory.

Of course, all governments' programmes evolve during their period of office. This is inevitable and desirable as governments react to emerging circumstances, pressures and occasionally crises, and as they learn from experience. However, the development of an effective discourse in social policy relies heavily on the electorate and other policy and political actors understanding that there is a clear and consistent answer to the basic question: what is this government about? A government's basic narrative has to resonate with the public and other actors or else people will become cynical and mistrustful as they perceive that government as opportunistic and lacking in clear principles. The key question this chapter seeks to address is: has the Labour government since 1997 had a consistent story to tell about what it stands for in relation to key areas of social policy? We address this question by first outlining very briefly the nature of public discourse in the UK, and more specifically under New Labour since 1997. We then examine how this discourse has been played out in welfare policy. We also look briefly at pensions and health policy. The substance of the debates in each of these areas is necessarily complex and what can be attempted here is only a sketch of how the discourse in these areas has evolved, so as to cast light on how Labour has governed since 1997.

The UK has often been identified as a country with a 'simple polity' where government has the ability to impose change, subject to the sanction of periodic general elections. The term 'elective dictatorship' was coined by Lord Hailsham, an Opposition Conservative politician, in the late 1970s to describe a form of government where a 'first-past-the-post' electoral system, combined with a relatively powerful executive and weak legislature, appeared to give the incumbent government significant power to put its policy agenda into practice. Of course, Opposition politicians' real gripe is usually that the wrong set of dictators is currently in power. Over the past 25 years, successive Conservative and Labour governments have done little to change the nature of the 'elective dictatorship' once in office. However, developments including the increasing assertiveness of the judicial branch, membership of the European Union and latterly the devolution of political power to Scotland, Wales and Northern Ireland have modified the rules of the game.

It is challenging to describe the nature of the discourse between political leaders and the public in the context of the Labour government. At the heart of the concept of a communicative discourse is the notion of a two-way conversation between the government and the governed, as the former seeks to secure legitimacy for its programme. There have been occasions when the government has sought to engage in constructive dialogue with the electorate, most notably through the so-called 'consultation exercise' entitled the 'Big Conversation' of 2004, but these have tended to be damp squibs. The overwhelming popular impression is of a government more interested in 'spin' than 'discourse', with the end result that popular disillusionment with politics and politicians has grown.

Labour's political strategy for winning power in 1997 involved distancing itself from certain popular perceptions of what it might mean to have a Labour government. Central to this was the objective of shedding Labour's image as a 'tax and spend' party. It was widely believed that proposals set out at the time of the 1992 election for increases in taxation to fund public spending had helped Labour to lose that election. It was also perceived that Labour had to show it could be trusted to manage the economy, and having a credible fiscal policy would be central to achieving that trust. The Labour Party that won the election in 1997 did so on the back of a rather cautious set of policy proposals communicated to the electorate in the form of a pledge card with five specific and modest proposals.

However, what the Labour government has actually done since 1997 is consistently raise taxes and, while from 1997 to 1999 Labour stuck to its pre-election pledge of adopting the previous Conservative government's spending limits, from 1999/00 it has been increasing public spending at a rate without precedent in peacetime. Between 1999/00 and 2005/06, public spending will have risen from 37.4% of Gross Domestic Product (GDP) to 41.9% of GDP, an increase of 4.5% of GDP in six years, paid in part by allowing the overall fiscal position to swing from modest surplus to modest deficit. Health spending has been the largest single beneficiary, but all main areas of public spending have seen their share of national income increase, with the exception of defence where spending as a proportion of GDP has edged down a little.

Welfare spending: not admitting what you are doing

Unemployment, measured using the International Labour Organisation definition, averaged a little under 5% in 2004, half the rate of a decade ago. But, despite falling unemployment since 1993, the social security budget has increased since 1998/99 as a proportion of GDP as the government has devoted significant resources to increasing tax credits and benefits for families with children. The government is spending more on children than ever before: there was a 53% rise in real terms in child-contingent support between 1999 and 2003 and this trend is set to continue (Adams and Brewer, 2004; HM Treasury, 2004). As a result of these rises in benefits and tax credits as well as the rise in employment and fall in unemployment (Sutherland et al, 2003), the government has made progress towards meeting its target to reduce child poverty by a quarter by 2004. However, this progress was more modest than many commentators had predicted. Figures released in April 2005 showed that child poverty had fallen by 16% since 1997, leaving just one year to reduce child poverty by a further 9% in in order to meet the target (National Statistics, 2005). Progress against this ultimate target of ending child poverty will be measured against the number of households with below 60% of contemporary median income. From 2004/05, child poverty will be measured in three separate ways (DWP, 2003b): an absolute, a relative and a combined material deprivation and low-income measure:

- Absolute low income: children are counted as poor on this measure if they live in a household with a before housing costs equivalised (taking account of household composition) income of less than 60% of the 1998/99 median income, uprated for inflation.
- Relative low income: children are counted as poor on this measure if they live in a household with a before housing costs equivalised income of less than 60% of the contemporary median.

- Material deprivation and low income combined: children are counted as poor on this measure if they live in a household with a before housing costs equivalised income of less than 70% of the contemporary median, and if they both lack material necessities and cannot afford them (Dornan, 2004).

In setting clear and measurable targets to reduce child poverty, the government is holding itself to account in a way that few governments have done before. Yet, in terms of how the Labour government has communicated this extensive policy of fiscal redistribution, it has first and foremost studiously avoided talking about redistribution at all. Phrases often used in the wider public debates such as 'redistribution by stealth' and 'stealth taxes' reflect an understanding that the Labour government has not wanted to be explicit about what it is doing.

Even in the autumn of 2004 when key ministers, including the Prime Minister, were rightly wanting to emphasise how much had been achieved in reducing relative poverty, they had written out of the script any mention of increases in benefits for adults with children where the adults are not in work, as this does not fit the narrative the government wants to highlight of an approach based on sharpening work incentives. In adopting a narrative of 'rights and responsibilities' to describe their approach to benefits policy, the government may have strengthened popular opinion that benefits discourage work (see Stanley et al, 2004). It is significant that the government has failed to generate widespread support for redistribution to create greater levels of equality. Survey evidence shows the proportion of people who support redistribution is lower now than during the Conservative governments of the 1980s and early 1990s (Taylor-Gooby, 2005).

There are two significant looming threats to the current strategy of quiet redistribution: reduced growth in public spending and levels of public support. After 2005/06, the rate of growth in public spending is planned to fall sharply. Health and international development will continue to receive generous spending increases for a while longer, with public spending on health rising from 6.9% of GDP in 2004/05 to 7.8% in 2007/08. However, in all other areas, growth in spending is set to decelerate and in some areas, like social care, the reduction in spending growth is quite large. Characteristically, this has not been communicated at all to the wider public; indeed, quite the opposite as the rhetoric remains focused on how much extra funding the government is continuing to commit in so many areas.

Childcare is an example of this. The government is keen to extend childcare in order to achieve its redistributive aims for at least three reasons. First, there is a robust body of evidence that demonstrates the importance of the early years of life for child outcomes in terms of health, educational attainment and labour market experience. High-quality childcare in the early years can improve child outcomes, and children from poorer homes stand to gain most from high-quality childcare experiences (Waldfogel, 2005). Second, the lack of affordable, high-quality childcare is one of the reasons lone parent employment rates in the UK are low compared to other European countries. By improving the availability of affordable childcare, the government believes it can also support increased levels of female labour force participation, particularly among lone parents, and so reduce poverty and improve child outcomes (DWP, 2005). Third, attitudinal evidence suggests that there are high levels of support for the government taking a role in helping with the costs of childcare, and particularly strong support for helping with the costs for lone parents with children under school age (Taylor-Gooby, 2005). These reasons caused the Prime Minister to describe childcare as "the new frontier of the welfare state" (Blair, 2004), and ministers have emphasised the government's ambition to extend the welfare state through a commitment to rolling out universal childcare and early years services.

There has already been progress in improving the availability of affordable childcare, but the 10-year childcare strategy announced in 2004 was intended to go much further and to embed childcare in the set of public policy priorities for the next decade (HM Treasury et al, 2004). In practice, however, the specific proposals are quite modest and fall far short of the childcare revolution that might have been signalled by the rhetoric; but then modest proposals were all that the government could realistically afford, as it had run out of fiscal room for manoeuvre. The Chancellor clearly struggled to find the £600 million by 2007/08 necessary to fund the initial stages of the government's childcare package.

The government is faced with considerable difficulties finding the resources to deliver on this extension to the welfare state, while at the same time making further progress in other areas. For example, we have already highlighted the need for further progress on child poverty. To meet its historic pledge to halve child poverty by 2010, spending of at least an extra £2 billion a year each year in the second half of the decade is needed (Brewer, 2005). Other analysis suggests that the government would need to spend an additional 1% of GDP on child tax credits, or achieve a substantial rise in parental employment, particularly among lone parents, to sustain progress and meet the 2010 target (Goodman et al, 2003). Other areas where resources are required include ending pensioner poverty, addressing poverty among adults without children, and tackling economic inactivity and poverty among sick and disabled people.

There is no explicit target for ending pensioner poverty, but further progress is needed if the Chancellor's broad aim to 'end pensioner poverty in our country' (Brown, 2002) is to be met. Resources have gone to poorer pensioner households and relative pensioner poverty has been falling but, while the extension of means-tested benefits and access to services such as long-term care has meant resources can be targeted at the poorest pensioners, the strategy has been hampered by low take-up. In 2004, approximately 1.25 million pensioner households were not claiming means-tested benefits to which they were entitled (DWP, 2004a). This suggests that there is a continuing need to enhance take-up or look again at the current less expensive but less effective means-testing approach in relation to pensioners. The falling value of private pensions, which we consider later, also poses a threat to continued progress (Hirsch and Millar, 2004).

There are also disadvantaged groups who have not benefited at all as a result of the government's welfare spending, such as adults without children who are out of work. They have been targeted by welfare-to-work programmes and will benefit from the National Minimum Wage and Working Tax Credit if they find work; yet, if they do not find work, their situation has barely improved since 1997. While the number of couples with children living in poverty – defined as below 60% of median household income – fell from 4.8 million to 3.8 million, on the same measurement the number of working-age adults without children living in poverty actually rose from 3.3 million in 1994/95 to 3.8 million in 2002/03 (Paxton and Dixon, 2004). The government's welfare policy is contributing directly to this problem as benefit rates for adults without children have not kept pace with average income; in most cases they have remained linked to prices rather than earnings. This group has slowly seen the value of their benefits eroded in comparison with other poor households and the population at large. Clearly, there is a need to prioritise spending and there are very good arguments to support the government's decision to support families with children and pensioners; however, there is a question as to how long the government can continue in the current vein while the numbers of adults without children living in poverty rise.

A further pressure on public spending comes from people who are economically inactive, and here too the government has set itself targets to meet. Sick and disabled people are by far the biggest group claiming out-of-work benefits and are more likely to have been in receipt of out-of-work benefits for longer periods than all other groups. There were 3 million people receiving the range of disability benefits in February 2004 (DWP, 2004b). At that time, 77% of those claiming disability benefits had been claiming for two years or more, compared with only 8% of those claiming unemployment benefits. Once a person has been claiming Incapacity Benefit (IB) for a year, the average duration of their claim is eight years (DWP, 2005).

The employment rate of disabled people has actually risen in recent years, but from a meagre starting point of 43.5% in 1997 to 49.1% in 2003 (DWP, 2003a). It has also been argued that this growth in the employment rate of disabled people has been among those already close to the labour market and who were most likely to have found jobs anyway, without government intervention, such as the New Deal for disabled people (NDDP) (Walker, 2003). The NDDP has been subject to the same criticism as the other New Deal programmes that it 'cream skims' those people who require the least support while offering little to those facing the most substantial barriers to work. However, there is some evidence of greater penetration than the idea of 'creaming' suggests (see, for example, Hills et al, 2001; Loumides et al, 2001). But, perhaps more significantly, there is a limit to what the NDDP might have been expected to achieve given that expenditure on this and other welfare-to-work programmes for sick and disabled people has been very low in comparison to the scale of the task. For example, spending on NDDP in 2002/03 was around £30 million; this compared with £80 million spent on the New Deal for lone parents and £270 million on the New Deal for young people (HM Treasury, 2003). It is clear that the employment of sick and disabled people has not been awarded the same level of priority as the employment of other groups, who may have been regarded as easier to help.

The persistence of the low employment rate and high claimant rate of sick and disabled people is a social justice issue. The benefit and welfare-to-work regimes have been failing sick and disabled people. In 2003, survey evidence showed that there were well over 1 million people claiming disability benefits who wanted to work and believed they could soon, but these people were not receiving the support necessary to help them move into work (Stanley and Regan, 2003). At the same time, the benefits system has been failing to offer a decent standard of living to those people who cannot work as a result of sickness and disability. Recent analysis has suggested that the weekly income of disabled people who are solely dependent on benefits is approximately £200 below the amount required for them to ensure an acceptable, equitable quality of life (Smith et al,

2004). The average IB payment is higher than Job Seeker's Allowance but, in 2002/03, it still only represented an annual income of £4,287, so many IB claimants experience poverty. In 2002/03, the average income of an IB claimant was 14% below the poverty threshold used by the government of 60% of median income (Stanley with Maxwell, 2004).

In 2002, the approach to sick and disabled people began to shift, and the government set a short-term target to increase the employment rate of disabled people and 'significantly reduce' the difference between their employment rate and the overall rate by 2006 (HM Treasury, 2002). Unlike the employment target for lone parents, no actual target employment rate was set. However, the emphasis on the employment of sick and disabled people has shifted up a gear again in 2004/05. The Prime Minister's Strategy Unit proposed a longer-term target for disabled people so that: "By 2025, disabled people in Britain should have full opportunities and choices to improve their quality of life, and will be respected and included as equal members of society" (Strategy Unit, 2004, p 8). Further, the Department for Work and Pensions' five-year strategy (DWP, 2005) announced the ambition of an 80% employment rate, and identified that this could only be achieved through a substantial increase in the employment of sick and disabled people.

This is another area where the government has bold ambitions, but the scale of the challenge of supporting significantly more IB claimants back to work cannot be underestimated and will require substantial resources. On current forecasts, IB spending is set to drop, but in the short to medium term these savings will be required to continue expanding welfare-to-work efforts and to improve the living standards of IB claimants. The government is right to identify that there is a need for reform in this area but it must recognise that it will cost money, at least in the short term. This is because it is not reasonable to expect to make significant savings on the rates of IB paid, and increased spending is required elsewhere, for example, in meeting the extra costs of disability and health problems. Many of the potential savings to be made in disability spending, and elsewhere within government budgets, will only be achieved over a relatively long timescale.

The second threat facing the government's strategy of quiet redistribution is how can you continue to maintain political support for a redistributive strategy that you have never been completely open about? The Chancellor worries specifically that the government's commitment to reducing child poverty does not have sufficient popular support. He is right to be concerned. Survey evidence shows that, while people in Britain do think poverty is an issue, it is not an issue they tend to feel very strongly about (Taylor-Gooby, 2005). In 2003, 42% of people surveyed agreed that 'the government should redistribute income to the less well off' and only 26% disagreed, while the rest were undecided. What is notable is that, while 80% of people believe income inequality is too large, only 42% would support government action to redistribute. It must be a difficult task to win the electorate around to support a policy of tax and spend and redistribution (that is not too different from that of earlier Labour governments) when you have never openly acknowledged that this is at the heart of your social democratic reform project. This is not what developing a progressive consensus is supposed to be about.

The prospect is for many of the government's ambitious social policy goals to be undeliverable because of the need to sharply slow the growth in public spending, unless the government is prepared to raise taxes to fund its social policy agenda, and it is not clear at this time whether or not the government is prepared to do this. But the point is that it is proscribed in putting forward the case for raising taxes to help fund a more socially just set of outcomes, because it has made no attempt to engender a consensus on the need to raise taxes.

Pensions policy: responding, or not, when circumstances change

In 1998, the newly arrived Labour government published a Green Paper (DSS, 1998) on pensions policy, against the background of concern over relatively high levels of pensioner poverty but continued satisfaction that the UK state pensions system was fiscally sustainable and that private pensions would not only remain strong but would grow in relative importance. The punchline to that Green Paper was that the current split in pensioner incomes between 60% coming from public sources and 40% from private sources could be reversed with 60% of pensioner incomes coming from private sources in the future, allowing state pension provision to shrink further to providing just 40% of pensioner incomes.

At the time only a few voices were heard expressing concern that the shift to private pensions might already have gone too far in the UK. The government – specifically the Treasury – put the emphasis on introducing more generous means-tested benefits to target support at the poorest pensioners to reduce pensioner poverty. There was no attempt to generate a consensus on this line of policy.

After 1998, the earth beneath the UK pensions system moved. This is the best example of a public policy area where a change in circumstances has forced a change in the nature of the public debate. The collapse in the stock market undermined the confidence of individuals in their own private personal pensions, but even more fundamentally it forced employers to look at the sustainability of the pension promises they had made to their employees, with the consequence that there was an acceleration in the move away from generous occupational pension schemes. Unlike the rest of the European Union (EU) where the sustainability of the public pensions system was under question, in the UK it was the sustainability of the private pensions system that now seemed questionable.

The government's focus on improving the generosity of means-tested pensions provision has had some success in reducing levels of relative pensioner poverty, but with increasing concern about the impact on the incentives to save of those currently in the workforce. The government's response to the 'pensions crisis' has been an incremental one, an approach that has tended to make an already complex pensions system more complicated still. The government finally resorted to that most favoured tactic for solving a technically and politically difficult issue – by launching a Commission. The interim report of the Pensions Commission in the autumn of 2004 (Pensions Commission, 2004) re-emphasised the scale of the problem and made it quite clear that the aspiration of the 1998 Green Paper to reverse the proportion of pensioner incomes coming from public and private funding was effectively dead.

The final report of the Pensions Commission is due in autumn 2005, after an election is likely to take place at which the government will put no specific new policies forward for debate, although it has put forward six 'principles for reform', the last of which is that 'reform should be based around as broad a consensus as possible'. This is the character of the attempt to build a progressive consensus in this area of policy, in a simple polity where the government, with a massive parliamentary majority, seemingly has the authority to impose change. The 'elective dictatorship' in the UK has found it no easier to create the political consensus and popular understanding necessary to deliver difficult reforms to the pensions system than other Organisation for Economic Co-operation and Development (OECD) countries with their more sophisticated checks and balances. It will be interesting to see after the election how far any attempt to build a broad consensus on pension reform will progress.

Health policy: doing the opposite of what you said you would do

The NHS is the iconic institution of the British welfare state. Its core principle of a tax-funded healthcare system largely free at point of use has more widespread political and popular support than any other part of the economic and social framework of the country. Together with pensions and education, the NHS has the highest level of public support as a spending priority.

At the 1997 election, Labour worked hard to convince the electorate that the NHS was not safe in Conservative hands and that Labour would preserve and enhance its central features. As part of this campaign, Labour criticised the structural reforms that the Conservatives had instituted to establish an 'internal market' where the commissioners or purchasers of healthcare would be separate from the providers, a reform designed to sharpen incentives within the NHS in a way that would increase efficiency and make services more responsive. The electorate in 1997 might have been confident that Labour would end the internal market, and indeed the early rhetoric of the Labour government suggested that they had done just this.

The Labour government in England has presided over the most fundamental changes to the structure of the NHS since it was created in the immediate post-war period. At the heart of these changes is a more ambitious version of the internal market featuring a clear split between the commissioners of care and the providers, with funding flows following patients based on fixed tariffs for different procedures and with explicit encouragement of the private sector and overseas providers to enter the healthcare market. These fundamental structural changes have been accompanied by the longest period of generous increases in funding in the service's history. This dual strategy of large-scale structural reform plus generous funding has been accompanied by ambitious targets to improve health outcomes, narrow health inequalities and improve the quality of the service as experienced by users.

A great deal of intellectual opinion is very much behind this strategy. However, it is not what Labour said it would do in 1997. In this case, the lack of consistency will probably not matter so long as the strategy is seen by the electorate to work and on that point the jury is still out. Health policy is given extra interest by political devolution, as health is an entirely devolved matter. The NHS in Scotland and Wales is evolving in quite different ways from the NHS in England, without the same fundamental structural reforms and without a place for an internal market, but with similar generous increases in funding and with Labour in government in Edinburgh (in coalition) and in Cardiff. This is a natural policy experiment that will give researchers much to write about.

The point about the public policy debate on health is how difficult it is to involve the public in a debate about the effectiveness of detailed and complex structural reforms when what matters to them is the quality of the healthcare they and their families receive and what they perceive is happening to their local hospital, GP services and other front-line provision. There can be and is a rich policy debate among academics, policy makers and others about the nature of these health reforms, but it is almost completely disconnected from the wider public debate. The wider electorate is not interested in the possible impact of the internal market on allocative efficiency, but this makes it difficult for the government to bring people around to support its approach. Against this background, there is evidence that, despite wide support for the NHS, dissatisfaction with it remains relatively high. Levels of dissatisfaction ran at 33% in 1998, rising to 41% in 2002, before falling back to 37% in 2003 (Sefton, 2003).

Conclusion

In 2004 – after seven years of government – several Labour ministers were starting to use the language of trying to ensure the permanent embedding of a progressive consensus that marries economic success and social justice as a way of describing the social democratic narrative of the administration. It is a neat formulation. It begs questions about what defines economic success and social justice, but these are not insuperable. A UK where GDP per head remained close to other major EU economies, employment rates continued to rise, regional economic differences were tempered, core public services were seen to improve and relative poverty and perhaps income inequality were falling, would satisfy a lot of people as constituting an adequate definition of a successful economy and a fair society.

The more difficult questions relate to these concepts of a 'progressive consensus' and its 'permanent embedding'. This is where the notion of a discourse is helpful. How can you permanently embed a consensus when you do not address explicitly in public key questions such as how you pay for social justice? Labour, at the time of the 1997 election, refused to enter into a discourse over the tax and spending implications of its vision. Labour will enter the 2005 election no better placed to have this necessary conversation with the electorate. If, after the election, a newly elected

Labour government is required to move quickly to raise taxes and/or scale back its social policy ambitions for lack of resources, the perception that the government has run its course may quickly gather pace. At a time when only 9% of people report that they trust the government a great deal to spend taxpayers' money wisely, this could pose a terminal threat (Taylor-Gooby, 2005).

However, Labour has benefited from two pieces of good fortune. One is a benign economic background: Labour inherited a reasonably well-functioning economy in 1997 and to its credit has maintained a sound economic performance. But, perhaps most importantly, it has faced an Opposition not seen as credible and with no better answers to the key questions of maintaining economic prosperity while delivering public services that are seen as adequate and social outcomes that are at least perceived to be fair.

There is a discourse that needs to be developed in the UK. A reasonably successful economy should allow Britain to aspire to match the social outcomes widely admired in some other European countries, which in intuitive terms amounts to a fair distribution of the outcomes of that economic success. But with the UK economic model delivering a much wider distribution of *market* incomes, with a particularly unequal distribution of earnings, the UK welfare state has to work even harder to ensure that the distribution of *final* household income, after taxes and benefits, comes closer to that achieved in other European countries. With the added pressures that stem from extra demands for healthcare and other services that people in the UK want to be funded collectively, the inescapable conclusion is that the progressive consensus the government wants to embed is one reliant on a lot of 'tax and spend'. This is precisely what the Labour government does not want to admit openly and is precisely why it is unlikely to engender the consensus it seeks. For, in the end, Lincoln is surely right: you cannot fool all the people all the time and, if you want to engender consensus around an economic and social model, the starting point is to be clear and explicit about what that model is, the challenges it implies and how it is to be paid for.

References

Adams, S. and Brewer, M. (2004) *Supporting families: The financial costs and benefits of children since 1975*, Bristol: The Policy Press.
Blair, T. (2004) Speech to the National Association of Head Teachers, 3 May (www.number-10.gov.uk/output/Page5730.asp).

Brewer, M. (2005) 'Maintaining momentum in tackling child poverty', in S. Delorenzi, J. Reed and P. Robinson (eds) *Maintaining momentum: Promoting social mobility and life chances from early years to adulthood*, London: IPPR, pp 104-9.

Brown, G. (2002) Speech to Labour Party Conference, 30 September (www.labour.org.uk).

Dornan, P. (2004) 'Defining income poverty out of existence?', *Poverty*, 117 (www.cpag.org.uk).

DSS (Department for Social Security) (1998) *Opportunity for all*, London: DSS.

DWP (Department for Work and Pensions) (2003a) *Opportunities for all*, London: DWP.

DWP (2003b) *Measuring child poverty*, London: DWP.

DWP (2004a) *The new Pension Credit: A review of the campaign to May 2004*, London: DWP.

DWP (2004b) *Incapacity Benefit and Severe Disablement Allowance quarterly summary statistics: August 2004*, London: DWP.

DWP (2005) *Five year strategy: Opportunity and security throughout life*, London: DWP.

Goodman, A., Brewer, M. and Clark, T. (2003) 'What really happened to child poverty under Labour's first term?', *Economic Journal*, vol 113, no 488, pp F240-F57.

Hirsch, D. and Millar, J. (2004) *Labour's welfare reform: Progress to date*, York: Joseph Rowntree Foundation.

Hills, D., Child, C., Blackburn, V. and Youll, P. (2001) *Evaluation of the New Deal for disabled people innovative schemes pilot*, London: DWP.

HM Treasury (2002) *2002 spending review. Opportunity and security for all: Investing in an enterprising, fairer Britain*, London: HM Treasury.

HM Treasury (2003) *Budget 2003*, London: HM Treasury.

HM Treasury (2004) *Budget 2004*, London: HM Treasury.

HM Treasury, Department for Education and Skills, Department for Work and Pensions and Department of Trade and Industry (2004) *Choice for parents, the best start for children: A ten year strategy for childcare*, London: The Stationery Office.

Loumides, J., Youngs, R., Green, A., Arthur, S., Legard, R., Lessof, C., Lewis, J., Walker, R., Corden, A., Thornton, P. and Sainsbury, R. (2001) *Evaluation of the New Deal for disabled people personal adviser service pilot*, London: DWP.

National Statistics (2005) *Households below average income 1994/95 to 2003/04*, London: Department for Work and Pensions.

Paxton, W. and Dixon, M. (2004) *The state of the nation: An audit of injustice in the UK*, London: IPPR.

Pensions Commission (2004) *Pensions: Challenges and choices, the first report of the Pensions Commission*, London: The Stationery Office.

Sefton, T. (2003) 'What we want from the welfare state', in A. Park (ed) *British social attitudes: The 20th report*, London: Sage Publications and National Centre for Social Research, pp 1-28.

Smith, N., Middleton, S., Ashton-Brooks, K., Cox, L. and Dobson, B. with Reith, L. (2004) *Disabled people's cost of living: More than you would think*, York: Joseph Rowntree Foundation.

Stanley, K. with Maxwell, D. (2004) *Fit for purpose: The reform of Incapacity Benefit*, London: IPPR.

Stanley, K. and Regan, S. (2003) *The missing million: Supporting disabled people into work*, London: IPPR.

Stanley, K. and Lohde, L. with White, S. (2004) *Sanctions and sweeteners: Rights and responsibilities in the benefit system*, London: IPPR.

Strategy Unit (2004) *The life chances of disabled people*, London: The Stationery Office.

Sutherland, H., Sefton, T. and Piachaud, D. (2003) *Poverty in Britain: The impact of government policy since 1997*, York: Joseph Rowntree Foundation.

Taylor-Gooby, P. (2005) *Attitudes to social justice*, London: IPPR.

Waldfogel, J. (2005) 'Social mobility, life chances and the early years', in S Delorenzi, J. Reed and P. Robinson (eds) *Maintaining momentum: Promoting social mobility and life chances from early years to adulthood*, London: IPPR, pp 31-55.

Walker, R. (2003) 'Employment, support and security: balancing the needs of disabled people', *New Economy*, vol 10, no 1, pp 50-5.

FIFTEEN

New Labour's family policy

Fiona Williams

The creation in 2003 of a new Ministry for Children, Young People and Families marked the emergence of an explicit, universal and child-centred family policy. Many policies have been unprecedented for Britain, and have moved from some of the earlier inauspicious moves, such as the cutting of lone parents' benefits in 1997, and the more conservative endorsements of married family life in *Supporting families* (Home Office, 1998). They have included a commitment to abolish child poverty by 2020; a National Childcare Strategy guaranteeing a place for every three- or four-year-old; a National Carers' Strategy; the development of Sure Start to support families with young children in deprived areas; a range of tax credits to help working families on low incomes and for working parents to pay for child care; extended maternity leave and pay and paid paternity leave; and the right for parents to work part time and to take unpaid time off to care for children. Policies have been wide ranging: at the liberal end, New Labour has promoted measures to equalise legal and social conditions for lesbians and gay men; at the disciplinary end, they have introduced the enforcement of parental obligations in relation to children's behaviour.

But the development of policies like these has not only been New Labour inspired. They find reflection in other European countries that have been subject to similar social changes and political pressures. Increases in women's employment, the inadequacy of a single income for households, increases in divorce, cohabitation and lone-mother families, and an ageing population, all point to what EU-speak calls the 'care gap'. And to some extent, too, policies around work–life balance have been shaped by EU policy directives. In addition, the combination of those policies which provide care receivers or care givers with cash to buy in services, which enhance opportunities for mothers and fathers to take paid work, or which involve the private and voluntary sectors in service provision, also reflects some of the more general features of welfare state redesign in Europe. By the end of their second term in 2005, New Labour's family policy had gathered speed. Below I discuss four of its key features: 'hard-working families'; its child-centredness; its focus on parental responsibilities; and its acknowledgement of diversity – identifying some of the key tensions that each bears.

Supporting 'hard-working families'

Commending his Budget to the House of Commons in March 2005, Gordon Brown concluded that it was "a budget for Britain's hard working families and pensioners". Encouraging and rewarding parental involvement in employment has been a central element in New Labour's family policy: it has been part of a strategy of combating poverty, especially for lone parents and other low-income families; of encouraging economic self-provisioning (for housing, pensions, care services); as embodying the shift away from a male breadwinner model for welfare; as the basis for a prosperous and economically competitive nation; and as the role model parents can provide for their children. As such, there have been three main elements affecting parents and children: financial support, support services and time to care.

Tax credits have been the centrepiece of financial support for parents and serve to help low-income families while encouraging and rewarding participation in the labour market. There are two key elements to the tax credit system. The first is the income-related Child Tax Credit, paid direct to the main carer, for which around 90% of families with children (in or out of work) are eligible. The 2005 Budget set to increase the child element of the credit in line with average earnings. The second is the Working Tax Credit for parents in work, which includes an element to help pay for up to 70% of the costs of childcare. The 2005 Budget also put this up, and added to it a tax subsidy, which allows employers to give employees a voucher to put towards the cost of a nursery, childminder, or, for the first time, a nanny who looks after a child in the parents' home (but not relatives). Associated with these financial inducements, measures such as the New Deal for lone parents provide advice for lone parents finding work.

The second aspect of support for working parents is exemplified by the National Childcare Strategy. Originally launched in 1998, this strategy combines aims for universal and integrated education and care with targeted help in poorer areas. It includes the promise of part-time nursery places for all three- and four-year-olds and out-of-school clubs for school-aged children. The latter increased from 3,000 in 1997 to around 10,000 by 2004. It also requires local authorities to convene partnerships to monitor and respond to childcare needs and supply in their areas. The development of Sure Start for parents of children under four and Children's Centres have provided services and support in areas of greatest deprivation. In 2004, the Treasury strengthened these developments with its plans for a 10-year childcare strategy (HM Treasury, 2004). This aims to increase the number of Children's Centres to 3,500 by 2010 so that parents in every community will have access to holistic centres offering childcare information, health services and support. The strategy also plans to extend free nursery care available to three- and four-year-olds to 15 hours a week for 38 weeks a year with greater flexibility as to how the time is taken. By 2010 all secondary schools are to be open from 8 am to 6 pm providing 'wrap around care', and all three- to 14-year-olds are to have access to an out-of-school childcare place.

The third area of support is in time to care. The 10-year strategy promises improvements in existing parental leave. Having extended maternity leave to a year, the government seeks to phase in an extension of statutory maternity pay from six to 12 months. Mothers will be given the option of transferring part of their leave and pay to fathers, and there are moves to extend the new right of workers to ask for flexible hours to care for dependants.

There can be little doubt that the combined effect of these three areas of development has been to transform the assumption of responsibility for childcare for working parents from an individual to a public responsibility, such that the Conservative Party's 2005 election manifesto was forced to address how it too would support working parents if elected. In addition, as far as the anti-poverty strategy is concerned, the poverty rate of lone parents has fallen from 28% to 20% since the mid-1990s, and the increase in value of benefits for non-working families with children has also improved their position (Millar and Gardiner, 2004). At the same time, however, the poverty rate of the 37% of couple families with fathers in low-paid work has not changed. Take-up of Working Tax Credits is lower in couple households (McKay, 2002): more breadwinners now are dependent on low-waged employment and the family-based means test to determine eligibility for tax credits creates a disincentive for potential second earners to take up work especially if there are high care costs involved (Hirsch and Millar, 2004). In general, for low-income families, it is less their income that has the potential to lift them out of poverty as the contributions they get from the state or from family and friends. The low-wage culture, poor future employment prospects and the lack of sustainability of many low-paid jobs make it difficult to make work alone pay. Also, for lone parents especially, the transition to employment can be hazardous with complex calculations needed about the relative costs of credits, childcare costs and travel. Childcare credits only cover 70% of childcare costs, which still places childcare beyond the reach of poorer families. Many families prefer to use relatives for care of younger children and childcare credits cannot be used this way. Partly as a response to care costs, in 2005 the government recommended an increase cover to 80% of costs and a pilot of a £40-a-week bonus for the first year of return to employment for lone parents to ease this transition. Elsewhere demands have been to increase the National Minimum Wage (NFPI, 2005).

There have been criticisms of a different kind of the 'make work pay' strategy. Qualitative studies of mothers of young children, lone or partnered, indicate that the differences that exist in mothers' decisions about how to combine childcare with paid work – whether to work full time, part time or not at all, and what kind of childcare support to use – are based less on a cost-benefit analysis of *what pays* than a moral understanding of *what matters* as far as the proper care of their children is concerned (Duncan et al, 2003; Williams, 2004a). These understandings of what it means to be a good mother are also influenced by social networks, class, ethnicity and culture, as well as by local conditions and customs. What impels women's decisions is the affective quality of care for their children as much as the possibility of financial betterment. It is an ethic of care as much as or more than an ethic of work that influences them. This suggests that policies have to put as much emphasis on the quality, flexibility, affordability and diversity of care options as financial incentives.

This concern about the *quality* of care has been expressed in other ways. One is that while tax credits have helped families in poverty, they are not the right instrument in the long term to generate affordable, quality care. This is because in funding the demand for childcare provision they have stimulated the growth of low-waged care in the private sector. Nor do they provide parents with scope to demand better quality provision; they can lead to an inflation of childcare costs, and they do not constitute a secure funding source for providers (Daycare Trust, 2005). Further, the effect of the increase in privately provided nurseries has done little to improve the status of nursery and childcare work, which still commands low pay and few qualifications, and this reflects the low value ascribed to care in society. Some have argued for a radical reform of the childcare profession with the introduction of the 'pedagogue' – a childcare graduate (Moss and Petrie, 2002). In response in its 10-year strategy, the Treasury promised to introduce a career structure and new qualifications.

A third concern is with the continuation of Sure Start programmes. These have been generally acknowledged to have provided highly innovative and intensive support for parents in deprived communities through grass-roots involvement and been responsive to local needs and conditions (ww.ness.bbk.ac.uk). The plan to 'roll out' the programmes into more universally available Children's Centres has raised concerns about spreading resources too thinly to sustain impact. Thus, the Daycare Trust has argued that the present commitment of £125 million to local authorities to deliver is 10-year strategy will be inadequate (Daycare Trust, 2005). There is pressure on government to develop an independent review of long-term ring-fenced funding for future childcare. Without this the costs of care will fall, as they do now, mainly on parents, especially for the under-3s where there are no plans for support. The argument is for making childcare not simply a *public responsibility* but a *public value* too.

Children as citizens of the present or the future?

"... we shall put children at the heart of everything we do. All our services must be planned, developed and delivered around the needs and wants of children, young people and their families." (Margaret Hodge, the first Minister of State for Children, Young People and Families, 8 July 2003)

In seeking to promote 'the best interests of the child' in matters of divorce and child welfare, New Labour has continued along the path of policies established by the 1989 Children Act. However, the publication of the Green Paper *Every child matters* in 2003 (DfES, 2003) – the precursor to the Children Bill – marked a much more child-centred family policy. The new Ministry for Children, Young People and Families is to join up children's services, family policy and law, policy on teenage pregnancy, and Sure Start, in the Department for Education and Skills. *Every child matters* sets out a more universal approach to children: it proposes universal prevention and early intervention, rather than just targeted protection, and draws these into the goal of ending child poverty and enabling every child to reach their potential. It argues for children to have a voice in the development of policies that affect them, and for a multi-disciplinary approach in children's services to be established within schools and Children's Centres with Directors of 'joined-up' Children's Services at local level and a Children's Commissioner at national level. It sets five key outcomes for children: being healthy; staying safe; enjoying and achieving; making a positive contribution; and economic well-being.

While *Every child matters* goes some distance in setting out structures of accountability to protect children, to recognise their needs and to create educational opportunities to enable them to become productive future citizens, it also sets up tensions. The first concerns how far every child matters as a citizen of the present or a citizen of the future. The balance of outcomes favours more the processes of *becoming an adult* than fostering the active enjoyment and negotiation of childhood and young personhood with friends and siblings (see Williams, 2004c). The leitmotiv in the document is towards education and the educatability of children – education as the pre-cursor to work, self-sufficiency and independence, just as social security and taxation policies have emphasised getting adults into paid work as central to an anti-poverty strategy. This approach has been identified by some analysts as part of a new design for liberal welfare states as 'social investment states' (Dobrowolsky, 2002; Lister, 2003; Fawcett et al, 2004). One of the dominant characteristics of the social investment state is the investment in the child as citizen-worker-of-the-future, achieved through anti-poverty and education measures in which a notion of partnership of the state with parents, business and the voluntary sector, is central. The overall aim is to maintain competitiveness in the global economy.

Certainly there are strong elements of this investment approach in New Labour's family policies. The location of the new Ministry for Children, Young People and Families in the Department for Education and Skills, and, with it, responsibilities that formally belonged to the Home Office and Department of Health symbolises the centrality of education, as do plans to make schools the new centres for new multi-disciplinary children's services. Yet in some ways this could be seen as a progressive move: schools represent a universal service, freed from the stigma of the social services offices. At the same time, however, the idea of education as the centre of a more holistic approach to children and their parents does not fit with recent policies. The thrust of education has been towards creating schools as centres of educational achievement. Head teachers have been encouraged to think of their schools as autonomous and competitive institutions, striving to meet exam targets and to attract good pupils. Now they are to open up their gates to other professional groups, to share pastoral care of their children with them, and to be open to the community. Recent proposals have already given head teachers the further responsibility of collecting fines from parents whose children stay away from school. This suggests an uneasy tension between achievement, accessibility and proscription that will not necessarily encourage trust among all pupils or parents.

The focus on schools may well reinforce the marginalisation of those who are excluded or who exclude themselves from school, such as

Travellers' children, children of asylum seekers and homeless families. Similarly, the argument for investing in children provides little rationale for attending to the needs of those who may not have an educational future – older people, disabled people and children with learning disabilities. It ends up identifying particular groups of children who pose some sort of risk to the investment project such as educational non-achievers (teenage mothers, disabled children, truants, excluded children, looked-after children, boys from some minority ethnic groups); or those such as looked-after children, young carers or unaccompanied child migrants, who have no 'responsible' parent (Fawcett et al, 2004). This obscures the experiences that children share *as children* vis-à-vis adults within generational social relations of power, and emphasises instead the particular characteristics of some groups of children that prevent them from becoming responsible future citizens. Nevertheless, it is possible to see these proposals in *Every child matters* as creating the political space to ask what education is for, and to reframe the testing and target-centred culture of education towards broader values of education as supporting children to develop their emotional, physical, intellectual and creative capabilities.

There is also a tension between the Green Paper's efforts towards protection of children and its endorsement of the punitive elements in the youth justice system. It did not respond to pressure from the Joint Committee on Human Rights (House of Commons and House of Lords, 2003) to increase the age of criminal responsibility from 10 to 12, and to condemn the use of custodial sentences for 12- to 14-year-olds even when they have not been persistent offenders, or to abandon the right of parents to use 'reasonable chastisement' on their children (smacking). (This contrasts with New Labour's policy public education campaigns against domestic violence.)

Balancing a respect for privacy and a need for intervention presents a third tension. Part of a universal approach to protect *all* children includes a proposal to introduce electronic dossiers holding every child's details (including whether they have been excluded from school, whether they are known to any of the agencies such as the police, youth offending teams and so on). This raises important issues of civil liberties as well as questions about the maintenance of trust with both parents and especially children who place a premium on confidentiality in their use of services. There are concerns that it represents a technological fix for deeper-seated issues of accountability and trust between different professional groups, and that it underlines the need for guarantees of confidentiality, for cultural respect for the diverse ways people may live their lives, and for the protection of the vulnerabilities of children to any misuse of information about them. It also reinforces the need for parents and children to be able to influence how protection policies and support practices are implemented.

These tensions find reflection in other parts of New Labour's family policy. Policy around divorce has continued to emphasise the need for parents to recognise their joint parenting responsibilities after divorce. Reform of the child support system introduced in April 2003 attempted to make it less conflictual and more transparent by simplifying support calculations, allowing the non-resident parents reduced rates according to parenting responsibility and circumstance, and instituting deductions for parents with care responsibilities on Income Support (Ridge, 2005). However, the net effect has been that a third of resident parents will be worse off. The more explicit linking of parental contact to the rate of payment creates the possibility for increased conflict between divorcing parents, as does the continued deduction of Child Support from resident parents who are on Income Support, and the move to recognise the rights to support of step children and biological children in second families has shifted the benefits in favour of second family and away from first family children. Making children the legal beneficiaries of Child Support in their own right, with rights to receive the payments directly as they get older, and direct payment of support from the state, which would bear the responsibility of recouping missed payments would, it is suggested, better promote the best interests of the child and reduction of conflict (Ridge, 2005, pp 136-7).

Responsible parents

Every child matters endorsed the 1999 Crime and Disorder Act that gave courts the powers to make parenting and child safety orders enforcing parental obligations in relation to children's behaviour. Parents can be fined and imprisoned for having a truanting child. The consultation paper, *Supporting families* (Home Office, 1998), the Green Paper, *Meeting the childcare challenge* (DfEE, 1998) and the White Paper, *Respect and responsibility* (Home Office, 2003) all emphasise parental responsibilities for children's upbringing, behaviour, educational success, emotional and physical health. This can be seen as part of the 'Third Way' philosophy in which entitlements and support are conditional on the exercise of proper individual responsibility. Behind much of the responsibilisation discourse lies a deficit model of family life and parenting capacity (Etzioni, 1993) –

an idea that families are being undermined by the decline in mutuality and growth of individualism. However, empirical research does not bear this out (Williams, 2004a). It shows that parents and children feel their responsibilities and commitments keenly; that although they may be anxious about their parenting and want support, this has to be the right sort of support – practical, non-judgemental, fair, respectful and practical (Williams, 2004b; Williams and Roseneil, 2004). Research suggests that the wrong sort of help can be damaging to people's self-esteem and their capacity for involvement with others (Ghate and Hazel, 2002) and that the development of trust between parents, children and services in local communities takes time, stability in funding and opportunities for involvement.

In some ways this nettle has been grasped in the development of Sure Start programmes where parental representation in management of the programmes has been given priority (see www.ness.bbk.ac.uk). Elsewhere, local partnerships have been the mechanism for materialising support and involvement of parents. But they have also been a way of devolving responsibility to local areas while government retains tight control over agenda setting and policy development (Newman, 2001). One analysis of local partnership workings in local childcare provision – the Early Years Development and Childcare Partnerships – provides an example of this (Penn and Randall, 2005). The Early Years Development and Childcare Partnerships set up forums for local stakeholders. In principle, this could provide opportunities for better coordination, responsiveness to local needs and 'community ownership'. In practice, however, the requirement to meet targets set by central government meant that it was difficult to attend to the task of working through conflicts of interest and tradition at local level. Targets and deadlines had to be met in order to secure funding, so the partnerships tended to be dominated by those who knew best how to do this – the local authority officers and the education sector, with voluntary sector members feeling left out. Tensions existed here between a target culture and a culture of integrating local communities into the assessment of needs, the development and management of services, and the training priorities of local professionals. Not surprisingly, in this situation the articulation of needs of those most marginalised tends to be overlooked: disabled and poor minority ethnic groups, for example, have less access to childcare provision (Grewal, 2004).

The relationship between responsibilities, entitlements and state intervention is a tricky matter. In the area of conception, those who conceive 'naturally' are generally at liberty to do so, although teenage pregnancy is discouraged, whereas those who adopt or seek donor-assisted conception are subject to regulation, even though they might avoid these through the private Internet market. In other areas, intervention hits a raw nerve of mistrust between parents and the state; the difficulties in trying to make compulsory the triple vaccination of children against mumps, measles and rubella, demonstrate this, making New Labour jumpy about appearing to be a 'nanny state', and leading others to push for a clear contract between parents and the state (Hendricson, 2003). In other areas, such as education, New Labour's conception of parental empowerment revolves around 'choice' of schools. By contrast, in 2005, the concern about child health took a quite different turn when, following a television programme fronted by celebrity chef Jamie Oliver, a high profile public campaign demanded state intervention to impose nutritional standards in school meals. The demand challenged all the main discourses about children and healthy eating: that it was individual parental responsibility; that the principles of the market, choice and efficiency should predominate in the organisation of school meals. The Department for Education and Skills responded by following Scotland's example, ring-fencing £220 million for improvements in nutritional standards, equipment and training.

Acknowledging diversity *and* inequalities?

While government debates on divorce and family change are usually framed in terms of how marriage might be strengthened (Lewis, 2001), there has been a move towards the 'normalisation' of homosexuality, and the equalisation of legal and social conditions for lesbians and gay men. The discriminatory Section 28 of the Local Government Act, which was passed in a wave of anti-gay propaganda by the Conservative government in 1988, was repealed in 2003, the age of consent for gay men was equalised with that of heterosexuals in 2001, measures to allow lesbians and gay men to jointly adopt were introduced in 2003, and there have been a number of openly gay members of government. Proposals for civil partnerships for same-sex couples emerged in 2004.

At the same time, other diversities have received less recognition. Heterosexual cohabitees do not have protection in law, and have not been recognised in either family policy or in the proposals for civil partnership (Barlow et al, 2001). On the other hand, cohabitees *do* have the same responsibility of being treated as a single earner and dependant when it comes to receiving state benefits. The joint assessment of cohabiting sexual partners is one area of welfare where the old principle of the main provider and dependent partner is still maintained.

As far as minority ethnic parenting and partnering is concerned, the 1989 Children Act and the 2000 Race Relations Amendment Act placed a duty on all public institutions to take measures to prevent racial discrimination, yet it is surprising how little discussion these issues command in policy documents such as *Supporting families* or *Every child matters*. This is in spite of the fact that research shows how racism, lack of respect for religious or cultural differences and material disadvantages continue to be part of the day-to-day lives of people of African Caribbean, Bangladeshi, Indian and Pakistani heritage (Becher and Hussain, 2003), and that there is an urgent need for sensitive strategies to track equality and anti-discriminatory practices through the services, training and recruitment of those who work in the services for children (Daycare Trust, 2003). While unaccompanied asylum-seeking children were highlighted as vulnerable in *Every child matters*, there was no mention of the children of asylum seekers; in fact, the Home Office in November 2003 proposed to take into care the children of asylum seekers who stay in Britain without legal permission. In addition, moves to ban forced marriages and marriages arranged abroad have been framed within demands to assimilate to 'British culture', rather than as a move for gender and/or generation equality.

The emergence of an explicit family policy has also been curiously spare in its mention of gender inequalities. Recent proposals have referred to the possibility of attracting men into the childcare workforce and extending fathers' entitlements to paternity leave, but in general the gender-neutral concept of 'parenting' tends to obscure the particular responsibilities and difficulties that mothers face. Men work the longest hours in Europe, and gender inequalities persist in care responsibilities, in pay, and in pensions (Rake, 2001). More generally, few policy documents provide a complex reflection of how inequalities operate across class, gender, age, ethnicity and disability. The main social justice issue is poverty, with education and employment the main vehicles for tackling it. Policies tend to position parents and children in terms of their access to educational qualifications and employment rather than the meanings that these give to their lives and the social networks of which they are part. While of great political importance, the target-investment-outcome approach it has generated tends to occlude a vocabulary and an analysis of cultural practices and injustices, and the way they are both part of, and distinct from, economic deprivations.

Conclusion

I have suggested that there are four key characteristics of New Labour's family policy. A moral and economic imperative of the importance of paid work for fathers and mothers has brought together *support for working parents, investment in children's opportunities* especially in education, and *parental responsibilities,* in the fight against child poverty and social exclusion. In addition, there has been greater acknowledgement of the *diversity* of partnership relationships that marks a waning influence of a morality 'from above'. However, these priorities have set up tensions – in the balance between work and life and the extent to which care and the quality of care provision is given as much value as paid work; in how far child-focused policies are about children's needs as citizens in the here and now or simply as well-behaved worker adults of the future; and in the balance between protecting children and punishing them. The emphasis on parental responsibilities still tends to outweigh involving parents and supporting them in the ways they think fit, and the move to acknowledge diversity has been variable, especially where diversity and inequality work hand-in-hand. The goal of eliminating child poverty has made progress, but its targets sometimes obscure rather than highlight those inequalities that provide its context and consequence – especially those of gender and of ethnicity. In so far as a new normative family is emerging, this revolves around the adult couple whose relationship is based on their parenting responsibilities, and whose priorities are rooted in work, economic self-sufficiency, education and good behaviour. The main challenges to this ideal have stressed the need for an ethic of care as politically strong and viable as the ethic of work (Williams, 2001, 2004a); a review of funding mechanisms for child care (Daycare Trust, 2005) and the role of the private sector (Land, 2003); a radical reform of the workforce (Moss and Petrie, 2002) and a reconsideration of the principles of both in work and out of work benefits (Hirsch and Millar, 2004; Ridge, 2005).

References

Barlow, A., Duncan, S., James, G. and Park, A. (2001) 'Just a piece of paper? Marriage and cohabitation in the UK', in A. Park, J. Curtice, K. Thompson, L. Jarvis and C. Bromley (eds) *British social attitudes: The 18th BSA report: Public policy, social ties,* London: Sage Publications, pp 29-58.

Becher, H. and Hussain, F. (2003) *Supporting minority ethnic families – South Asian Hindus and Muslims in Britain: Developments in family support*, London: National Family and Parenting Institute.

Daycare Trust (2003) *Parents' eye: Building a vision of equality and inclusion in childcare services*, London: Esmee Fairbairn Foundation.

Daycare Trust (2005) *Day Care Trust's consultation on 'Choice for parents, the best start for children: A ten-year strategy for childcare'*, London: Daycare Trust.

DfEE (Department for Education and Employment) (1998) *Meeting the childcare challenge*, London: The Stationery Office.

DfES (Department for Education and Skills) (2003) *Every child matters*, London: The Stationery Office.

Dobrowolsky, A. (2002) 'Rhetoric versus reality: the figure of the child and New Labour's strategic 'social-investment state'', *Studies in Political Economy*, no 69, pp 43-73.

Duncan, S., Edwards, R., Reynolds, T. and Alldred, P. (2003) 'Motherhood, paid work and partnering: values and theories', *Work, Employment and Society*, vol 17, no 2, pp 309-30.

Etzioni, A. (1993) *The parenting deficit*, London: Demos.

Fawcett, B., Featherstone, B. and Goddard, J. (2004) *Contemporary child care policy and practice*, Basingstoke: Palgrave Macmillan.

Ghate, D. and Hazel, N. (2002) *Parenting in poor neighbourhoods: Stress, support and coping*, London: Jessica Kingsley Publishers.

Grewal, H.K. (2004) 'Childcare "fails to reach poor and disadvantaged"', *Society Guardian*, 11 October (www.society.guardian.co.uk/children/story/0.1074.1324648.00.html).

Hendricson, C. (2003) *Government and parenting*, York: Joseph Rowntree Foundation.

Hirsch, D. and Millar, J. (2004) *Labour's welfare reform: Progress to date*, York: Joseph Rowntree Foundation.

HM Treasury (2004) *Choice for parents, the best start for children: A ten-year strategy for childcare* (www.hm-treasury.gov.uk).

Home Office (1998) *Supporting families: A consultation document*, London: The Stationery Office.

Home Office (2003) *Respect and responsibility*, London: The Stationery Office.

House of Lords and House of Commons (2003) *The government's response to the Committee's tenth Report of Session 2002-03 on the UN Convention on the Rights of the Child*, HL Paper 187, HC 1279, London: The Stationery Office.

Land, H. (2003) 'Leaving care to the market and the courts', Paper presented to the ESPAnet Conference: 'Changing European Societies – the role for Social Policy', 13-15 November, Danish National Institute of Social Research, Copenhagen.

Lewis, J. (2001) *The end of marriage? Individualism and intimate relationships*, Cheltenham: Edward Elgar.

Lister, R. (2003) 'Investing in the citizen-workers of the future: transformations in citizenship and the state under New Labour', *Social Policy and Administration*, vol 37, pp 427-43.

McKay, S. (2002) *Low/moderate income families WFTC and childcare in 2000*, DWP Report No 16, Leeds: Corporate Document Services.

Moss, P. and Petrie, P. (2002) *From children's services to children's spaces*, London: Routledge Falmer.

Millar, J. and Gardiner, K. (2004) *Low pay, household resources and poverty*, York: Joseph Rowntree Foundation.

Newman, J. (2001) *Modernising governance: New Labour, policy and society*, London: Sage Publications.

NFPI (National Family and Parenting Institute) (2005) 'NFPI signs up to end child poverty', Press release, 19 January (www.nfpi.org).

Penn, H. and Randall, V. (2005) 'Childcare policy and local partnerships under Labour', *Journal of Social Policy*, vol 34, no 1, pp 79-98.

Rake, K. (2001) 'Gender and New Labour's social policies', *Journal of Social Policy*, vol 30, no 2, pp 209-31.

Ridge, T. (2005) 'Supporting children? The impact of child support policies on children's well-being in the UK and Australia', *Journal of Social Policy*, vol 34, no 1, pp 121-42.

Williams, F. (2001) 'In and beyond New Labour: towards a new political ethics of care', *Critical Social Policy*, vol 21, no 4, pp 467-93.

Williams, F. (2004a) *Rethinking families*, London: Calouste Gulbenkian Foundation.

Williams, F. (2004b) 'Care, values and support in local self-help groups', *Social Policy and Society*, vol 3, no 4, pp 431-8.

Williams, F. (2004c) 'What matters is who works: commentary on the Green Paper, *Every child matters*', *Critical Social Policy*, vol 24, no 3, pp 406-27.

Williams, F. and Roseneil, S. (2004) 'Public values of parenting and partnering: voluntary organisations, intimate and family life and welfare in New Labour's Britain', *Social Politics: International Studies of Gender, State and Society*, vol 11, no 3, pp 181-216.

www.ness.bbk.ac.uk – National Evaluation of Sure Start at Birkbeck College, London.

Index

Page references for notes are followed by n

competitiveness 214–15
Conservative Party
 choice 167
 family policy 291
 Local Government Act 298
 New Deal 246
 NHS 58, 283
 Northern Ireland 110
 think-tanks 148
 welfare state 242, 257–9, 260, 261,
  263, 265, 267, 269, 270
consumerism 178–80
 see also choice
Coulter, C. 108, 111, 121
Council of Mortgage Lenders 72, 73
Cowan, D. 70
Crime and Disorder Act 1999 296
Crisp, Sir Nigel 51, 52, 54, 56
Crouch, Colin 161, 164, 237, 238, 244

D

Daly, M. 244
Dangerous Dogs Act 1991 10
Daniel, C. 239
Darby, J. 111
Darling, A. 220
Dasgupta, P. 89
David, M. 225n
Davies, B. 86
Davis, Tom 141
Day, P. 63
Daycare Trust 292, 293, 299, 300
de Gier, E. 126
Deacon, A. 17, 256
Deacon, B. 204
Deeming, C. 65
Democratic Health Network (DHN)
 147, 148, 149, 159, 160
 ownership 153
 patient involvement 155, 156
Demos 147, 148, 149, 158, 162, 163
Denham, A. 147, 148, 162, 163
Denmark 246
Department of Education (DoE)
 (Northern Ireland) 118
Department for Education and
 Employment (DfEE) 44, 211, 217,
 218, 296

Department for Education and Skills
 (DfES)
 Apprenticeships 34–5
 discipline 37
 Educare 39
 EMA 36
 Every child matters 224n, 293–4, 295,
  296, 299
 higher education 46, 214, 215
 leadership 44
 Ministry for Children, Young People
  and Families 294
 performativity 40, 41
 Savings Gateway 221
 school meals 298
 secondary education 41, 42, 43
 skills upgrading 212
 workforce reform 44–5
Department of the Environment,
 Transport and the Regions
 (DETR) 76, 79
Department of Finance and Personnel
 (DFP) (Northern Ireland) 122
Department of Health (DH) 2, 52, 57,
 58, 61–2, 160, 294
 GP fundholding 61
 measuring outputs 195, 198
 Personal Social Services 85, 91, 92,
  93, 95, 96, 97, 98
 public health 64, 66
Department of Health, Personal Social
 Services and Public Safety
 (DHPSS and PS) (Northern
 Ireland) 117
Department of Health and Social
 Security (DHSS) 150
Department of Social Security (DSS)
 15, 16, 17, 18, 20, 25, 281
Department of Trade and Industry
 (DTI) 243–4, 247
Department for Work and Pensions
 17, 18
 child poverty 275–6
 childcare 277
 disabled people 279, 280
 employment services 212
 Housing Benefit 28, 29
 Incapacity Benefit 23
 lone parents 24